Futures we are in

International series on the quality of working life

Vol. 5

Futures we are in

Fred Emery
Centre for Continuing Education, ANU, Canberra

In co-operation with
Merrelyn Emery
Geoff Caldwell
Alastair Crombie

Martinus Nijhoff Social Sciences Division
Leiden 1977

ISBN 90 207 0662 4

Printed by Mennen, Asten, the Netherlands.

This study arose out of the interest and stimulation of Qantas Airlines.
They impressed us with the urgency of an Australian view of the future, even if it turned out to be no different to anyone elses: they provided us with a valuable set of guidelines and questions about the future.

Foreword and acknowledgements

This study is but one further step in an effort to understand the kinds of social environments that men create, and the ways in which these evolve or regress. The following listing indicates the series of which it is the latest member:

1963 Second progress report on conceptualization, Doc. T125 Tavistock Institute of Human Relations, London.

1965 With E. L. Trist: The causal texture of organizational environments *Human Relations*, 18, 21-32.

1967 The next thirty years: concepts, methods and anticipations. *Human Relations 20*, 199-237.

1972 With E. L. Trist: *Towards a Social Ecology*, London and New York, Plenum.

Each succeeding step has carried forward a great deal of the preceding step, particularly with regard to theory and methodology. The same is true with this step. I still find that a basic part of the theory and the methodological considerations are viable and relevant. The very considerable additions and revisions that have more than doubled the size of the statement are due to two developments. My work with Russell L. Ackoff, *On Purposeful Systems* has made it possible to extend the analysis of what system characteristics are necessary for adaptation to different environments. In particular that collaboration and the work of Eric L. Trist has made it possible to tackle the question of what ideals can aid adaptation to turbulent environments: till now I did not feel that there were to hand the conceptual tools to tackle this job. Also the work that I began with Trist 1951- and Einar Thorsrud, 1959-, on 'democratization of work' has now reached such a degree of fruition that one no longer needs to pussy-foot in print. Any hope that I had that the systems thinking derived from the U.S. space programme would provide an alternative route to de-bureaucratization has pretty well faded. The approach Trist pioneered in 1951 has been proven over a very wide range of technologies and cultures (O'Toole, 1972). This time I have been prepared to spell out what this could mean for the evolution of our societies.

Other additions have arisen from various tasks with which I have been involved since returning to my country. Thus the study of Mao's document was much aided by Ian Wilson, a specialist in China affairs. The comments on planning owe much to the challenge of a new educational authority emerging in Australia's Capital Territory. The comments on education owe a great deal to continuous engagement with Chris Duke and his Centre for Continuing Education at the A.N.U. In other matters it is more difficult to identify the persons, the occasions or issues that contributed more than I did. My feeling is that they are innumerable. More than that I feel that these wide ranging, often heated, and little remembered discussions are the seed-bed for 'discoveries' that one thinks that one has made. One such I do remember clearly. After returning from a year at the Centre for Advanced Studies, Palo Alto, I was enthusiastically espousing the significance of the distinctions Ackoff and I were drawing between functional, goal-seeking, purposeful and ideal-seeking systems. Hans van Beinum simply asked 'Isn't there a relation between this and the concept of environmental levels?' We have still not ceased to explore this relation.

The second new set of inputs has come from my collaborators. Alastair Crombie's concern with 'Planning for turbulent social fields' gave us, in particular the concept of 'active maladaptive responses'. This was a critical contribution for our efforts to understand the transitional stage where men were seeking to control turbulence. Geoff Caldwell's special concern with leisure and 'leisure co-operatives' (1972) made it possible for us to grasp the degree of change that can be expected in this field. More importantly his studies enabled us to appreciate that changes in leisure could not be predicted outside of a tight context of leisure, work, family and education. Merrelyn Emery's particular contribution was to our concept of recurrent education (see Butterfield, 1970) and particularly its interface with changes in the family, and in community settings. Beyond this she acted as editor, secretary-organizer and court-critic.

The work of the group was greatly aided by the very active intellectual participation of Chris Duke and Chris Berry in the 'Tuesday sessions'.

In reflecting on this study there seem to be two general questions that I may not have given enough space to. First I have not dwelt on 'man's inhumanity to man'. There was no intent to evade or play down the significance of Freud's contribution in *Civilization and its Discontents*. It was simply that I proceeded from different premises. I believe that the key to man's inhumanity to man lies in the quality of his 'group life' – the consistency of the demands and nurturance available to the individual in his 'panorama of significant personal ties' (Greco, 1950; Laing, 1960; Emery, Emery and De Jago, 1973). Secondly, I should perhaps have spent more time refuting Kahn's thesis that employment in manufacturing will become as much a minority problem as agriculture in the U.S.A. or Australia (1972). This is no place to go into this in depth but I think the tenor of our discussion conveys our beliefs. I see the tertiary occupations moving closer to the work-face, not continuing to separate off. Just as at the moment we are seeing a return to the land by wealthy tertiary and quaternary workers so we can expect, with the change in nature of industrial work, a marked tendency to return to the excitement and experimentation that is inherent in the industrial work-face.

Production of this work is especially due to Kathy Parish and those other members of the Centre for Continuing Education who never failed to give willingly of their time and energy.

F. E. Emery

Contents

FOREWORD AND ACKNOWLEDGEMENTS   VI

LIST OF TABLES   XII

INTRODUCTION   XIII

1. FROM EVOLVING SYSTEMS TO EVOLVING ENVIRON-
MENTS   1

1.1.1. Type 1: Random, placid environments   5

1.1.2. Type 2: Clustered, placid environments   6

1.1.3. Type 3: Disturbed, reactive environments   8

1.1.4. Type 4: Turbulent environments   9

1.2.   The May-Ashby model   11

1.3.   Trends towards the emergence of turbulent environments .   13

1.4.   An historical view of the transition to turbulence   16

1.5.   Bureaucratisation as a fifth major contributor to the
transition to turbulence   20

2. THREE PATTERNS OF MALADAPTIVE RESPONSE TO
TURBULENCE; THREE POSSIBLE SCENARIOS   31

2.1.   Superficiality: Marcuse's scenario   33

2.2.   Segmentation: the Orwellian scenario   40

2.3.   Dissociation: Neumann's scenario   43

3. THE DOOMSDAY SCENARIOS   48

4. ACTIVE ADAPTATION: THE EMERGENCE OF IDEAL
SEEKING SYSTEMS   67

4.1.   Turbulence, values and ideals   67

4.2.   A theoretical note on the parameters of choice (and hence
       decision making)   81
4.2.1. Ideals and the parameters of choice   85
4.2.2. Choice, environment and ideals   89
4.3.   The embodiment of ideals   91
4.3.1. Two basic organisational designs   91
4.3.2. Democratisation of work   100
4.3.3. The assembly line: its logic and our future 102
4.3.4. The historical significance of democratisation of work . . 115
4.3.5. Matrix organisations   121
4.3.6. Adaptive planning   123

5. THE MOST PROBABLE FUTURE FOR WESTERN SO-
   CIETIES   132

5.1.   Probable futures in work   132
5.2.   Education   137
5.3.   The family   145
5.4.   Life patterns: security, mobility and leisure 147

6. A SCENARIO FOR ASIA AND THE WEST   155

6.1.   China as the leading part in Asia   156
6.2.   China and the leading role of the West   173
6.3.   China and the U.S.S.R.   177
6.4.   China and the rest of Asia   179
6.5.   Japan   180
6.6.   'Maphilindo'   182
6.7.   India   183
6.8.   India 1976: a new path?   185

7. NOTES FOR A WORLD SCENARIO 190
   7.1.   The 'Third World' 193
   7.2.   International co-operation about international concerns   195

8. EPILOGUE: SOCIAL SCIENCES AND SOCIAL FUTURES   198

   8.1.   Social science roles 200
   8.2.   Examples of ethical problems 202
   8.3.   Conclusions 205

APPENDIX I. SOCIAL FORECASTING 207

A.   Methodological premises of social forecasting 207

B.   Forecasting social futures as a problem in reduction of complexity 213

C.   The problem of detecting emerging processes 214

BIBLIOGRAPHY 219

INDEX 224

List of tables

1.5.1.   Indicators of scale of production, U.S.A. 1880-1905   . . .   21
3.1.   Estimates of deficiency in the nutrition of the average
           inhabitant of India   50
3.2.   Food consumption, income and body weights of different
           castes in an Indian district   51
3.3.   Underestimation in some food supply statistics   52
3.4.   Estimated consumption (calories/day), (developed coun-
           tries and an Indian district)   53
3.5.   Consumption trends in industrial and post industrial
           societies   56
3.6.   Estimates of what Australians live on and what the species
           homo sapiens live on   57
3.7.   Significant break throughs in plant breeding   61
4.1.1.   The parameters of choice and related ideals   70
4.2.1.   Human ideals: past, present and future   77
4.2.2.1.   Environmental levels and salience of parameters of choice   90
4.2.2.2.   Environmental levels and salience of ideals   90
6.1.1.   Elements of two models of the future: Soviet and Mao's . .   169
8.1.1.   Levels of mutual engagement, task content and outcomes   201

Introduction

After explicating the analytical framework I will proceed to develop scenarios as follows:

1. General scenarios – maladaptive and adaptive.
2. The future for the Western group of societies. Within this will seek to identify the main changes in the natures of work, leisure, family organisation, education and life styles.
3. The future for the major Asian powers, China, Japan and India.
4. A world scenario centred about the first two scenarios but also aimed to locate within this pattern the most probable future for sets of the smaller societies and under-developed countries.

The scenarios will be developed in that order, for good reasons.

Sociological forecasting has to deal, in the first instance, with sets of societies that are closely interdependent, each with the other. A scenario for Western societies generally is required before one can hope to write one for the individual countries, e.g. France, Australia, because they are not evolving independently. The widespread upsurge of student revolts in 1967-68 well illustrates this interdependence.

Some writers, like Stevens (1970) have taken the U.S.A. as the model of the future for the other smaller Western societies. There is some justification for this as the U.S. has certainly been the 'leading part' in the West for some decades. However, there is danger in assuming that that will persist. A change in the near future in the problems that commonly confront Western societies may make the U.S. example 'depasee', old hat, if not down-right misleading.

In concentrating on a scenario for the Western society, rather than one for each individual Western society, I am accepting the same methodological restrictions as have scenario writers as diverse as Bell, Drucker, Kahn, Jungk, Galtung, McHale, Buckminster Fuller, Marcuse, McLuhan, Stevens.

As the general scenario is developed it becomes possible to make some predictions about the different rates at which parts of the 'Western set' change, and special disabilities and capabilities with which they confront the changes, perhaps creating unique national solutions.

Proceeding then to develop an Asian scenario should enable us to get the main outlines of a world scenario. Only within this is it possible to make plausible sociological predictions about the futures of the smaller and under-developed societies. They are not likely to be able to develop along their own courses, in splendid isolation.

Herman Kahn obviously has a similar strategy of proceeding from wholes, or partial wholes, to analysis of parts:

'We should very soon complete Hudson Institute's second study of the 70's and 80's – that is, a study of the general environment and its interactions with individual nations and special issues, all with an emphasis on this transition to a post-industrial culture. We hope then in our 70-71 study program to do new 'country studies', and 'issue studies' – to reexamine a number of separate countries and issues, *but now in the overall context set by the new study of the 70's and 80's* (1970, ix).

Kahn goes out of his way to explain the apparent inconsistency of producing the case study of Japan in 1970 (*ibid.*, x) and in fact centres this study on economic and demographic projections. He sees his *sociological* forecasting about Japan as dependent on analysis of the general phenomena of 'postindustrial culture' (*ibid.*, vii).

These methodological restrictions on sociological forecasting would not seem to apply so rigorously to demographic and economic forecasting. Data on these matters are collected on a national basis and invite national projections. Cultural mechanisms and state machinery for intervening in these matters exist at the level of the nation-state. Whether and when these mechanisms are set in motion, and for what purposes, may, however, depend very much on international developments.

The methodological principle that we are invoking can be stated more generally. It arises from the situation where two social processes '*A* and *B* are coextensive in time but *B* is a part process of *A*. One would expect that predictions about *A* would be theoretically easier than predictions about *B* taken alone. The basis for this expectation is the general property of part-whole relations. *A* sets some of the parameters of *B* and hence, whatever one knows of the values likely to be taken by *B*, one knows more if one knows how these parameters might change. The future of B is dependent upon the future of A in a way that A is not dependent upon B. At the same time, predictions about A will be less specific than could be predictions about B' (Emery, 1967).

The discussion around this methodological principle in Appendix I may, hopefully, explain the course followed by these sociological studies, as distinct from demographic studies, and the manner in which they will be reported. It by no means exhausts the methodological problems of forecasting social futures.

Introduction to the 1976 revised edition

There have been two major revisions to the 1973 edition.

The dismal picture I then painted for India has changed. For many in the western world, and in the universities and press of India, recent events may seem to have fulfilled our forebodings. I think not. As I try to explain in the text, Mrs Gandhi's Emergency may have given India it's second wind. If this is so then I think it will not be long before more optimistic scenario's can be written for Africa and Central and South America.

An additional chapter has been included to discuss the premisses of the Doomsday scenarios. I had hoped that their shallowness would be the death of them. Apparently not. Even with the much mellower Second Report to the Club of Rome (Mesarovic and Pestel, *Mankind at the Turning Point*, 1974) it is evident that we in the 'West' are victims of assumptions grown out of our past centuries of military superiority. With this new chapter I hope to challenge some of these assumptions. In some small way this challenge might give some added determination to the Third World countries to find their futures in a past that has long been denied to them. The challenge might even provoke a little more discussion in the West of the alternatives open to man.

The persistence of the Doomsday scenarios is disquieting. They are obviously put forward to induce change. They are obviously the sort of message the mass media love to propagate. Why? They seem to carry the message that with a little more intelligence and western type scientific know-how the world could be brought to rights, without changing the status quo. The world's difficulties lie apparently with the crass greed of western industrialism and the ignorance typified by India's sacred cows, and, of course, the Third World's indiscriminate breeding habits!

The section on active adaptation to turbulent environments has been considerably expanded. This is not unexpected. My own work and thoughts have been, I hope, consistently oriented to this end.

1. From evolving systems to evolving environments

I will argue that the future will be largely shaped by the choices people make, or fail to make, and it will not be moulded simply by blind forces of technology, economics or biological reproduction. Hence I will be looking at the present to try and identify the ends that people are pursuing that will lead them to make those choices over the next thirty years. I will be looking for something more than demographic projections or projections of G.N.P., resource limits and pollution levels. I accept that these and other matters will constrain human choice, that is, that:

1. people can proceed only from the objective conditions of the present.
2. they tend to pursue only those ends that appear from experience to be approachable; and hence be blind to possibilities that have newly emerged.
3. the means they choose and the effort they put behind those means may frequently have unanticipated consequences for the pursuit of other ends.

On this basis I shall seek to identify current developments which are changing the conditions within which men can make their future, and shall look at these both in terms of the challenges they pose and the opportunities they create for further human development.

The overriding questions that are raised in appendix I, on the methodology of social forecasting, are 'Where to look?' and 'What to look for?'. The suggested answer to the first question is that 'the unit of analysis must be the environment that includes the set of institutions and organizations with whose changes we are concerned'. The suggested answer to the second question is that we seek to identify phase changes in those environmental features that of fundamental significance in determining its overall characteristics. In living systems the most fundamental characteristics are the system-environment relations that determine survival, *i.e.*, continued survival and reproduction. In populations of living systems capable of active adaptation each system is part of the environment of the others and they constitute together a social field in a shared natural environment. As one actively adapting system becomes sensitive to the role that another may play in the same natural setting so it becomes sensitive to how that system may have acted in the past to bring about the present situation *i.e.* whether there are implications of intended harm or benefit to oneself. Similarly, questions arise about how choices made now may change or re-inforce past relations. Each of these temporal perspectives has similar implications for the others with whom each of these systems is involved. These interdependencies are 'directive correlations': the choices of the many systems in their shared environment are co-related and they are directed, at least, to harm or benefit each other and oneself (Sommerhoff, 1950; 1969). The multiple short and medium term directive correlations that thus emerge, constitute an *extended field of directive correlations*: a social field within a shared natural environment. Such environments have properties that persist in the absence of any one of their constituent systems and at the same time determine critical conditions for adaptation and survival of these systems.

The environment, the field of directive correlations, of a set of institutions we are concerned to study will thus include less than the social environment that includes all possible institutions and organisations we might wish to study; and even less of the total natural environment. Nevertheless, we think that it is only by such a method of approximation that we can find a unit of analysis that meets the logical requirements of system analysis and is yet graspable.

This is not an arbitrary reduction of the total field of possible environmental influences. Most of the conditions determining what people can and will choose are established by the vast array of institutions and organisations that they have brought into being. This is true even of man's ability to use physical and biological resources. To insure their survival and reproduction people seem always to have placed great reliance on organised forms of group life. Organised people can exert a much greater moulding force on the natural environments within which they seek to survive and reproduce. Hence my concern to define a *social* environment, an environment that is delimited by what social choices are possible, and not run into geological, geographical or climatological theories of man's future.

However, within the vast array of institutions and organisations not all can be expected to be equally significant in determining the changing patterns of directive correlations over the next thirty years. Some parts of the social environment will undoubtedly play a more leading role than others. I assume that the leading part is, and for some time will be the productive systems of society: the complex of interrelated socio-technical organisations concerned with the social (not household) production of material goods and services. It is in these systems that we get the most direct and deepest interpenetration of the social and natural environments. The conditions for human survival and reproduction hinge on these productive systems. It would not, however, be enough to trace out the phases in the evolution of technology or in the evolution of the social forms of relation to the means of production. What is required is no less than a model of the evolution of the environmental features that fundamentally determine the conditions required for survival and reproduction of human systems. Our general proposition is that in order to understand any human system we require some knowledge of each member of the following set, where L indicates some potentially lawful connexion, and the suffix 1 refers to the system and the suffix 2 to the environment:

$$L_{11} \quad L_{12}$$
$$L_{21} \quad L_{22}$$

L_{11} here refers to inter-dependencies within the system; L_{12} to the actions or the planning of actions by the system out into its environment; L_{21} to the goals and noxiants presented by the environment for the system (and these will not be the same for different systems with different requirements for survival and reproduction) *and* the flow of information from the environment about the availability of these goals and the threat offered by the noxiants.

Clearly the availability of goals or the threat of noxiants is not just a question of the properties of the goals or noxiants in themselves but also of the environmental barriers and constraints that surround them (Chein, 1954). L_{22} refers to the *causal texture of the environment*: the ways in which the parts of, and the processes in the environment causally deter-mine each other independently of L_{12}, processes independent of what individual systems or sets of systems try to intentionally impose on the environment.

The traditional contention has been that the history of man has been the history of the evolution of the L_{11} relations (L_{11} being taken as man and his institutions) and hence of man's ability to impose his will on the environment (L_{12}) and wrench from nature its secrets (L_{21} seen as L_{12} – otherwise known as 'the experimental method').

It is within the framework of this traditional contention that is has seemed reasonable to trace past evolution, and hence the likely futures of man, in terms of the L_{12}, the extensions of man in his technologies and his theories for economic planning.

My contention is that the L_{12} and the L_{21} are at least as much deter-mined by the character of the L_{22} as by the L_{11}.

This could be true but not very important if the L_{22} was a steady and to all human intents and purposes an unchangeing ground. Under those circumstances the study of the L_{22} could well be left to those who study human reflexes and instincts, geology, meteorology and the like. Those who study the history of man's actions in his technologies or his institu-tions could breeze along on the *ceteris paribus* clause.

So, I am further contending that the L_{22} has been evolving in ways that significantly change what is possible and probable in the L_{12}'s and the L_{21}'s and hence determine the survival or reproducibility of the particular classes of systems that inhabit those environments.

I am not for one moment denying that the changes in the L_{22} of human systems have arisen largely from their action on their environment. What I am stating is the belief that once these changes are wrought on our environments, social and natural, they tend to take on a life of their own. The obvious mythical parallel is Frankenstein.

The evolution of institutional and organizational environments is an evolution in the causal texture of those environments. An evolution in which those things that are supportive or destructive of system survival or destruction are more or less closely related to each other and more or less available to or avoidable by the class of systems we are con-sidering (Terreberry, 1968; Simmonds, 1975).

There is a discernable continuum from one level of causal texturing to the next. This is a continuum from a level at which the environment and its elements are only randomly related to a level at which they are all imbricated in a closely woven causal texture. We will see, however, that if this progression were described in the terms of information theory it would appear as curvi-linear, not linear.

1.1.1. Type 1: Random, placid environments

At one extreme there is what we have labelled a type 1, *random, placid* environment.[1] In this type of environment there is a random distribution of the goal objects that are necessary to the survival of the system and its reproducibility, and of the noxiants that threaten survival. In this kind of environment the system cannot know what will turn up next, when or from where.

For an individual it would be like being dropped for the first time into a tropical jungle. He would probably be able to recognize what are fruits, nuts, water, tubers, snakes, spiders *etc.*, but, not knowing this habitat, would not know where to look for them, or where to look out for them; and not know what was a fruit but also poisonous, *etc.* A very disturbing environment in which many men just die, as did most of Chapman's companions (Chapman, 1963).

However, as Chapman observed, in time to save his own sanity, 'the jungle is neutral'. In our terms, *placid.* The goals and noxiants that relate to human survival in a true jungle are typically very randomly distributed but this environmental arrangement is not in any way intentionally arranged to destroy a man or to sustain him. The next step toward survival in a type 1 environment is to learn that no strategy can be better than the best tactic. If walking to the north-west brought one to wild bananas and water today then this cannot be taken as the 'best hunch' for tomorrow's direction of travel. The best tactic, and hence the best strategy, would be toss a coin, allowing the north-westerly direction no

---

1. The first three levels of causal texturing are described in *Towards a Social Ecology* and the sources documented. Here we will seek only to convey the basic notions needed to understand the fourth level of turbulence.

more chance of being selected than any other quarter of the compass. The guiding principle is 'catch-as-catch-can' and the characteristic forms of behaviour will necessarily be exploratory and trial-and-error, vacillating from one hunch to another, even switching to contradictory hunches rather than being persevering or parsimonious.

Learning in such cognitively undifferentiated environments cannot be much more than reflex formation and conditioning. In the pure form of the random, placid environment the notion of learning has no more survival value than the idea that a person learns from having watched the dice fall in thousands of dice games. Such an experienced dice player is very likely to be conditioned to believe that certain runs in the play increase the probability that the next cast will yield a given value. He has been conditioned but he has learnt nothing. He can be wiped out on the next throw without there being any change in the laws of probability.

In postulating random, placid environments as one extreme we were well aware that this was largely theoretical. It seems most unlikely that any living systems evolved from such environments. The only practical relevance appears to reside in the fact that people are sometimes accidentally stranded in such wildernesses, societies sometimes incarcerate people in institutions that are more or less deliberately designed along these lines *e.g.* concentration camps intended to induce a high rate of 'natural' attrition, and many of the findings from psychological laboratories have emerged from placing volunteer subjects in such peculiar conditions.

1.1.2. Type 2: clustered, placid environments

There are obviously degrees of randomness. With every decrease in randomness there is an increasing flow of information available to systems living in that environment. New forms of L_{12}, behaviour, planning and L_{21}, learning, become possible. To mark off an identifiable point on this continuum we have postulated a type 2, *clustered*, *placid* environment.

The essential features of a clustered placid environment are that, like type 1 it is placid and unlike type 1 it is non-random. The goals and noxiants cluster in ways that are lawful but their ordering carries within it no intent to benefit or harm the systems that live in it. Most of the collecting, hunting and early agricultural societies appeared to have lived in such environments. Many areas of modern societies are still like this.

In a clustered placid environment the information flow permits *meaningful learning*, as in the learning of a poem and as distinct from rote learning of a list of nonsense syllables. Intelligence, or the rate of learning the relevant structuring of the environment, becomes critical to survival. As the structure is apprehended it no longer follows that 'the bird in the hand is worth two in the bush'. A distinction between tactics and strategy necessarily emerges as what is immediately presenting has to be discounted for what might be attained by proceeding to further parts of the environment offering a richer cluster of goal-objects. The overriding planning objective in this sort of environment is to achieve 'optimal location'; that location where there is maximum access to goal-objects and minimum exposure to noxiants.

The characteristic behaviours in this type 2 environment are persistence and step-by-step testing to add to the existing body of knowledge about the clustering in the environment. The behaviour appropriate in a type 1 environment would be self-defeating in a type 2 environment. It would inhibit learning when learning was possible and prevent the emergence of life saving strategies. One further point is of interest. Given that things hang together in a lawful way it becomes possible for man in such an environment to increase his survival chances by becoming symbol-user and toolmaker. In an environment where things are clustered together in time and space it is possible for some things to act as cues for the co-occurence or subsequent appearance of other things and for others to be seen as co-producers, with man, of certain desired effects *e.g.* the use of fire.

An adaptive system in these environments needs to be at least a goal-seeking system.[2]

2. A goal-seeking system is one that is able, in different situations, to choose paths that lead to a common end.

1.1.3. Type 3: disturbed, reactive environments

The next clearly distinguishable level of causal texturing is one that we have called the type 3, *disturbed, reactive* environment. The disturbed, reactive environment is no more than the clustered placid environment inhabited by two or more systems of the same kind. This may seem a small difference and in fact in a type 1 environment would make no difference: the presence of other like systems in a type 1 environment would only mean more befuddled systems adding to the randomness. In a type 2 environment the presence of other systems of like nature has critical effects. The optimal location for one is also the optimal location for the other. The elements of a competitive, zero-sum game, have been introduced as it is not likely that the optimal location is big enough for all, and certainly not big enough for the future aspirations of all. When competing systems emerge in a placid, clustered environment it becomes disturbed and reactive. What one system can learn of the environment can be learnt by others. A move by one system towards what it conceives of as a more optimal location can be disturbed by the reaction of another system to pre-empt that location. Between tactics and strategy there emerges another level of *operational planning* devised to out-manoeuvre the other in order to achieve the strategical end. Development of the art of operational planning requires a deepening knowledge of how the system functions, not just of how the environment is structured. By deeper knowledge of itself an organisation is better able to guess what tactics will be adopted by competing organizations that are like itself. Perhaps it is there that we have the birth of organisational theory and the so-called management sciences?

Learning in this type of environment is not simply a matter of learning and remembering how things go together. The background environment is stable but there is always the problem of what the others will do; will they just do their own thing? will they re-act to block one's own move? will they act to pre-empt options; will they one-up their competitor? Problem solving is the kind of learning that has greatest survival value. This problem-solving learning has the characteristics of syllogistic reasoning and the solving of chess problems. As defined in the O.E.D. problem solving starts from a set of givens, what is problematic is so within that framework.

The characteristic behaviour in these environments is simulated behaviour. The other must always be kept in a state of misunderstanding if one is to proceed unmolested towards one's ends. To this end interest must be simulated when no interest exists, disinterest must be simulated when there is a real concern, and so on. Behaviour becomes an opaque and inauthentic screen for motivations that are serious and of long-term consequence.

The instruments that men try to create in these environments share a common principle, namely that they will be variety-reducing. Whether the instruments are machines or human organisations they will be expected to be *fool*-proof. They must be a reliable means of carrying out what is tactically necessary regardless of the reason why. To provide the perfect medium for translating strategic goals into reality the elements constituting the instruments must be standardised, interchangeable and to all intents and purposes indistinguishable from each other.

These meccano-like organisations seek to concentrate the maximum reserve powers at the top, as little power as possible is delegated downwards. The possession of these reserve powers enables an organisation to adapt to the unexpected contingencies that arise from the actions and counter-actions of others: to purposefully choose between tactics that seem, in the short run, equally good. Because of the potential others have for disturbing one's own plans, strategic objectives need to be formulated more in terms of power to meet competitive challenge than simply in terms of achieving optimal location.

1.1.4. Type 4: turbulent environments

We have used the term *turbulence* to describe the next level of causal texturing. Like the disturbed, reactive environments these are dynamic environments, not placid ones. Unlike the disturbed, reactive environments the dynamic properties do not arise just from the interaction of particular systems but from processes that are set off in the environment itself. The environment ceases to be a stable ground on which organisations can play out their games and counter-games. With shifts in the ground the ground-rules change in unpredictable ways.

Simple examples of how disturbed, reactive environments can be transformed into turbulent ones may be seen in the whaling industry where intensified competition triggered off disastrous processes in the whale populations. What was assumed to be a stable environment turned out to have its own dynamics. The recent work of ecologists and the catastrophe theory of Rene Thoms have made us more aware of these processes. It is not difficult to see that even more complex processes are set off in human populations and their institutions.

When institutions and organisations are large enough and powerful enough, their efforts at producing planned changes in the environment can trigger off social processes of which they had no fore-warning, in areas they never even thought to consider and with results they had certainly not calculated on. Massive efforts at planned change like President Johnson's War on Poverty just seep away in the sand; minor miscalculations, like the Watergate burglary, spread like wildfire to paralyse the political life of a nation and overthrow a president.

The position of the turbulent environment in the series we have outlined can be summed up in the following table:

Environment	Focus for adaptation
1. random, placid	L_{11}
2. clustered, placid	$L_{11} L_{12}$
3. disturbed, reactive	$L_{11} L_{12} L_{21}$
4. turbulent	$L_{11} L_{12} L_{21} L_{22}$

In the random, placid environment survival is dependent simply on the resources the system has in itself (L_{11}), and luck. In the random, clustered its survival depends also on its ability to reach out into the environment for what it wants and to avoid dangers (L_{12}). In the disturbed, reactive environment there must be a response to the intentions and capabilities of the competing others, as these are revealed in their actions (L_{21}). In the turbulent environment adaptation is not possible unless somehow one comes to grips with the L_{22}. These are the most complexly textured environments in which adaptive behaviour is possible, as distinct from sheer survival tactics. They are the environments into which most modern countries appear to be moving and it is not sure whether adaptation is very probable. Certainly it is doubtful that individual systems can by their own efforts successively adapt to such richly textured fields. The forms of strategic planning and collusion that aided survival in disturbed reactive environments would be no more adequate than tactics alone would be in clustered placid environments. We will come back later to the planning question.

1.2. The May-Ashby model

An encouraging confirmation of some of our propositions about turbulent fields has emerged from the work of Ashby, Gardiner and May on instability in large complex systems. May's instability equation is as follows:

$$\alpha < nC^{-\frac{1}{2}}$$

where
n = number of components
C = probability of a pair of elements interacting
α = average strength of interaction

These are basically the conditions we hypothesized to explain the transformation from the type 3, disturbed, reactive environment to the type 4 turbulent environment. Namely, that organisations in adapting to type 3 environments, have become so powerful that their actions set off autochthonous processes in the extended social field (*i.e.* α).

It will be noted that n is not independent of C; if for any element C drops to zero that element cannot be regarded as a component of the system, *i.e.* the system becomes n-1; and vice versa for any element for which C becomes greater than zero. C is thus a communication index. For our 'model' it spells out the simple implication that the reduction in numbers of independent organisational components in any given territory may be offset by emerging communications with other territories. Becoming a big fish in a small pond an organisation may find itself small fry on the multinational scene. At the level of individuals every increase in the value of C tends to be empirically associated with an increase in n, *i.e.* as we make it technically more feasible for any two persons to interact more persons are drawn into communication.

By themselves n and C measure only complexity. The α term, on the left side of the equation, introduces the critical element of 'relevant uncertainty'. If α is low nothing much in the way of relevant uncertainty is likely to be generated (α cannot take a zero value as then 'interaction' and probability of interaction, C, would be without meaning). As α increases 'relevant uncertainty' increases. In our explanation we saw this in the increase in 'average strength of interaction'.

Computer simulation of this mathematical model revealed (over the range simulated) that when the inequality was reached *the transition to instability was extremely rapid.* This makes prediction very difficult. A country like New Zealand might have all the outward appearances of 'an anaethetized society' and yet the values of the above variables be at a point where almost overnight, at least in one or two years, the society finds itself in the turbulent state.

It is perhaps not completely idle to speculate on what happens if the uncertainty and complexity of a turbulent environment is compounded by the prevalence of maladaptive responses. Theoretically one would expect something like the type one, randomized environment to emerge where there is no longer any hope for a strategy for survival. Edgar Allen Poe imaginatively posed and confronted this question in his short story *Into the maelstrom*. Amazingly he found a survival tactic: behave like an inanimate object and do not struggle. In the language of the animals I guess it could be called, 'playing possum'. Note, however, that this is a denial of purposefulness and Poe made no pretence that in the face of the immense forces of the tidal vortex he was writing about (the L_{22}) there were any adaptive *strategies*. This would suggest that failure to quickly evolve adaptive strategies to emerging turbulence could seriously lessen the chances of subsequently coping. It is rather like the boxer who is a slow learner. If he only learns his opponent's style by the ninth round he may by then be too weakened to take any advantage of the knowledge.

Two corollaries of the mathematical model are relevant. Large complex systems, that can be characterized by the above equation, can move toward stability by:

1. lowering the number of other elements with which they interact, i.e. the mechanism of segmentation which we will discuss; or
2. lowering the strength of interaction with other elements, *i.e.* the social mechanism of 'superficiality' or the more personal mechanism of 'dissociation'.

Theoretically one could also reduce C, the probability of interaction, *i.e.* communication. In our non-mathematical model we did not allow this as a real possibility: to stress the significance of the change in communication we used a bit of poetic license, namely that the effective difference between our species now and 100 years ago is greater than if by mutation we were now growing two heads, with four eyes, ears *etc.* At least if that mutation had happened we would be a little more conscious of the differences, and perhaps a little more willing to take it into account. We did not see any chance of men going back to the 'pony express' level of communication. We do recognize that the biblical story of the Tower of Babel may carry a relevant moral by the 1990's.

One restriction on the mathematical model is that the elements were not attributed to the characteristics of 'purposeful systems' and hence no corrollaries emerged that correspond to our notions of active maladaptive responses or adaptive responses.

If I was to go into the business of mathematical modelling it would be simple to replace the one unity expression in May's equation with the function that we introduced to express the properties of purposeful systems (Ackoff and Emery, 1972). This could take a range of values: $1 > \pi > 0$.

Passive adaptation, as distinct from passive maladaptation, cannot be expressed in this way but then we do not think this possiblity is real under these conditions (*i.e.* when n and C cannot be more than temporarily changed).

1.3. Trends towards the emergence of turbulent environments

I have identified five trends that have greatly enhanced the complex interdependencies and the sheer amount of relevant uncertainty in our societies. There can be no doubt but that I have overlooked others. However, these trends have been so pervasive and of such consequence that even if only these trends had occurred our disturbed, reactive environments would have been transformed.

1. The sheer growth in organisational size and concentration of power. This is inherent in a disturbed, reactive environment because maximization of power is the basic adaptive strategy. Beyond a certain point this concentration of power undermines the very thing it was meant to do *i.e.*, to reduce the relevant uncertainty in the organization. The power becomes so great that the exercise of it sets off all sorts of autochtonous and unpredictable processes in the environment. As someone said of General Motors, 'if it sneezes the nation gets a cold'. More recently it shut its eyes for a moment, and got Ralph Nader.

2. The growing interdependence between all sectors of society. The productive sector is increasingly enmeshed in social responsibilities as citizens assert their role not just as producer but as consumer, inhabitant and as a social and political entity. Much of this arises from growing affluence and education but in itself it is a transformation from man-as-a-tool to man-as-a-citizen. A transformation that is less reversible than affluence or education and has wider significance than either of those taken in themselves.

For organisations these changes mean primarily a gross increase in their areas of relevant uncertainty, not just complexity *per se*. They find themselves losing their grip on both their internal worlds and the L_{22}.

This point cannot be stressed too much. Many writers have suggested that turbulence is simply a result of the sheer complexity of modern life, in large part generated by affluence, with its enlargement of areas of individual choice, and by the rapid increase in rate of change. By these criteria many periods in the past might be rated as equally turbulent as the present, and yet were coped with without institutional revolution. One has only to recall the tremendous amount of change that was taking place in individual lives in most of the world in 1945-1947. Tens and tens of millions were faced with being socially uprooted, resettled, demobilised *etc*. Whole economies and governments were being turned around, and many turned over. Yet the immediate post-war institutions were not radically different (although they were often new to a particular country *e.g.* Eastern Europe). Most of the Western countries were able to move firmly and confidently with their plans for post-war reconstruction. Most people seem to have survived the psychological shock of the changes. We simply do not believe that individuals or organisations are 'future shocked' into inadaptability by decreases or increases in their range of choice (*i.e.* hardship, success or good luck). It is my contention that change only begins to have this effect when it increases the degree of 'relevant uncertainty'; unsureness and consequently anxiety about what can be expected in areas that really matter to the person or organisation. Our cultures and our institutions constitute vast aggregations of knowledge about how people and institutions can relate and adapt to each other and to their environments, except when their social environments take on the self-moving character we postulate as turbulence.

3. The harnessing of scientific research and development to the pursuit of competitive organisational power. This has fed on itself. No organisation can afford to see its power evaporate overnight because a competitor has emerged with a technical break-through. Not only does this increase the areas of relevant uncertainty but it deepens the interdependence between organisations and their environments. Others demand that organisations assume responsibilities not only for what they are currently doing but for the futures they are trying to produce.

4. The revolution in communications. This has been a century of unabated technological revolutions in the means of communication, the collation of facts for communication and the transport of people to communicate face-to-face. There is no doubt that this has aided the growth of organisations and the emergence of the multinationals but it also transformed their environment. The great increase in the flow of information has not reduced uncertainty, instead it has created problems of information overload. The greater speed of information flow has created problems of over-sensitivity, greater temptations to act before the picture has become clear. In this kind of electronic environment it becomes increasingly difficult to prevent matters of concern flooding over to other areas, and increasingly difficult to try something

out before being forced to a conclusion. The L_{22} starts to re-act before
the organisation has a chance to test out its strategies let alone justify
them. These circumstances invite radical counter-measures which tend
to be maladaptive and increasingly unpredictable in their consequences.

5. Increasing bureaucratisation of all walks of life. In 1896 Webster's
   dictionary could dispose of the word as simply a way the government
   does its business; in the 1964 edition bureaucracy had become the way
   any large organization does its business and it had become 'a system
   of administration'.

The previous four trends have been well documented and publicly discussed. This fifth trend has been more the subject of abuse than analysis
and yet it is the one trend that might be reversable and hence the one
trend that might provide the means of stopping the drift into turbulence.
We propose to go back over the history of this drift into turbulence in
order to better understand the role of bureaucratisation.

1.4. An historical view of the transition to turbulence

We look back in order to get a better future perspective.

The growth in size of organisations to better compete for market power
is well illustrated by figure 1.4.1. The data are for the U.S.A. but parallel
the waves of growth in the other major western countries.

As these waves of acquisition built on each other, and on the internal
growth of the acquiring organizations, the significance of the build up of
the 1950-1968 wave can be readily appreciated. It is directly reflected in
the statistics published annually by *Fortune* on the top 500 Western
corporations.

Each of these waves reflects the inter-relation between size (α) and
communication (C) that was referred to in the discussion of the May-
Ashby model.

The 1895-1890 wave was unique in the history of western society and
represents, we argue, the point of emergence of the disturbed-reactive
phase (ironically the economists were then busy establishing as their

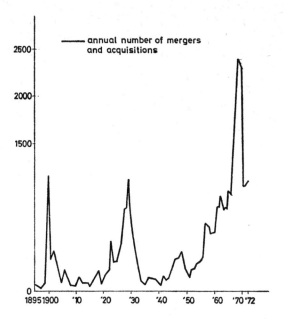

Figure 1.4.1. Acquisitions of manufacturing and mining companies, 1895-1972, U.S.A.

(Adapted from graph of *Fortune*, April 1973 p. 71)

doctrine a theory adequate to the preceding phase *e.g.* Marshall). As we will discuss in more detail later, the immediate *stimulus* to this wave of mergers was the technical break-through in energy-generation. Between 1880 and 1900 the practical output of a stationary steam engine rose more than 1600 per cent. It was possible to realize the economics of this only because the railway, telegraph and telephone network provided the first truly national markets. Not unnaturally the focus of corporate growth was on those basics that entered into production of most other commodities or into the sustenance of the labour force *e.g.* U.S. Steel, Standard Oil, International Harvester, National Biscuit Co., American Tobacco.

The second wave both grew on the production of new kinds of products and was made possible by them. The radio added a new dimension to advertising that favoured the big advertising budget. The truck and car

brought a flexibility to product distribution that destroyed the insularity
of local markets with respect to most products. Great new corporations
grew up about the combustion engine (Chrysler), the diesel (Caterpillar),
radio (R.C.A.) and also perishable commodities (National Dairy Products).

That something new was emerging in the way of an extended, highly
interactive social field, with new properties, was reflected in 'the economics of imperfect competition' (Chamberlain and Robinson) and Keyn-
sianism. In a word, macro-economics.

It is the third phase that interests us most. The subphase 1950-1966 built
up inexorably against a background where television was coming to
dominate the media-mix; research and development was increasingly
seen as the means to ensure new markets; with the government as a major
purchaser of defence oriented products and with the increasing affluence
of the individual consumers the old segregation of private enterprise was
being eroded. The final dramatic peaking in 1967-1969 may be regarded
as a concomitant of the information revolution and the jet aircraft. From
Chester Barnard through to the Carnegie school of Simon and March
there appeared to be a growing body of scientific management theory of
general applicability. The computer offered to create an information
base that would enable these principles to be realistically and hence
effectively applied to organisations of previously unimagined scale and
complexity. The jet aircraft offered the possibility of the essential ingre-
dient of face-to-face confrontation of top managers no matter where in
the world operations were located.

It was, we believe, this final phase 1967-1969, that marked the undenied
significance of 'turbulence' in Western societies. (Although a sensing of
this transition was reflected earlier in such diverse sources as Jack
Kerouac, McLuhan, Marcuse, and the economic controversies following
Sraffa.) Our first formulation of the concept of type 4 environments, *i.e.*
turbulent, was Emery, 1963.

However, before concentrating on this transition, and on turbulent
environments themselves, there are some insights, and questions, that
arise from considering the whole period.

First, these peaks have occurred only at intervals of 30-40 years. It would seem unlikely that we will see another wave-producing the super-super-multinationals, that Perlmutter and others have envisaged, until about 2000 A.D.

Second, these peaks have occurred with dramatic suddenness and lasted about two-three years. This strongly suggests that the existing system absorbs the strain of technological change, without adequate piece-meal adaptation, until, on some stimulus, radical restructuring occurs – unplanned and unpredicted.

However, some strange features mark the third phase of growth. The first two produced organised political and social reaction, e.g. the Sherman and Clayton Anti-Trust Acts and, much later, 1950, the Amendment to section 7 of the Clayton Act. The first wave made the American Federation of Labour, the second the C.I.O.

First, the third wave does no appear to be producing a direct reaction to simply limit the power of the new giants, the conglomerates. The reaction appears to be to redirect the exercise of power by all such bodies, public as well as private. 'Consumerism', 'conservationism' and the movement toward 'participation' all seem to be less worried about size *per se* than with enforcing the premise that the resources they are using are still in some sense social resources. (Something like this was emerging after the second wave, but it was a very narrow concern.)

Second, each of the first two waves seems to have given greater economic viability to the 'victors'. It may be reckless to judge the conglomerates to soon but their initial promise seems to have died very rapidly and their overall economic effect seems very neutral. An economic report of the U.S. Federal Trade Commission on the performance of nine such conglomerates through the sixties concluded they had neither improved corporate efficiency nor reduced market competition.

Third, the first wave had amply confirmed the economic value of Taylor's 'scientific management' and the second had reconfirmed this with the Bedaux system, O and M and the growth of 'modern organisation theory'. The third wave, in contrast, gave rise to sharp challenge to the 'management sciences' that were a major part of its rationale.

What I am suggesting is that *another such wave may not occur, not even in thirty years time.* The qualitative differences in this third wave may indicate the end of the conditions that led up to it; an end to the disturbed, reactive environment.

It seems obvious to me, as to Galbraith, (1969, pp. 359-360) that sheer concentration of capital is no longer the answer to corporate viability: 'In the present day economy capital is, under most circumstances, abundant', ... *The crisis is an organisational crisis* (*ibid.*, 359).

More specifically I think we can identify a fifth trend making a major contribution to the emergence of turbulence, and to the special characteristics of the transitional phase we are now experiencing.

1.5. Bureaucratisation as a fifth major contributor to the transition to turbulence

The period 1880-1900 saw not only the emergence of the giant corporation and the revolution in transport and communication. It also witnessed the emergence of so-called scientific management.

A basic development was that whereas 400 hp steam engines were common in 1880, by 1900 steam engines of 8,000 hp were common (Forbes, 1968, p. 54). By 1905 steam *turbines* were taking over the generation of electricity and the internal combustion and the diesel were coming into the picture. On the principle that the availability of energy becomes the stimulus for new and better ways to apply it there was a revolution in the economic scale of production. The small human scale of production that had dominated throughout most of history was displaced from central position by the large mass production units. Several crude but enlightening indicators are given in table 1.5.1.

Growth in scale in the decades immediately preceeding 1880 was impressive in percentage terms but after 1880 the organisational problem was unavoidable. On the one side the legal problems arising from the growing divorce of ownership and managerial responsibility were finding some sort of solution in the device of the corporation. On the other side the quite fundamental task of creating stable productive organisations of men-about-tasks was being taken in hand by men like Taylor and Gilbreth. It was they who focussed on the interface where human efforts interact with material and inanimate energy sources to yield a product.

Table 1.5.1. Indicators of scale of production, U.S.A. 1880-1905.*

	Iron and steel Tons/establishment	Electrical machinery Value of products/ establishment	Agricultural machinery Value of products/ establishment
1880	8,200	35,000	35,300
1890	22,600	101,100	89,300
1900	44,100	159,100	141,500
1905	57,500	179,600	172,800
% increase 1880-1905	705%	414	490

* From van Hise, 1912.

Most attention has been given to the emergence of the great overarching corporations like United States Steel, I.C.I., I.G. Farben, partly due to the liberal and marxist critique of monopolies. The work of Taylor and Gilbreth has been regarded as being of limited historical interest at the stage of imposing industrial discipline on migrant peasants and subsequently just a narrow discipline concerned with the details of work organisation in some industries.

Looking back from our present position in time I think it is easier to see that it was Taylor, Gilbreth and subsequently Ford (with his first car assembly line in 1912) that shaped the industrial society of today. The economies of scale that were made possible by the large steam engine could not have been achieved by the traditional forms of work organisation. The traditional forms were typically craft centred or a loosely organised gang system. In both cases a boss conveyed what he wanted done and the workers decided how they went about the job, the tools they would use (often their own) and the appropriate speed of working. This was a proven way of working in small establishments where a modus vivendi could be established on face-to-face terms between boss and worker. In the large establishment there was no such social mechanism to control the exchange of labour for wages and typically no time honoured local standards of what constituted 'a fair day's work' (each new technological change created new kinds of work). In these establishments systematic 'soldiering on the job' was the order of the day. As Taylor put it, 'It is well within the mark that in nineteen out of twenty industrial establishments the workmen ... deliberately work as slowly as they dare'. (Taylor, 1911, p. 33) The self-reliant craftsman and the multi-skilled semi-autonomous group that were the source of efficiency in small scale industry (and agriculture, forestry, mining and fishing) were the bane of large scale enterprises.

There is widespread understanding of the general contribution of Taylor and Gilbreth to founding industrial engineering and its parellel in the office, O and M. However, I suggest we take heed of Taylor's insistence that he was advancing a new philosophy for organisational design, not just a set of mechanisms or techniques. This implies looking closer at what Taylor means by 'scientific management'. The essential components, or steps, as he outlines them can be summarised as follows:

1. Determine as objectively as possible the quantity and skill level of work that has to be done to achieve the designated task goal.
2. Break this total work load down into *one man shift units* such that:
   a. all control and coordination functions are concentrated in staff and supervisory roles (*e.g.* work planning, task allocation, records, allocation of rewards and punishments).
   b. concentrate skilled operations in specialised roles from which non-skilled tasks have as far as possible been removed (*e.g.* Gilbreth's classic redesign of the bricklayer's job; Taylor, 1911, pp. 77-85). That way one pays skill rates only for skilled work.
   c. specialise the remaining semi-skilled and unskilled work roles so as to minimise the training required for efficient performance.
3. Ensure that for each work role, staff, supervisor or operator there are:
   a. unambiguous job specifications for each individual.
   b. clear and measurable standards of *individual* performance (group or gang working being proscribed, Taylor, 1911, pp. 72-73).
   c. contemporaneous records of individual performance with a mechanism for regular feedback from supervisor to the individual.
4. Selection of people to fit the roles that have thus been designed, *i.e.* 'donkeys for donkey jobs'.

I agree with Taylor that there is a design *philosophy* in these prescriptions, and a philosophy at that which brooks no marriage with the tradition of 'initiative and incentive' existing at the Midvale Steel Works when he started in 1878 (Taylor, 1911, p. 48). I do not believe that it was a *new* philosophy. Later I will argue in more detail that there are only two basic design principles for adaptive systems. Redundancy is essential for adaptiveness. This redundancy may be gained from designing in redundant, easily replaceable parts *or* from designing potentially redundant functions into the parts; functions that can come into play if some other part loses the capability for this particular function. Put more simply, an organisation can be designed to be adaptive by strengthening and elaborating special social mechanisms of control *or* by increasing the adaptiveness of its individual members. The former design philosophy has some advantages when the cost of individual parts is low, when skills are scarce and relatively expensive and when shared values about the organisation's goals are weak. It has not got the learning capabilities or range of adaptiveness provided by the latter design philosophy.

Taylor makes it very clear that he was espousing the design philosophy based on 'redundant parts'. He seemed somewhat unmoved by what this choice implied: 'As the workmen frequently say when they first come under this system 'Why, I am not allowed to think or move without someone interfering or doing it for me'. The same criticism and objection, however, can be raised against all other modern subdivision of labor' (*ibid.*, p. 125). He has made a dramatic statement of his personal and danger-ridden crusade to eradicate the alternative design philosophy from the work place (*ibid.*, pp. 48-52). This should be judged against a societal background in the U.S.A. circa 1890 that favoured industrial designs based on the concept of 'redundant parts', cheap migrant labour, and offered real prospects of greater wealth for all.

The next step in my argument is that *Taylor's 'scientific management' was not only not a new design philosophy; it was an adaptation of the basic bureaucratic model developed by earlier Asian civilisations* for their great engineering works, widespread administrations and their military. As Mumford quotes from Petrie

'We know from mummy records how minutely work was sub-divided. *Every detail was allotted to the responsibility of an individual*; one man prospected, another tested the rock, a third took charge of the products. There are over fifty different qualities and grades of officials named in the mining expeditions' (Mumford, 1967, p. 193).

Whilst the measurable man-shift unit was *the brick* from which these bureaucratic organisations arose, *the basic design module* was the section wherein a number of workers, few enough so that they could be directly overseen, was under a section boss whose own performance could be overseen, measured and recorded by the next level of supervision. Behind all this overseeing, measuring and recording was of course a system of coercive measures exercised from above as with the systems evolved by Taylor, Gilbreth and Ford. About this organisational module Mumford observes of ancient Egyptian and Mesopotamian bureaucracies that:

'the fundamental unit was the squad, under the supervision of a gang boss ... 'The Egyptian magistrate' Erman observes 'cannot think of these people otherwise than collectively: the individual workman exists for him no more than the individual soldier exists for our higher army officers.' Precisely: this was the original pattern of the archetypal megamachine and has never been radically altered' (Mumford, 1967, pp. 192-193).

Weber makes the connection more explicit,

'To this day there has never existed a bureaucracy which could compare with that of Egypt ... it is equally apparent that today we are proceeding toward an evolution which resembles that system in every detail, except that it is built on other foundations (than slavery) on technically more perfect, more rationalized, and therefore much more mechanized foundations' (in Coser, 1957, p. 472).

Taylor *et al.* brought this ancient Asiatic model into the main stream of Western society by showing how even the newest kind of work emerging from technological change could be standardised into average man-units of effort, and coordination centralised into management hands. Particularly they showed that where 'scientific' methods of measurement and selection were adopted controls over individual effort could be so finely tuned that the gross methods of coercion used by the ancient 'mega-machines' and Hitler's slave labour factories were unnecessary. Threat to job security and money largely sufficed. At the time that they did this the bureaucratic model was a fringe element of western society. It was established in the small standing armed forces and in some of the then small governmental administrative bodies.

Thus, even when England and Wales had a population of fourteen million in 1832 the central government employed only 21,000 civilians, of whom 15,000 were in Customs and Excise (Roberts, 1960, p. 9).

From World War I on, the massive temporary recruitment of civilians into the armed services created a major feedback of bureaucratic concepts of organisation into industrial and commercial life.

Before considering the impact of military bureaucratic concepts on social organisation let me make a brief comment on the mass assembly car line that Ford introduced in 1912. By relating inanimate energy sources to the transport of materials and parts as well as to their physical transformation, Ford did to industrial and machine production what Gilbreth had done to bricklaying. Practically every skilled task was reduced to a quanta of unskilled components, including supervisory skills. The speed of the line standardised the effort of the individual and coordinated their individual contributions. Special inspectorial control systems were needed for control over the quality of individual efforts, but more about that later. *The special significance of the assembly line is that it epitomised the logic of the design based on redundant parts.*[3] Ironic, perhaps, that it was a Western innovation but then we had the surplus energy to replace what is probably the most natural contribution of man to production: just moving himself.

Coming back to my main theme, the bureaucratisation of our work organisations, I think it is arguable that 'Taylorism' received a major impetus from the military from World War 1 onwards.

After World War I, the so-called new science of organisations was replete with concepts of 'line-staff' relations, 'chain of command', 'span of control'. Post World War II the emphasis has been on coordination problems and the weapon system related techniques of PERT, PPBS, network analysis *etc.*

I think I have said enough about this point. In the period 1880-1900 the major western societies were faced with a dilemma as to how they effectively organised the large productive organisations that had then become possible with our new capabilities for energy generation, materials processing and distribution. The brutal coercion of ancient bureaucracies

3. See Appendix 2.

and early British industrialisation were not possible choices. 'Scientific management' was a realistic alternative. This path was taken and heavily re-inforced by the experience that civilians had of the wartime mobilization of the first half of this century.

Now let us take our stand in the present and take an overview of what had happened since 1880-1905.

My view is that three major developments had arisen out of the success of the contributions of Taylor, Gilbreth and Ford, and the militarisation of our organisational thinking:

1. we had cauterised the connection between the workers (office or industrial) and those at the bottom of the executive structure. (As Wilfred Brown would put it, we had increased the gap-at-the-bottom of the executive chain.) As a result organisational change was becoming more dependent on bureaucratic coercion.
2. an organisational form for control and coordination had emerged that seemed to make it entirely feasible that 300 odd corporations could in the near future do most of what is needed in the Western, non-communist world. An Orwellian prospect for the individual.
3. The bureaucratisation had proceeded to the stage where even top management echelons were divorced in critical ways from ownership. Their performance was judged against decision rules which concerned the narrowly defined and preferably quantitatively defined, interests of their particular bureaucracy. This in no way reduced the impact each giant had on the other. On the contrary, it increased 'relevant uncertainty' for all as each giant sought to move on its own narrowly defined terms.

This brings me to the nub of my argument. It seems to me that the bureaucratic solution had not only brought Western society to this, the transition to instability, to the turbulent social field; *it had sapped society's ability to resolve the business, to map and determine constructive futures.*

Let me explain what is in my mind when making that last charge against the bureaucratic model. I do not think a foreign technique of organisation can be introduced into a culture without creating pervasive and potentially shattering effects, any more than we can avoid this when introducing steel axes into a stone age tribe. It is many years ago that Ralph Linton gave us a detailed study of the Madagascan tribe that went from dry rice cultivation into wet rice cultivation with all of its greater productive potential. They moved back to dry cultivation because they were not prepared to sacrifice their values and way of life. We did not seem to have widely appreciated this message, although Chaplin's 'Modern Times' had continued to haunt us over more than thirty years. There had obviously been a sense that something was wrong with the emerging picture of industrialised society. Perhaps we had been overimpressed by the great changes that have taken place in the external conditions of work. Very few in the work force in the midsixties worked in the sheer bullocking, exposed and dangerous conditions that were the lot of the majority before World War I, and for great numbers up to the late 1940s (Emery, 1976).

This overlooks the more vital question of the clash in values inherent in choice between the two basic design models outlined earlier. Asian states have typically favoured the design based on 'redundant parts'. Even with Mao's revolutionary doctrine and emphasis on group working in agriculture and industry the emphasis is on the fact that the individual should be related to the group as the tool is to the user. Western cultures and the traditional forms of work organisation that Taylor set out to destroy have typically favoured the design based on the multi-skilled individual, some of whose skills are at any time redundant to the task in hand. Their work groups were the means, the tool, for achieving their jointly agreed ends (Ackoff and Emery, 1972, Chap. 13). Taylor (1911) is replete with observations on this relation between western men and their groups. Forbes, in his reply to Ellul's argument for technological determinism, puts his finger on this value clash:

Roman agronomists regarded animals and slaves as interchangeable 'pieces of machinery'. This concept was tacitly rejected by the idea of the inherent dignity of man that came with an introduction of Christianity (Forbes, 1971, p. 94).

I think the break was at Thermopylae but that is of little moment here. What is of considerable importance is that the bureaucratic model in its day-to-day operation conveys a value message to all and sundry who work in such organisations or have significant dealings with them. And that means practically all citizens in western nations. The message is that *you* do not count, *you* can be rubbished, *you* are replaceable. All of which is a bit contrary to the Western culture. The contradiction has only been exacerbated by the bureaucratisation of educational institutions to allow for economic processing of masses of students. This rather makes one wonder which is the 'counter-culture' in our present society.

Just how bureaucratic structures convey the value message can be much more closely pinpointed, and it is not simply by use of unemployment. We have firmly based scientific knowledge of what a job needs to provide if a person is to develop greater self-reliance, self respect, in a word, dignity. The job must provide optimal variety, opportunity to learn on the job and go on learning, adequate area for decision making, mutual support and respect from co-workers, a meaningful task and some sort of desirable future (see Emery and Thorsrud, 1976, Appendix). It is precisely these things that are negated by a bureaucratic organisation of work.

- 'Optimal variety' is knocked on the head by standardisation of effort;
- 'continued learning' is defeated by job simplification;
- elbow room on the job is restricted by shifting all possible controls and coordination to the supervisors and staff planners;
- 'mutual support and respect' is replaced, not by the impersonality with which bureaucracies are usually charged (by customers rather than employees?), but by invidious interpersonal comparisons as individuals seek to ease or improve their personal lot, and self-serving cliques in cohesion to improve their lot vis-a-vis their co-workers;
- meaningfulness of the individual's task tends to disappear in the interest of job simplification and the centralisation of responsibility for 'whole tasks' in supervisory hands;
- the 'desirable future' of job security and promotion that the industrial and administrative bureaucracies hold out to middle level and lower employees becomes something of a Pilgrims Progress in the light of the preceding comments (Emery, 1976).

I suggest that when people spend their lives in these kinds of jobs they are very likely to respond to the challenges of our current turbulent environment in maladaptive ways. If they are ordinary cogs they will favour passive maladaptive responses. In a way one might dismiss this as the 'TV and beer can' response, but this misses the social significance of what we can actually see about us. The groundmovement of masses of people, similarly disposed by their lot in work life, whether blue or white collared, is shaking the basis of our society and rendering precarious even our most ancient religious institutions. Briefly, these people will be sorely tempted to simplify the world about them by adopting a more superficial stance (Marcuse's 'One Dimensional Man'), denying concern for all but their own kind and adopting an attitude of 'I'm alright Jack'. These attitudes, or social orientations, are of temporary protective value to the individual but reduce the chances of people becoming involved in jointly shaping their futures. I will expand on this in the next section.

From the leadership, the big wheels in the bureaucratic organisations, we are probably faced with an active, but no less maladaptive, response to our present circumstances. The selection of leadership in a bureaucratic structure suffers from an inherent fault. At any point in the executive structure the would-be successors are specialists in their function and are neither learned nor tested in the other functions that, together with theirs, define the managerial responsibility of their superior. In practice it means that in selecting for instance a new managing-director, one has to decide whether the organisation, in its next phase, needs to be strong on production, marketing, financial control, or capital raising.

The only general criteria that can over-ride the qualifications of specialist skills are those that mark the good bureaucrat: getting standard effort out of his subordinates under varying circumstances without introducing additional variance into the system (or 'rocking the boat'). This implies a lot of loyalty and commitment to the larger system when subordinates believe that changes in circumstances justify changes in standards. Because the latter are general criteria they will tend to override, on average, the special skills argument. This is why I think that, in general, the leaders in bureaucratic organisations will seek to find answers in their past, where they made no detected mistakes. As Crombie (1972) describes them, these active maladaptive responses are of basically three kinds (corresponding to the same system dimensions on which passive maldaptive responses are classified). First is *synoptic idealism*, the belief that if we can cram everything into a computerised model of reality the experts will come up with our future (*e.g. The Limits to Growth*, 1972). Second is *authoritarianism*. 'If the whole society is properly organised (bureaucratised) we will have an end to this counter-culture nonsense.' Third is *evangelicism*. We can put aside the Billy Graham version. The most relevant form of this response is that if we keep the G.N.P. growing all else will fall into place (which is remarkably close to Taylor's justification for bureaucratising work; See Taylor, 1911, pp. 141-143).

I have delineated the passive and active maladaptive responses that bureaucratic employment tends to generate. I shall take just a glance at the effects on those that are not directly employed in bureaucratic organisations. Firstly, there are considerable areas of employment where the traditional Western workshop practices prevail. However, when one looks closer at petrol service stations, sub-contract engineering plants and farms, the overwhelming impression is that they are sorely pressed by the large bureaucratic organisations that control their critical inputs and their output markets. Their economic viability is increasingly dependent on a 'spare parts' attitude toward their staff and even themselves. We have already mentioned what we think has happened in our educational institutions (for a more detailed statement see Emery, 1972). For the Western type nuclear family structure the situation has been potentially even more disastrous. It is hard to separate the basic Western notion of 'individual dignity' from the socialisation that is possible only in the nuclear family. However, crucifying this family on the demands brought home by bureaucratised breadwinners and bureaucratised students leaves us with a, not surprising, high casualty rate. Rates of divorce, 'suburban neurosis' and schizophrenia reflect this imposition. It would be difficult to argue that they reflect inherent defects of this family system. The same may not be true of our traditional back-up systems of religious beliefs. However, it may be.

This may seem a dismal prospect, one that inevitably lands us in the future land of Clockwork Orange, 1984, Karp's Number 1, and all that. I do not think there is any real chance of this. However, I will not try to spell out my reasons until I have more fully spelt out the nature of the maladaptive social responses that currently hold the centre of the social stage.

2. Three patterns of maladaptive response to turbulence; three possible scenarios

If the transition to turbulent social fields is the most general characteristic of Western societies then we can expect the next decades to be shaped by the endeavours of people to adapt to or to reduce turbulence.

I have suggested that for the great mass of people the almost automatic unwitting response to 'future shock' will be to degrade their social fields. The May-Ashby model clearly indicates several strategies; elsewhere Angyal has presented a systems model yielding a remarkably similar set of strategies. I will, however tie my remarks back to the Ackoff-Emery model because it is more fully developed and the concepts more rigorously defined as 'ideal operational definitions'.

The quality and complexity of a social field is determined by the purposeful choice of co-production with others for mutually agreed ends. Where choice thus becomes too difficult and too anxiety laden, and yet choice is unavoidable, we can expect the effects to be manifested on one or more of the three dimensions of purposeful choice, *i.e.*

1. Probability of choice; other things being equal, the probability of choosing one course of action rather than some other because it seems more fitting to oneself or one's, idea of himself.
2. Probable effectiveness; knowledge of what courses of action are most effective, least effective etc.
3. Relative value of the intention leading to choice.

A fourth dimension derives from 1 and 2.

4. Probable Outcome $= f$ (Prob. choice $\times$ Prob. effect.)

On the first dimension, probability of choice, the escape from the demands of choice is manifested by *segmentation*. There is an enhancement of ingroup-outgroup prejudices as people seek to simplify their choices. The 'natural' lines of social division that have emerged historically become barricades. Co-production tends to be restricted to the people one knows and can trust. To all intents the social field is transformed into a set of fields each integrated in itself but poorly integrated with each other.

The manifestation of reduction of choice on the second dimension (probable effectiveness) is *dissociation*; denial that what others do or could do as co-producers would enhance what one could do if guided by selfishness. This anomie is characterized by indifference, callousness and cynicism toward others and to existing institutional arrangements.

Reduction with respect to value of intentions manifests itself in *superficiality*. The amount of relevant uncertainty is reduced by lowering emotional investment in the ends being pursued whether they be personal or socially shared ends. This strategy can be pursued only by denying the reality of the deeper roots of humanity that bind social fields together and on a personal level denying the reality of their own psyche.

These three strategies may all be described as *passive maladaptive strategies*. Passive because they are directed only at reduction of the immediately confronting uncertainties. Maladaptive because they actually lessen the chances of changing the sources of turbulence. While it is possible to conceptually distinguish the three strategies in reality all will tend to be present in any Western society in transition to social environmental turbulence. Some circumstances in a society may favour one rather than the others but it would be unrealistic to deny that all modern Western societies offer opportunities for and inducements to use all the strategies. However, there are two reasons for going further into each of the strategies. First each seems to have attracted its own particular *active* maladaptive strategy. Secondly each has tended to be the primary focus for influential scenarios of the future.

For each of the passive maladaptive responses it is possible to identify in Western societies a corresponding *active* maladaptive response. Thus the passive maldaptive response of superficiality has the corresponding active maldaptive response of 'synoptic idealism'. Segmentation that of authoritarianism. Dissociation has its correlate in 'evangelicism'.

These pairs can be spelt out as logical correlates in terms of the definitions given above.

What is relevant is that:

1. the correlates tend to appear together in scenarios of the future. Thus when Marcuse assumes that superficiality will be the dominant mode he postulates 'synoptic idealism' as the accompanying form of societal organisation. *Clockwork Orange* assumes that dissociation will be contained by 'winning in hearts and minds' (admittedly by the wiring in of hearts and minds!).
2. this correlation appears to arise from the masses indulging in passive forms of maladaptive and the leaders seeking to meet the social breakdown with appropriate active behaviours.
3. in this case of transition to turbulence the masses appear to be more sensitive in their behaviour to the transition (*e.g.* 'the pop phenomena'). The leaders typically react as if the problems were still being played out in a type 3 disturbed, reactive environment.

2.1. Superficiality: Marcuse's scenario

Marcuse's *One Dimensional Man* is probably the most influential scenario based on superficiality as *the* response to what we have termed turbulent environments. We can readily grant that this is the dominant mode of response in countries like U.S.A., Canada and Australia where the culture is heterogeneous or historically shallow. Under these circumstances the joint pressures of bureaucratisation and affluence might well cause the social system to break with its cultural roots and shift to 'outer-directedness'. Why something is done is no longer particularly relevant, as personal reason or excuse or justification of another's behaviour. As deeper motivations are denied their relevance, widespread permissiveness will co-exist with marked tendencies toward surface conformity. Toffler presents a welter of evidence on this trend in his chapters on transience.

Three attitudes associated with this lack of depth of concern are highlighted by Marcuse (pp. 226-227). These can be paraphrased as follows:

− Instead of the critical 'is this necessary' the bland acceptance that 'this is the way things are'.

– Not 'what should be' but 'grateful for small mercies'.
– Not leisure as free uncommitted time but as relief from bad feelings.

These attitudes are a denial of individual character, whether of a person or an organisation. They constitute a tactical retreat from an environment that is seen as too uncertain and too complex to cope with. It is almost as if environmental evolution had come full circle to confront some people with a type 1 environment, admittedly one that that was richer in 'goodies'. Choice between 'goodies' becomes meaningless when one does not know what if anything follows. When the environment takes on this character for an individual it matters little whether he is offered a wide, cafeteria like, range of choices. If he feels unable to bind together his choices over time into something that is recognisably him-self then choice becomes pretty meaningless, and the momentary ex-perience becomes all. In stressing this point Marcuse was at pains to make clear that this was not just an epi-phenomenon of the involvement of people with the mass media:

'The pre-conditioning does not start with the mass production of radio and television and with the centralization of their control. The people enter this stage as pre-condi-tioned receptacles of long standing; *the decisive difference is in the flattening out of the contrast (or conflict) between the given and the possible, between the satisfied and the unsatisfied needs*' (Marcuse, *ibid.*, p. 8).

What will happen in a society when the relevance of the possible, and of the unsatisfied needs is denigrated? At the very least one would expect a marked decline in support for institutions, organisations and individuals who are seeking to realise what has become possible. One would expect also an increasingly blind eye to those claiming that they are being denied satisfaction of their needs. Of course neither of these are very new phenomena in the history of man. I am merely suggesting why such phenomena are so persistent in societies that are better placed than ever before to realize the possible (in more ways than landing on the moon) and to meet unsatisfied needs.

I would expect also that where superficiality is a dominant mode of response to turbulence there would be a paradoxical response. Even though behaviour is less and less indicative of deeper concerns and of individual character it will increasingly be the criteria for thrusting others aside. The mere fact that others indulge in drugs, sexual perversions, intellectualising or dropping-out is enough reason to try and exclude them regardless of why they so behave. Conformity in behaviour is enough for acceptance, without knowing why the conforming behaviour is displayed. This is literally a social process of *'fractionation'*. Society is torn apart along superficial lines of difference, like the breaking of a glass not the deeper communal lines we will be discussing next. This matters little when superficiality is the dominant mode. The overriding concern is the reduction of environmental variance, particularly that variance which might force one to examine the roots of one's own behaviour. It is little wonder that Fred Skinner's 'scientific proof' that everything begins and ends with behaviour was selling out of the shelves of U.S. supermarkets. In his theoretical framework, as in a one dimensional society, deviant human framework was no challenge to the rethinking of the motivational roots of one's own behaviour; it was simply a challenge to our skills in engineering the deviants back to normal.

Thus far we have considered the aggregate response to superficiality.

The active response of societal leaders to the emergence of superficiality amongst the masses is seen by Marcuse as simply giving them more of the conditions that produced their superficiality: an ever more effective administration of good affluent life.

'The enchained possibilities of advanced industrial societies are: development of the productive forces on an enlarged scale, extension of the conquest of nature, growing satisfaction of needs for a growing number of people, creation of new needs and faculties. But these possibilities are gradually being realized through means and institutions which cancel their liberating potential, and this process affects not only the means but also the ends. The instruments of productivity and progress, organized into a totalitarian system, determine not only the actual but also the possible utilizations'.

'At its most advanced stage, domination functions as administration, and in the overdeveloped areas of mass consumption, the administered life becomes the good life'. (1964, p. 255)

Crombie has termed this 'Synoptic Idealism'. It is not necessary, from this point of view, for the individual to wrack his wits about what is best. With the planning techniques of the 'optimiser' (Ackoff, 1969) the relative cost/benefits can be designed into welfare schemes, consumer goods, towns by experts with more knowledge at their disposal than an ordinary individual could hope to muster.

The conjunction of these passive and active maladaptations seems to Marcuse to produce a future steady state:

'We are again confronted with one of the most vexing aspects of advanced industrial civilization: the rational character of its irrationality. Its productivity and efficiency, its capacity to increase and spread comforts, to turn waste into need, and destruction into construction, the extent to which their civilization transforms the object world into an extension of man's mind and body makes the very notion of alienation questionable. The people recognize themselves in their commodities; they find their soul in their automobile, hi-fi set, split-level home, kitchen equipment. The very mechanism which ties the individual to his society has changed, and social control is anchored in the new needs which it has produced' (1964 p. 9).

I challenge this belief in the strength of the new rationality, 'the new utopians' (Boguslaw, 1965).

Despite the great advances in providing data based on human behaviour, beliefs and needs, and parallel computer facilities there seems little chance that this style of planning could avoid the consequences of the mass of its citizen's adopting the maladaptive life strategy of superficiality.

If the optimiser is to utilize his skills for determining optimal allocation of resources he must know beforehand what are the alternatives to be examined and, more fundamentally, alternatives serving what human ends. For technical reasons the end must be so defined that one can derive a measure of what would constitute progress to that end. If more than one end is involved, as is usual in such human affairs as education, then they must be so ordered, hierarchically, that a single overriding measure can be calculated. Given such a measure the optimiser can hopefully proceed to determine the best path by which to pursue the chosen end, provided he has a further measure for comparing all the significant resources that would be required for any of the possible paths. In other words, it is not enough to be able to measure the benefits that will follow from pursuing different paths. It is also necessary to be able to determine the cost that would be incurred. If the benefits and the costs can be put on the same scale of measurement (*e.g.* money or time saved) so much more power to the planner.

The specification of such an overall measure of achievement must challenge the balance of power between institutions and social groups that have formed around values of their own: values which serve their function best by not being too closely analysed. Conflict will also be generated within institutions and groups because no single measure, or hierarchical set of measures, is going to give adequate representation to the very many things that people are committed to doing. This will be very much the case in psycho-socially oriented systems like consumer markets, education and community development where encouraging, trying, commitment and involvement seem to defy quantification, and yet are essential to the democratic process.

In the struggle to assert this style of planning there tends to be a pre-occupation with the numbers game, *e.g.* military concern with 'bangs for a buck' and body counts, T.V. concern with ratings, marketers with percent of market share, and educationalists' concern with staff student ratios. Somewhere the individual becomes an integer.

This search for explicit definition of the objective can involve the optimiser in some deeply conservative assumptions which could nullify his very radical proposal to objectively examine any probable course of action, provided it is measurable. This risk arises from the fact that only a very powerful set of interests could force diverse interests to agree to plan for achieving a single measurable objective. Clearly they are going to prefer a measure that will give good weight to the resources they control. The planners may therefore get their explicit definition of the objective but be implicitly constrained to look at those sorts of futures most likely to maintain those currently holding the power, *i.e. planning for the best of a conservative set of futures.*

Turning now to the problems of choosing paths of action and allocating resources we find the planning activities of which the optimiser is most proud. There are grounds for pride. Without these planning skills it would not have been possible to plan the massively complex construction and operational tasks of the space missions. However, there are certain limitations that are significant in planning for people because then we are not engineering inanimate matter but elements that are quite capable of doing their own planning or counter-planning. The critical limitation is the optimiser's need to deal with commensurate, quantifiable variables. Thus the selection of paths must be restricted to those that show significant variation on a few measures that are relevant to the criterion of change and can themselves be reduced to a single measure. Thus time and people may be reduced to a money measure and hence made comparable and substitutable for computer simulation exercises. The various courses of action will not be considered in themselves but in terms of the resources they require and the effects they have. No weighting will be given to the fact that some of these paths are more familiar to the actors and some more in character with the institution. The fact that some paths have goal qualities, satisfactions of their own, is an added complexity that will usually be avoided. Finally, for technical reasons, the optimiser will tend to ignore courses of action that are likely to involve any but the simplest organisational changes. His mathematics just won't cope with them. Insofar as organisational structure embodies the past history of an institution this constitutes a further conservative tendency or at best pressure toward a simple centralised organisation.

We find a similar situation with respect to resources. The optimiser will be concerned with those resources he can measure in common terms and hence will be very much inclined to think in money terms. Human resources will come into his planning as costs for training, maintaining and replacing. Their morale, creativity and cooperativeness will not be represented in his model except possibly as estimated costs for the absence of these qualities, *e.g.* costs of labour turnover, absenteeism, time wasted on the job. This concern with money will extend to the optimiser's planning for implementation. The skeleton of the plan will be the series of nodal points at which decisions must take effect to release money for the resources required for the next steps. In similar fashion the controls will tend to be based on the flow of monies. When the planned funds do not suffice for a given step, or leave a surplus, the discrepancy will trigger off a review mechanism.

This is a familiar enough picture. Unfortunately we are equally familiar with what happens in practice. No matter how sophisticated the critical path planning, PERT's or PPBS's, reality always manages to be a bit richer than predicted and human nature a bit more cunningly perverse than expected. To the first criticism the optimiser replies that the increasing sophistication of his planning concepts and tools are constantly reducing the gap. In addition to the planned commitment of resources he can, if the client is so worried, build in contingency plans for the slippages that might be expected from past experience. This is true but ignores the increasingly significant role, in a changing society, of what is genuinely new; emergent opportunities and obstacles and unpredicted restructuring of the situation in which the plan is being implemented. Pursuit of the predicted 'best path' may be proceeding according to plan, and hence not triggering off the review mechanisms, at the same time as a new and better alternative has become possible or the original relation between the path and the objective has changed.

The blind eye of the optimiser is turned to the fact that his plans for social change are going to be implemented by others and for others. These may be people who have never shared the planners enthusiasm for his overriding objective; they may be people who come to see a conflict of interest only as the plan materialises; they may simply be indifferent to the plan.

One thing is certain, namely that the divergence of the plan from reality will provide all the excuses and opportunities that people will need to subvert and sabotage it, if they so desire. Tighter, centralised authority will be the planners recommendation. If he does get his 'overlord' he is even less likely to get the commitment and involvement of people who will be affected and the implementation will be increasingly blind and insensitive to what is happening at the work face. That such 'command planning' sometimes appears to be effective seems to be due to either measuring effectiveness in terms of reducing sins of commission or to operating within a defence context that permits drastic overshooting of costs in order to get the weapon system in question. Neither of these conditions is very relevant to planning for human needs in a society that is changing rapidly in unpredictable ways. Costs to individuals are not going to be allowed to over-run too far and if sins of *omission* are too prevalent there will be little that is adaptive. In assessing the social control value of planning a distinction must be maintained between what is effective and what is efficient; a sledgehammer is undoubtedly a very effective way of killing a fly, but hardly efficient. Command planning in a society could be an unwieldy sledgehammer. Perhaps we are guilty of using a sledgehammer on this aspect of Marcuse's scenario. We think not. The scenario developed by Marcuse in his trilogy (*Soviet Civilization*, *Eros and Civilization* and *One Dimensional Man*) is perhaps the most pro-

found of modern, nonfictional, contributions. His theme comes to an
apex in the 'Political Preface, 1966' to a new edition of *Eros and Civilization*:

'The very forces which rendered society capable of pacifying the struggle for existence
served to repress in the individuals the need for such a liberation. Where the high
standard of living does not suffice for reconciling the people with their life and their
rulers, the 'social engineering' of the soul and the 'science of human relations' provide
the necessary libidinal cathexis. In the affluent society, the authorities are hardly forced
to justify their dominion' (p. xi).

I think it will be admitted that Marcuse is projecting a 'Brave New World'.
A world that seems to many to have practically become the reality. I do
not wish in anyway to denigrate the depth of analysis, only its width.

Much of which Marcuse takes for granted are now clearly computer
myths of managers, political as well as industrial. Much of what he
thinks to be generally applicable to Western societies is true only of the
U.S.A.

One may well doubt that the scene in U.S.A. is still that presented by
Marcuse. Superficiality is still rampant, as note the Toffler data, but
other trends have emerged that show a determination to assert the relations between actions and motives, social behaviour and social ends.

2.2. Segmentation: the Orwellian scenario

This second way of simplifying overcomplex turbulent environments is
to segment society into meaningful parts that are of a size that one might
be able to cope with. Thus some Bretons feel that the problems that
confront Brittany might be better coped with if they were extracted from
the matrix of French society. Some Scots obviously feel the same way
about the United Kingdom. This path toward reducing uncertainty is
only maladaptive if there is no emergence of common planning bodies
like the E.E.C. or O.E.C.D. that enable the separating parts to re-relate at
a higher level. Typically such superbodies are slow to emerge and slow to
identify their role. However, the segmentative processes we have observed
in the last decade or so seem to be pregnant with adaptive possibilities.
They bring people closer to the historical and cultural roots of their own

behaviour, thus lessening the tendency toward superficiality. The segmentative process becomes maladaptive only when the struggle against
segmentation becomes so fierce that it inhibits re-integrative processes
e.g. Algeria, Ulster and the Jordanians. In these cases there is no question
of superficiality. It is the very roots of their individual behaviour that are
at risk; hence they find no behaviour so extreme that it is unacceptable in
pursuit of a segmented existence that is their own. The violence they can
exercise in pursuit of their ends is dramatic but trivial compared with
the violence of nuclear destruction that can be exercised by the great
powers who are threatened by some loss of power by segmentation.

If segmentation proceeds without parallel efforts at re-integration it
may be a more serious obstacle to active adaptation than the more visible
forms of superficiality and dissociation. Thus if it takes the form of
'apartheid' in a turbulent environment the boundaries between the
segments are likely to be the source of serious unpredictable disturbances.
Vortical process typically emerge at the boundaries between systems when
one is moving much faster than the other. We are suggesting that there
may be a parallel phenomenon in social fields leading to events like the
urban negro riots of the late 1960's in the U.S.A.

These tendencies generate their own *active* maladaptive response. As
the U.S.A. moved 'Beyond the Melting Pot' (Glazer and Moynihan, 1967)
and as Negroes and Chicano's asserted new identities a mass movement
developed for 'law and order' and back to the old America of the silent
majority. The atmosphere in the Presidencies of Johnson and Nixon was
one of siege and grim determination to force the pieces back into place.
(The author was a consultant to President Johnson's Kerner Commission
on riots from September 1967. By November 1967 it was clear that the
President no longer had a need for the Commission's Report; he had
decided to meet the wave of riots expected in summer 1968 by military
means.)

The most significant scenario based on segmentation and its authorita-
rian response is George Orwell's *1984* (1949). He sees segmentative tendencies harnessed by three very similar super states engaged in constant
pseudo war.

'The war is waged by each ruling group against its own subjects, and the object of the
war is not to make or prevent conquests of territory but to keep the structure of society

intact' (p. 160) ... 'In principle the war effort is always so planned as to eat up any surplus ... And at the same time, the consciousness of being at war, and therefore in danger, makes the handingover of all power to a small caste seem the natural, unavoidable condition of survival' (p. 155).

He provides also those other ingredients that make up so many of the scenarios produced in the fifties and sixties: the new aristocracy based on bureaucrats, scientists, technicians and the like: T.V. as the ultimate in surveillance and persuasion; the masses as 'the proles' under masses of petty bureaucrats imbued with the war mentality.

Just as Marcuse assumes an omnipotence on the part of 'the planners' that we cannot identify in real life so the Orwell class of scenario's assumes a Skinnerian psychology of man '(Planned) environmental contingencies now take over functions once attributed to autonomous man, and certain questions arise. Is man then 'abolished? Certainly not as a species or as an individual achiever. It is the autonomous inner man who is abolished, *and that is a step forward*'. (p. 205), our emphases). This model of man is simply that of a goal-directed system, like a radar controlled AA gun; although hidden in Skinner's social engineering are his engineers acting as purposeful systems. We have already indicated that in bureaucratised environments some of the behaviour of purposeful systems can be degraded, some of the time, to that of a human cog. Neither Skinner nor any other 'social engineer' has proved any more than that (Ackoff and Emery, 1972; Chein, 1972).

However, the main reason why we cannot rest with the Orwellian thesis has been put for us by I. G. Sharp (then Industrial Registrar, Australian Arbitration Commission).

When George Orwell wrote his novel in the 40's he was tremendously influenced by the events that had just occurred: by the dictatorship in Nazi Germany, the then continuing Stalinist dictatorship, and other things. He could see the sheer conformity that wartime enforced on people...

'I would have agreed with him that this was a tenable thesis up to the mid sixties, but from about '68 onwards I think I have been unable to accept the thesis... The outstanding influence in world affairs in the most recent years has been the emergence of individual conscience as an effective counter-force to legal/political domination...' (1972, p. 75).

I will consider these 'active *adaptive* responses' after analysis of the third pair of maladaptive strategies.

2.3. Dissociation: Neumann's scenario[1]

This third form of passive adaptation is the retreat into private worlds and a withdrawal from social bonds that might entail being drawn into the affairs of others. On the job the person strives to 'keep himself to himself' and not get involved with others; in moving himself around he avoids public transport; in his leisure he seeks the solace of television in his private lounge room; community, social and even family life are left to others to manage.

This has always been a fairly prevalent mode of adapting to the mass conditions of city living. In turbulent environments dissociation is more a product of the increasingly unpredictable nature of what might follow from even a trivial involvement with others. It offers some immediate ease for the individual but is maladaptive in its consequences. Dissociation means a lessening of an individual's responsibility for coordinating and regulating his behaviour with respect to others who remain potential co-producers of his desired ends. It is not just a private choice. In fact it would seem that it is at the interfaces between private and public life that dissociation is most manifest: where the citizen is confronted with aiding the police; being considerate to fellow motorists; honest in his tax accounting; scrupulous in his commercial dealings; willing to do his bit in community matters.

When many lower their sense of responsibility, even fractionally, there is a marked multiplier effect. Special and massive social regulatory bodies have to be brought into being to carry responsibilities formerly implicit in the web of mutual support. Such external and official regulation does little to restore a sense of responsibility.

I have already suggested that the response of dissociation is different from the 'strategies' of superficiality and segmentation. It tends to be a personal response rather than a cultural change, *e.g.* 'everyone does it', or a social change, 'let us get together against them'; it tends to manifest itself by amplifying the other strategies. A more profound difference is that dissociation induces, almost creates, its own active maladaptive response; it does not just stimulate others to act against it. Erich Neu-

1. This maladaptive mode is considered in relation to the use of television in *A choice of Futures*, Leiden, 1976.

mann has gone as far as any to spell out this as the scenario of our future, although it has never been far from the wings of the stage since Eric Fromm's production of *Escape from Freedom* (Neumann, 1954).

As Neumann sees it 'the process of mass aggregation (bureaucratisation and urbanisation) has undermined the significance of the family and the smaller groups with whom the individual was bound by historically evolved canons of mutual responsibility (pp. 436-437). The resulting *mass man* 'is psychically a fragment, a part personality' (p. 439); 'In these circumstances the disoriented, rationalistic consciousness of modern man, having become atomized and split off from the unconscious, gives up the fight because, understandably enough, *his isolation in a mass which no longer offers him any psychic support becomes unendurable*'. (p. 439, our emphases).

The 'process of mass aggregation' increases, a pace, in all countries except possibly China not just in the Western societies. 'The four phenomena – aggregation of the masses, decay of the old canon (value – structure), the schism between conscious and unconscious, and the divorce between individual and collective – run parallel to one another'. (*ibid.*, p. 383). All told, Neuman's deeply argued scenario predicts that Western societies will move once again to the perverse 'inhumanity of man to man' that particularly characterized Nazism; not, mind, the suffocating or brutal models of imposed controls that Marcuse and Orwell envisage.

Neumann's scenario is paralleled by that of the historian Norman Cohn, *The Pursuit of the Millenium* (1957). Cohn's concern was with 'the tradition of revolutionary millenarianism and mystical anarchism as it developed in western Europe between the eleventh and the sixteenth centuries' (*ibid.*, p. 9). Neumann's concern was as deep as the history, or mythology of man but Cohn's work invites us to extend the *concrete* historical base of our predictions. Turbulence is not a new condition for the human race. The drastic rise in sea level in the eleventh century not only disrupted the salt market but also brought out the Vikings and a new and extensive pattern of trade routes. The evangelical response was clearly limited to areas most affected by these changes,

'areas which were becoming seriously overpopulated and were involved in a process of rapid economic and social change' (*ibid.*, p. 53). In these areas affluence made its mark, 'there were, however, many who merely acquired new wants without being able to satisfy them; and in them the spectacle of a wealth undreamt-of in earlier centuries provoked a bitter sense of frustration' (*ibid* pp. 5-8) '...such people, living in a state of chronic frustration and anxiety, formed the most impulsive and unstable elements in medieval society. Any disturbing frightening or exciting event – any kind of revolt or revolution, a summons to a crusade, an interregnum, a plague or a famine, anything in fact which disrupted the normal routine of social life acted on these people with peculiar sharpness and called forth reactions of peculiar violence. And one way in which they attempted to deal with their common plight was to form a salvationist group under a messianic leader' (*ibid.*, pp. 59-60).

Cohn's is a history of four centuries when dissociation was probably the dominant response to an environment that was to large degree turbulent. The conditions leading to turbulence are now different but as Cohn concludes:

'...during the half-century since 1917 (the Bolshevik revolution) there has been a constant repetition, *and on an ever-increasing scale,* of the socio-psychological process that once joined the Taborite priests or Thomas Muntzer with the most disoriented and desperate of the poor ... revolutionary millenarianism and mystical anarchism are with us still' (p. 286).

This dynamic of dissociation – evangelicism, must be expected to operate into our future. It does not show the forms that Neumann and Cohn expected of Nazism, Fascism or Communism. These forms appear to have been relegated to the museum. The content of 'inhumanity to man' appears to thrive in the widespread acceptance of routine torture, 'accidents' like My Lai and indiscriminate high altitude bombing; but we wonder whether these are not but by-products of bureaucratisation. Moral Rearmanent, the Billy Graham movement, the Hare Krishna and Jesus Freaks seem more like the emergent form of reaction to dissociation. Most striking of all in the western societies is, to quote Carl Rogers (1970), 'in my judgement, the most rapidly

spreading *social* invention of the century, and probably the most potent – an invention that goes by many names, 'T-group', 'encounter group', 'sensitivity training' are amongst the most common' (1970, p. 1).

As the reasons for this mass phenomena (in the U.S.A.) Rogers refers, as have I, to the bureaucratisation/affluence syndrome but also to the critical psychological need to replace anxiety and unpredictability in interpersonal relations with 'trust and caring'. In the absence of any evidence that this mass movement changes the conditions that lead to turbulent environments it would have to be classified as evangelical, an active but still maladaptive response. The linking of this movement with the so-called 'Organizational Development' movement in organisational studies makes no substantive difference. The latter again does not challenge the conditions of turbulence. It may, however, reflect a widespread shift in values regardless of current use or misuse.

The fictional explication of a future based on this strategy did not achieve prominence until Burgess' *A Clockwork Orange*. Significantly this came out in 1962 but hit the highlights about 1972 when it went into film and paperback. Few films can be credited with directly instigating individuals with emulating the violence they depict. This film appears to have done so. I suggest that this was not because of any particularly novel form of violence that was portrayed but because the film successfully conveyed 'dissociation' as a fact of life. A majority of the people uselessly engaged in 'schooling', a few engaged in soul-destroying trivial labours, and a society, up there somewhere, who run it like a zoo (or like Harlem). Only one thing is lacking – the self generative properties of evangelicism: 'Music and the sexual act literature and art, all must be a source now not of pleasure but of pain' (p. 122). Orwell only went so far as to predict that in 1984 you would not get good sex or good food.

Before leaving this scenario it is worth noting that:

1. Neumann in 1954 was as hopeful as Marcuse in 1956 that active adaptive strategies would emerge, that 'the collapse of the old civilization and its reconstruction on a lower level to begin with, justify themselves because the new basis will have been immensely broadened' (*ibid.*, p. 393). This reconstruction he sees as the re-emergence of the historical 'group man' as distinct from the 20th century 'mass man'.
2. McLuhan sees the new era of the T.V. world as the re-emergence of Neumann's 'group man' in a 'world village'.

The point I wish to make by these references is that the dominant scenarios that emerge from consideration of the strategies of superficiality and segmentation are pessimistic; amongst those that arise from consideration of dissociation there is optimism. I would add that the former give the appearance of predicting that the future will be a continuation of the recent past and present, only more so. That is, the disturbed – reactive environment developed to *its* logical conclusions. Only with Neumann and McLuhan do we get a sense that the disturbed, reactive environments are transforming into quite a different type of turbulent environment. Only in these scenarios, for all their fatalistic 'acts and scenes' do we sense that there may be optimistic possibilities of 'downgrading' turbulent environments to type 2 'clustered environments', not just returning to the jungle of the type 3 disturbed, reactive environments of self-determining power seeking giants.

Aldous Huxley's idyllic scenario of *Island* (1962) is no exception. He leaves his Island at the point where it is impotent in the face of regression to a disturbed-reactive environment. However, his discussion of the new model family foreshadows our own (section 5.3, below).

3. The doomsday scenarios

Some of the maladaptive scenarios that were discussed in the previous chapter have exercised a remarkable grip on the imagination of people, others have exercised their influence less directly through their influence on other thinkers and writers. However, they have in common the fact that the futures they describe are ones that they see people bringing into being through their own social and political processes. In contrast we have had a recent avalanche of 'Doomsday scenarios' which see man's future as being shaped by biological, technological and economic processes that have got out of hand.

The most common feature of these scenarios is the 'population explosion'. Population growth, as this argument goes, is so far out of hand that the world food supplies will not be able to keep up. Hunger will become the daily lot of the great majority of the worlds population. Hunger on the scale envisaged is politics. War is 'the continuation of politics by other, more violent means'.

The most powerful statement of this future is Heilbronner's *Human Prospect*. Although predicting much the same as *Limits to Growth* he gives far more attention to the socio-political probabilities. He argues strongly that famine and war will be the answers to overpopulation, not human planning. The population forecasts he uses could well mean this type of future: twenty billion in the Third World by 2050 and something like two billion in the industrialised world. He assumes a doubling of population in the Third World every 25 years (an annual growth rate of about three per cent).

That assumption goes directly against the evidence:

1. *Birth rates.* The World Bank report on the *Limits to Growth* showed that of 66 countries for which good data existed, 56 showed falling fertility rates. Of course it is the industrialised countries that tend to collect good data. However, China, for which data are not good,

developed oral contraceptives very quickly and now probably has as
high a proportion of its women on these as any major western country.
Furthermore it appears to have markedly raised the age of marrying.
India and Brazil both fell many millions short of predicted population
in their last censuses. The Roman Catholic Church's hard line policy
and the official Communist line have both been broken.

2. *Rate of decline of birth-rate.* The evidence here is that once declines
   start they now take place more than twice as fast as they did historically
   in the Western industrialised nations, and the higher they are the faster
   they fall.

Against these trends is the very substantial increase in *expected length of
life* in the Third World. This trend, however, flattens out fairly fast when
DDT, *etc.* have done their job and nutrition levels remain where they
are.

The net effect is that there is a 'braking distance' within which the
world's population will still increase for a while. There is no evidence that
it will increase to Heilbronner's monstrous level.

What we have been seeing all around the world is that parents do not
need a college education in order to calculate that if death rates are
down they do not have to produce so many babies; if their mode of production starts to include labour-saving devices or effective labour pooling,
they do not need as many sons or daughters. As Carr Saunders suggested
in 1924 human populations have had built-in ways of adapting to pressures on food resources before the problem gets to Malthusian proportions. He thought this capability might have been eroded by agriculture
and closer settlement. The evidence given above suggests that it has not
entirely disappeared. There appear to be built-in socio-psychological
mechanisms against every family turning itself into a tribe.

Another important side to the Doomsday scenario are the assumptions
that have been made about human nutritional requirements. Such calculations had become a very serious business for the blockaded nations of
the two World Wars and for the rationing of mass armies (who could
not be expected to live by foraging). On the basis of such calculations
Lord Boyd-Orr, as retiring Director General of the U.N. Food and

Agriculture Organization, declared that 'a life-time of malnutrition and actual hunger is the lot of at least two-thirds of mankind' (1950). By 1957 F.A.O. had reduced the estimate to one half of the world. When they published their *Third World Food Survey* in 1963 it was revealed that they were defining malnutrition as eating less than what was recommended for the average English or French person.

In the following table we look at a couple of facts that suggest a rethink of the so-called facts proving that Doomsday is upon us.

Table 3.1. Estimates of deficiency in the nutrition of the average inhabitant of India.

	1953	1958	1964	1968(a)	1968(b)
U.S. official estimates of 'calorific requirements' for U.S. inhabitants	2500	2500	2275	2175	(1,945)[1]
Estimates of average actual calorific intake in India	1700	1700	1700	1700	1700
Percent deficit in average Indian diet	32%	32%	25%	22%	11%

1. Indian equivalent.

Note that the reduction from 32 per cent deficiency in 1958 to a 22 per cent deficiency in 1968 was not achieved by a green revolution or any such change in the real world. It results simply from a change in concepts about nutritional requirements. Pravda might describe this as a capitalist trick to minimise the reality of poverty in underdeveloped countries. However, the figures for U.S. requirements result from serious attempts to provide for the health of the inhabitants of the U.S.A.

Indians differ from the U.S. inhabitants in body size, environmental temperature and in days worked per year. If the usual allowances are made for these differences (*e.g.* Farnsworth, 1975, p. 90) the average Indian deficit is only 11 per cent, a far call from 32 per cent.

Similar calculations for the other great deficit areas of South America and Africa would undoubtedly show the same gross overestimation of

THE DOOMSDAY SCENARIOS   51

deficit. Margaret MacArthur, the Australian anthropologist, has already shown how grossly the Western nutritionists have overestimated the calorific requirements of the Japanese people. And this during a period when the Japanese had the extra money to spend on food if they so desired.

In presenting these calculations I am not for one moment denying the medical evidence we have for the presence of pellagra, kwasikor, *etc.* in these countries, nor am I denying that sections of the populations in these countries are thrown into dire poverty by failure of the monsoons or drop in world market prices for their exports.

What is being suggested here is that we have been sold a picture of underdeveloped nations as being grossly deficient in nutrients or the means to produce their necessary nutrients. I suggest that the much more serious problems for these nations lie in

1. their social distribution of food and the means to produce it, and
2. the imposition of mono-cultures on the agriculture of these countries to supply the armies of individual workers and clerks in the Western nations.

As if to add insult to injury the post-war aid programs of the West have tended to give temporary relief and yet exacerbate both problems.

To illustrate the first problem let us take some figures from a very in-

Table 3.2. Food consumption, income and body weights of different castes in an Indian district.

	Calories/ person/day	Average body weight (kgs)		Average income Rs/person/month
		men	women	
Harijans	1940	46	40	7½
Fishermen	1580	48	41	6½
Miscellaneous castes	1960	48	41	10
Agricultural castes	2440	49	41	8
Brahmins & Vaisyas	2720	51	45	18

(Swaminathan *et al.*, 1960).

tensive study of the 'nutrition of the people of Ankola Taluk, N. Kanara', India, 1960.

This district, as described by Swaminathan and his colleagues, was not particularly prosperous by Indian standards. Yet, when we look at the food that actually gets into the house we get an average figure quite a bit higher than the 1,700 calories that the F.A.O. experts calculated from available government figures on production and exports. Even the Harijans, the night-soil and garbage collectors, get substantially more. The official estimates of the western bureaucracies tend to grossly underestimate the significance of home-grown produce in nonindustrialised, nonurbanised societies. This applies not only to what is consumed by the producers but to what appears on the local markets. The official statistics, even of a country like India, with a very sophisticated body of statisticians, are at a loss in these matters.

An idea of the magnitude of underestimation that can be involved is well illustrated in a study by the Indian Council of Agricultural Research into just this problem with respect to two of their important fruit crops, mango and guava.

Table 3.3. Underestimation in some food supply statistics (hectares under crop).

		Official estimates	Detailed sample survey	underestimated
Mango	District 1	3862	9414	59%
	District 2	35	9583	99.9%
Guava	District 3	1612	2262	29%

(Seth *et al.*, 1971).

Apart from the fishermen in Ankola Taluk none really get less than the 1,945 calories we calculated as adequate on comparable standards (allowing for size, *etc.*).

There is more to the picture than that. The fishermen appear to be in a poor way but the average weight of fishermen and their women was the same as the agricultural castes. One must assume that the diet of the fisherfolk had a higher protein content from eating out of their catch. The Harijans show the clearest evidence of malnutrition, weights 46 and 40 respectively, despite the calorific intake of 1,940 per day. This caste is almost always landless and this fact gives us a clue as to why, with an income almost equal to that of the agricultural classes their consumption is only 1,940 compared with 2,440 and the average weight of their men 46 compared with the 49 kgs of the agriculturalists. The Brahmins are well into a money economy but the figures on intake of calories and their average weight hardly constitute an ideal for India to pursue.

This problem of maldistribution is by no means confined to the under-developed countries. It is obvious in the degree of *over*feeding in the western countries.

Table 3.4. Estimated consumption (calories/day), (developed countries and an Indian district).

Developed countries (1968)		Indian district	(1960)
U.S.A.	3,200	Brahmins	2,720
U.K.	3,180	Agric. castes	2,440
Australia and		Miscellaneous	1,960
Sweden	2,820	Harijans	1,940
Estimated level			
of requirement	2,175		1,945

The Indian pattern of distribution has probably existed for centuries and yet each social group has managed to reproduce itself. The Western pattern is probably very recent, probably very irrelevant to human needs and hence probably very transient. Epidemiological studies suggest that it is not just irrelevant but positively dangerous. The transience is well indicated by the reduction in scientifically constructed levels of nutritional requirements (Table 3.4.).

The most widespread nutritional problem in the world appears to be the over-eating of the West. The internal distribution question is the perennial of all of the great areas of deficit, Asia, Africa and South America. It is not a question that will be solved by anything we do in the

west to produce more agricultural commodities for export or more sub-
sidies for such exports. Whatever we send in or grant to the receiving
country would be distributed in similar fashion. That is the way they
have ordered their social affairs and they would not be changing this
just because of gifts their nation receives.

The second problem is equally challenging. Mono-culture in the underdeveloped countries came into being to serve the mass markets of the
industrialised work forces of the developed countries. Once the appropriate technologies developed, Australia, Canada, Argentine and the
mid-west U.S.A. were the great suppliers of grain and meat. From the
tropical countries came vegetable oils, tea, coffee, bananas, sugar and
spices.

Mono-culture did not come into being to serve the underdeveloped
countries. In these developments little or no consideration was given to
what the peoples of those countries required. I suggest that much of
the poverty that exists in the underdeveloped countries has arisen from
the imposition of these mono-cultures. Many of the local agriculturalists
were separated from their land to permit economies of scale for the
companies marketing into the metropolitan nations. The resulting landless people provided the necessary work force. Their subsistence required
the marketing of the cheapest forms of calories. Cut off from the land and
forced into the cash nexus their traditional diets were drastically modified.
In the traditional subsistence mode just about anything edible, plant,
animal, fungi or insect, was pressed into service to provide a balanced
diet. In her *Plague of Corn* Daphne Roe has traced the long social history
of such a dependence on a cheap mass nutrient and its disastrous effects
on the health of the agricultural labourers. F.A.O.'s study of *The World
Banana Economy* shows the breadth of dependency that is created.
The plantations, in contrast to subsistence and mixed farming by peasants,
create dependence on imports of agricultural equipment, pesticides,
fertilisers, transport equipment and scientific and managerial know-how.
The very scale and time-table of activities is geared to the whims of the
metropolitan markets; certainly not to the time-table required for local
food production.

To summarize: I think the Doomsday scenario is based on a misreading of population trends and a gross overestimation of the food requirements of the underdeveloped countries. More than that. It dangerously distorts the facts of our relations with these countries. If we followed the Dooms-day scenario we would be tempted to buy time by pouring in our surplus grain as aid, assist them in further cheap forms of industrial processed food and, the ultimate benefit, introduce them to very cheap single-cell protein cultures grown on petroleum. We would be better off to fix world prices for their agricultural exports that enable peasant production to be profitable. In 1971 for instance only about 25 cents of the retail dollar spent on bananas in Europe and the U.S.A. went into circulation in the producer countries. We would likewise be better off providing them with technical, managerial and scientific assistance to shorten their own food-chains by readapting to their local resources and traditional diets.

The future for nutrition or agriculture in the West seems to be a very different one to that which would follow a population explosion.

World population growth will require considerable development of our food production. These pressures are likely to be particularly great during the 'braking period' of population growth. This braking period may well run to year 2000. *After the year 2000 it seems pretty certain that different dynamics will be operating in all our societies.* The demands on the West as a food producer and our own pattern of consumption will both be quite different by at least the year 2000.

If the West adapted to the problems of the braking period without foresight to the period beyond then we could expect trouble. This is probably the main watershed between the predictions we would make and those that might be made by others.

Nutritional requirements for 2025 are therefore likely to be dominated by choice, not rationing, nor political concern. It is to this future that we direct our subsequent remarks.

If this particular future evolves from the choices of people then what are they likely to choose, from what options?

Let us first consider what pattern might be emerging in the domestic market by the year 2000.

Basically we expect very substantial reversals in that post-industrial society of the trends that flourished in industrial society. The trends in industrial societies have been amply documented in John Burnett's

Plenty and Want: a social history of diet in England from 1815 the present day (1966). What emerges is a picture in the first phase of industrialisation remarkably similar to what we discussed with respect to the underdeveloped countries. Marked maldistribution of nutrients, except that the Harijans of the Indian village are replaced by the vast armies of industrial workers and clerks in the urban conglomerations of the West. These industrial armies were separated from the soil and worked on a time schedule that made little allowance for their growing food even if they had the land. To feed and drug these armies there emerged the food industry to process, standardise, can, freeze or dry and to distribute the

Table 3.5. Consumption trends in industrial and post industrial societies.*

Past trends	Expected (by author)
1. Fat calories increase from under 15% to 30-40% (despite absolute decrease in consumption of unseparated fats from cereal, nuts and oilseed).	1. Decrease in fat caloric intake; higher proportion of this from cereal, nuts and oilseed.
2. Carbohydrate calories decline from 75% to 50-60%.	2. Increase in relative carbohydrate intake.
3. Change in ratio of sugar to starchy staples (cereals, roots, tubers, plantains & pulses). From 1:14 to 2:3.	3. Reversal of this ratio to about 1:3 or 1:5.
4. Protein intake steady at about 11% of total calorific intake but ratio of animal to vegetable changing from 3:8 to 7:4.	4. Reversal of this ratio to 50:50 or less.

* Based on F.A.O. survey of the national food balances of 85 countries at different levels of industrialisation, *Ceres*, 1973.

rations; the plantation system in underdeveloped countries; the food sciences to create yet cheaper forms of mass fodder and factory forms of animal husbandry.

As the industrial armies change their nature so will these trends be reversed. Table 3.5 indicates the basic reversals we would expect.

These trends can be highlighted by comparing estimates of the present Australian nutritional intake and the average intake of the human species.

Table 3.6. Estimates of what Australians live on and what the species homo sapiens live on.

	Australians[1]	Homo sapiens[2]
Livestock	34	11
Sugar	17	7
Fats, oils	10	9
Fish	1	1
Cereals	28	52
Tubers, fruit, vegetables	10	20
	100	100
100 =	3165 k.cals	2175[3]

1. Report 18. Australian Academy of Science.
2. Lester Brown's estimates.
3. This is the current estimate by the U.S.A. government of the requirements of their average citizen.

The estimates for the human species are obviously very rough. Nevertheless they are in the right direction and probably of about the right magnitude.

Our prediction is that as we free ourselves from the abnormalities of industrialisation we will exercise our freedom of choice to move back toward the dietary pattern from which we arose: a decline in over-eating and a restoration of plants as a source of calories and proteins.

We can also expect further movement away from the industrialised food concept. This concept has remorselessly pressed us to an ever lengthening food chain from the palate back to the most generally available cheapest source. Taken to its extreme the scientific-industrial complex would have us eating sand sandwiches (enriched, of course).

Part of the changes will arise from increasing awareness of the link between coronary disease, over-eating and in particular overeating of meat and animal fats.

A large part will arise as our societies replace the great bureaucratic structures with more humane participative forms of local democracy.

In this period we are very likely to have arrived at a point where mass destruction of mammals for human consumption will be discontinued. It will be generally felt as too close to cannibalism.

Large segments of humanity have highly valued traditions against such practices e.g. Hindus re cows and Mohammedans re pigs. Amongst the young generation and the old we have seen a mass movement to vegetarian health foods. Scientifically we have had an increasingly precise identification of the amino acids provided by meat proteins and an identification of vegetable sources of these amines.

The steak eating big strong male beast will be just a symbol of a past culture. More importantly the image of 'man the hunter' will be as de passe as the image of Cain. By the year 2000 our image of man will be that of 'man the gardener'. This corresponds to an ideal of nurturance and cultivation in all of the affairs of man. It is contrary to notions of dominating and devouring others. Contrary to the notion that weaker others are there simply as things to be made useful by rendering down for fat, etc.

This concept is so different from where we are today that we must go back to the intervening period 1975-2000. How is it possible that we could change so much?

There are two basic ways in which living organisms get about their business of living together: They establish areas of their own or they establish pecking orders.

We have over the past 70-80 years gone a great distance in establishing 'pecking orders' (bureaucracies) in every conceivable nook and cranny of our social life. The response of the mass of individuals has been to privatise an area that he can call his own, including a private box for driving around in (Pawley, 1973).

I suggest that this trend will be thoroughly reversed before the year 2000. Already there are powerful pressures to debureaucratise our society and clear demonstrations of the greater efficiency of organising work around groups with their own territory and without an internal status hierarchy (Emery and Thorsrud, 1976). In other areas of life we see profound and parallel revolutions in school, family and church. It seems very likely that these changes will flow over to revolutionise the style of urban life. We expect that many more people, including children, will spend much more time in their neighbourhood, working at home or learning at home. We expect that the notion of a neighbourhood will be transformed from that of fenced-off individual cells to various forms of 'cluster housing' with some significant shared community facilities. With the fences down and the pooling of some land useage we would expect to see not only shared recreational facilities but a widespread resurgence in local horticulture, orchards and poultry raising. It seems to us that these activities will largely replace lawns, flower gardens and ornamental shrubs as the social pecking orders go by the board and people become more immune to being shamed and humiliated by appearances. We are not suggesting that this local food production is likely to achieve the very high level of significance attached to the private plot in the collectivised agriculture of Russia and China. We do think it will be significant in the move away from our past heavy reliance on meat. It would also reinforce a movement away from reliance on mass produced processed foods.

We have seen a massive development of processed and convenience food industries. The major stimulus to the processed food industries has probably come from the requirements of war, from the American-Spanish war on. They have fought off the challenge of refrigeration and deepfreeze not only by price but by building in convenience of preparation for the housewife and by 'health contribution additives' to offset resistance to their low quality levels. There are grounds for believing that these forms of food have only made such inroads into the diet because civil life was becoming almost as bureaucratised as the army and the notions of caring and nurturance even in the family were being eroded. The strength of these notions was still such that the designers of convenience foods had to be careful not to make them seem too convenient; the housewife had to be given the creative role of breaking an egg into a cake-mix.

The rapid rise of the health food market and concern for macrobiotic foods coincided in the U.S.A. and Europe, with rejection of bureaucratic forms and dropping out of the 'industrial army'. These particular forms of protest against processed convenience foods may be short lived but not, we think, the general revulsion against eating such foods or providing them to the family. The ideal of nurturance is likely to be far too pervasive and too strong.

There is another major aspect of food intakes that is likely to be greatly effected by the changes in life and life style we have predicted. This is the use of food intakes to control the experience of affects rather than to service the physiological requirements of hunger and thirst. As people are able to relate positively to each other and are less subject to social shame and humiliation or to distress, we expect that they will be significantly less prone to turn their food inputs to non-physiological purposes. There are two sides to this. On the one side we believe that the ritualised over-eating to be found in the wealthy Western societies will become markedly less frequent. Some people will continue to overindulge themselves, that is obvious as there are more reasons than what we are discussing for this sort of behaviour. We are simply suggesting that there will be fewer people seeking substitute satisfaction in eating. The other side is the massive consumption of food inputs that is motivated by their sugar, salt or caffeine content. It is difficult to believe that the consumption of these commodities will remain as high as they are if people are freer to meet their affectual requirements in social intercourse.

The West is an important producer of food for the third World. As a secondary consequence it is a potential producer of know-how on food production.

There are alternatives in the way Australia for instance could respond to world food requirements in the braking phase. It could for instance further develop its agriculture along present lines and seek to sell its meat, milk, cheese and other livestock products to emergent middle class markets in Asia and the Middle East. The sorts of social changes I have referred to are general in Western countries and not irrelevant in Japan or India. For this reason we do not think there is any likelihood of a world meat market growing at the sort of rate implied by the notion of every developing nation pushing on to American levels of per capita meat consumption.

Conversion of grains to livestock products is grossly inefficient. Livestock eat up four to seven times as much energy as they provide. Fine if what they eat is inedible by humans and growing on land not suitable for cultivation of human foods. In that case it does not make sense to talk about inefficiences. However, when they consume grains and oil seed cake, the inefficiences are social, political and economic questions.

We think those questions will gradually shape our agriculture towards plant production and away from livestock production. As our agricultural research is also gradually shaped by the same questions we can expect that the grains and pulses we feed into the world food bank will be increasingly rich in protein, particularly those amines they currently lack. Over 70 per cent of mankind's protein intake comes from plant sources. If we can improve the protein content of plants, as has already been done with high-lysine corn, we can help improve the lot of the great masses in the Third World who are basically hungry because of money shortages, not food shortages.

This should be an achievable goal for agricultural researchers. As the following table shows the rate of significant break-throughs in plant breeding has been stepping up.

Table 3.7. Significant break throughs in plant breeding.

1933	hybrid maize
1957	hybrid sorghun
1959	hybrid pearl millet
1961	dwarf wheat
1963	dwarf wheat ('photo-insensitive')
1965	dwarf indica rice
	high lysine maize
1969	hybrid barley
	'hiproly' barley (high protein – high lysine)
1970	hybrid upland cotton

Developments along these lines will tend to reduce the dependence of the Third World on countries like Australia, Canada and the U.S.A. Increasingly their grain and pulse production will come to have a back-up function, just as the 'world food bank' will tend to adopt the functions of a reserve bank. The future of their grain and pulse export will depend (as usual) on its price. It seems certain that the necessary low prices will be achieved by a revolutionary scaling-up of size of the farm operation.

Two things are critical for this revolution. They exist and the need is there so the revolution will probably be completed in ten years. The first thing is the technology. The vehicle technology that revolutionised civil engineering and open cut mining has come into agriculture. This is the GOER concept based on very large low pressure tyres, articulation and positive power on all wheels. It is the concept that produced that weird family of monsters we have all seen dragging tons of burden through fields of mud on construction sites. Now, with prime movers like these even the very hard soils of Australia can be ploughed up whenever required, not only after a little rain, at rates like 200 acres in twenty four hours.

The other thing needed for the revolution is a social innovation. The tractors and their specialised equipment are so costly that some form of agri-business would seem to be needed. The other side of the question is the size of fields and property needed to achieve the economic advantages. The reluctance of farmers to lose their connection with the land and the difficulty of buying other land are likely to hinder the emergence of agri-business. What we are more likely to see is the wide scale emergence of production cooperatives. In this case the pooling and joint planning of land working and financing of equipment would be the prime bases for co-operation.

Beyond this 'industrialized agriculture' concept is an even more futuristic concept of 'industrial food' a science-based food industry that does not just process agricultural food but displaces agriculture by originating food.

Industry has a powerful impetus of its own. There is nothing it would like better than a solution to the world's food problems that was based on capital tied to its technical know-how. This plus-scientific hubris has fostered 'industrial foods' as the ultimate answer. At the extreme is S.C.P., single cell proteins (microbes) grown on the n-paraffins, natural gas or carbohydrates, in the form of algae, fungi or yeasts. This is a case of n-steps backwards to the source. The first steps forward have already been taken. 30,000 rats, 1,000 chickens and over 100 pigs over several generations have done alright on diets containing 10-15 per cent of S.C.P. from paraffins.

Less extremely, soya beans have been proposed as a food resource equivalent to bauxite in the metals industries. T.V.P. (textured vegetable protein) from soy could theoretically release man from meat dependence. It is already being used to 'extend' the humbler forms of meat such as sausages, hot dogs and hamburgers. Similar research programmes have developed around F.P.C. (fish protein concentrate, Peruvian anchovies).

Despite the international weight behind this 'industrial food' strategy I do not think it will be much in evidence after the next decade. The technical problems of acceptability of 'ersatz' food are unlikely to be solved in the low mobility, culturally defensive populations that make up most of the Third World. The critical fact is, however, socio-economic. The industrial food strategy is based on capital and technical know-how. Following this strategy would even further increase dependency on the industrial nations and even further exacerbate the common crisis of urbanisation in Third World nations. Massive urban concentrations of unemployed are growing in these countries. Thus in South America there are now 17 cities of over a million inhabitants as against 9 in 1960 (the U.S.A. at present has 7). The viability of local food production for local markets would be undermined even further. Cash cropping for international markets controlled by 'multinationals' would be further increased, in those areas suitable to the particular crops required for industrial processing. Mono-culture on an economic scale would drive people to the cities from even those areas. In the cities and the areas under monoculture it could be expected that nutritional standards would decline for the great majority. In the remaining agricultural areas the undermining of the traditional area markets by industrial foods would probably force the villages back to a level of subsistence agriculture inadequate to their nutritional needs.

Under colonialism these countries had little choice. Over the next decade we can expect them to exercise choice and one certain choice will be to negate the industrial food strategy and even to limit the growth of the more traditional food processing industry. Their preferred strategy will be to constantly seek out and adopt '*the shortest and most effective route*' between the production decision and the consumption tradition. This implies maximum use of local resources (particularly labour) and the feedback mechanisms of the traditional regional markets. It is in contrast with the food industry approach that constantly seeks '*the most value-added path*' it can find between a supplier and a consumer.

The 'shortest' path involves the least number of steps in movement, physical/chemical transformation or preservation/protection in the chain from deciding to produce, preparing the land, through to the meal.

The 'most effective' means are the ones, of those available, that are most likely to produce the desired results. Thus this strategy is *not* a strategy of moving toward the most *efficient* means for the best results.

When industry (including the food industry) speaks of efficiency it is basically talking about the efficiency with which it uses its paid up workforce (*e.g.* measures of output per man). This is simply not the problem in the Third World. Their agriculture is 'labour intensive' not 'capital intensive'. The relevant calculations start like 'cost-plus' production, from the required end, and then move back to what productive resources are available. In the Third World that is usually labour.

The pursuit of the 'best' products in traditional food markets is nigh on irrelevant. Such markets have historically evolved standards of what is available and acceptable, of what is good. Their own food preparation and dietary practices are built around their expectations. Throughout history they have usually evolved nutritionally adequate diets. The role of fermented fish products in the diets of south-east Asia is a classic of such adaptation. The primary objectives they will wish to achieve are those of getting back to these diets – at adequate levels of provision.

For the countries of the tropics and sub-tropics, in Africa, Asia, Oceania and America, this 'return to the villages' is no counsel of despair. I have mentioned some of the major forces that have disturbed and distorted these subsistence economies. There should also be some mention of the gross distortions in the picture of these subsistence agricultures that has traditionally been painted by Western trained agriculturalists and economists. The falsely assumed superiority of animal protein and fats has already been alluded to. The absence of these from the diets of New Guinea Highlanders has been found not to be associated with widespread deficiency diseases but with higher levels of active health than is to be found in the white Australian population, whose diet is presented in table 3.6. Second has been the assumption that high levels of productivity could be achieved only by following the lessons of Western agriculture:

'The two principal characteristics of this contemplated type of agriculture were the complete clearing of the soil, including the removal of all roots and other obstructions beneath the soil, and the maintenance of pure stands of each crop' (Jones, 1959, p. 94).

Only now is it being learnt that the subsistence farmers of the tropics have not survived for all these thousands of years without some deep understanding of how to grow in the hot, hot sun, and in their relatively poor soils. For good reason they have learnt not to expose these soils unnecessarily to the sun, nor subject them to continuous cropping. Clearing and tillage is kept to a minimum and a mixed culture of plants is followed to provide a vertical array of growth that will filter the sunlight, minimise pest infestation and provide insurance against failure of any one crop due to pests or climatic variation. It is this fundamental principle of mixed-culture that leads Westerners to underestimate the nutritional standards of village life and to overestimate their need for sophisticated fertilisers and pest controlling chemicals. Third has been the assumption that energy is naturally cheap in an advanced economy (since put in doubt by O.P.E.C.) and hence the rational and efficient forms of agriculture must be the high energy systems. To the meticulously cleared and tilled fields must be added the machines for all phases of cultivation and cropping, and the chemicals for fertilising and pest control.

A classic example of this mode of thought has been the scorn poured on India for her sacred cows. When Odend'hal added up the facts he found that in the West Bengali district he studied the cattle's gross energetic efficiency, defined as the useful calories produced, less the calories consumed, was 17 per cent. On the western American range country it is estimated at 4 per cent! The lesson is simply that in a low-energy subsistence economy man, beast, and plant, are more closely attuned to the multiple ways they can serve each other.

Attention could be drawn to more such assumptions but I hope that I have made the points that I think are of particular relevance. Namely, that many of the Western doomsday scenarios display ignorance of the adaptive capabilities of the agriculturalists of the tropic and subtropic regions. Furthermore those countries are at risk if they rely on the guidance of their countrymen who have become respected members of the scientific world of Western agriculture (a profession which did not even realize that in the tropics blue-algae, not the bacteria of the temperate zone, adds nitrogen to the soil).

I think the West will increasingly understand and respect these trends in Third World countries and not be a party to undermining their local agriculture whilst at the same time helping to maintain world food reserves against climatic or pest disasters.

4. Active adaptation: the emergence of ideal seeking systems

Men are not limited simply to adapting to the environment as given. Insofar as they understand the laws governing their environment they can modify the conditions producing their subsequent environments and hence radically change the definition of 'an adaptive response'.

'Such possibilities are present in turbulent environments. There are some indications of a solution which might even have the same general significance for these turbulent environments as the emergence of strategy (or ultrastable systems) has for clustered and disturbed reactive environments. Briefly, this is the emergence of ideals which have an overriding significance for members of the field. Values have always arisen as the human response to persisting areas of relevant uncertainty. Because we have not been able to trace out the possible consequences of our actions as they are amplified and resonated through our extended social fields, we have sought to agree upon rules such as the Ten Commandments that will provide each of us with a guide and a ready calculus. Because we have been continually confronted with conflicting possiblities for goal pursuit, we have tended to identify hierarchies of valued ends. Typically these are not just goals or even the more important goals. They are ideals like health and happiness that, at best, one can approach stochastically. Less obvious values, but essentially of the same nature, are the axioms and symbols that lead us to be especially responsive to certain kinds of potentialities' (Emery and Trist, 1972).

4.1. Turbulence, values and ideals

The social environments we and our institutions are trying to adapt to are turbulent environments. Massive unpredictable changes appear to arise out of the causal texture of the environment itself and not just as planned, controlled actions, not even those of the superstates or the multinational corporations.

Our patterns of morality and our sense of common ideals have not been immune to these kinds of changes. Traditional patterns of morality appear to be deeply eroded. Yet, man's greatest hope for coping with uncertainty lies in the emergence of widely shared values and ideals (Emery and Trist, 1972).

There is a dilemma here. We appear to be losing our values just as we

need them most. Certainly the demise of old values and ideals might help
to clear the way for the emergence of new values and ideals, if the reason
for them being discarded is because they are irrelevant. We are still left
with grave uncertainty about what new values and ideals could emerge
that would be appropriate to the task of curbing our turbulent state. And,
how could they possibly emerge quickly enough to prevent us irremedially
damaging ourselves by our short sighted and basically maladaptive responses to the turbulence, *e.g.* by our retreat into hedonism, law-and-
order, and life-boat concepts of the international order?

My first attempt to find a way out of this dilemma was to occupy the
middle ground between, on the one side, ideals and codes of great anti-
quity, like the Ten Commandments, and on the other, daily life. The
suggestion was that man could move toward some semblance of a common ideal by consciously confronting the basic choice that is always
present in social architecture: to use the whole person as the building
block or to build on a multiplicity of individuals, each a specialised functional bit, and anyone bit having a high order of redundancy (Emery,
1967; Mumford, 1967). At the time I made that suggestion my colleagues
and I were very busy creating a new order of morality in the daily life of
Norwegian industry. We translated the ideal of humanity into a set of
workable and relevant values by identifying what seemed to be a minimal
set of requirements that humans valued in their work activity:

1. Freedom to participate in decisions directly affecting their work
   activity.
2. A chance to learn on the job, and go on learning.
3. Optimal variety.
4. Mutual support and respect of their work colleagues.
5. A socially meaningful task.
6. Leading to some desirable future (Emery and Thorsrud, 1969).

We had found in practice that these things are valued in work regardless of
sex, nationality or race. They are also valued as much in working at an
education or working for a family or a community as in working for
money. Like any values they are given different weight by different persons, at different times and in differing circumstances.

Even a very tenuous formulation of an ideal proved a great aid in identifying relevant values. However, it was still a very tenuous formulation of what man might strive to make of himself. We had then no conception of any manageable *set* of ideals whose pursuit would guide man toward his own self-fulfilment.

Such a conception emerged only whilst Russell Ackoff and myself were struggling to formulate a model of man as a purposeful being. As we got on top of that problem we realised that we had the germ of an idea for formulating a model of man as an ideal seeking system. Our greatest efforts had been to break away from models of man-as-a-machine and cybernetic models of man as a pseudo human. Once free of these, the next few steps were relatively easy. The key to identifying purposeful systems had been the choice between alternative *goals*, simultaneously present. The next step was to recognise that purposeful systems could be confronted by choice between *purposes* or the objectives of those purposes. It seemed to us that that was what ideals are about. Endlessly approachable but unattainable in themselves. Ideals enable people:

1. to maintain continuity of direction and social cohesiveness by choosing another objective when one is achieved, or the effort to achieve it has failed; and
2. to sacrifice objectives in a manner consistent with the maintenance of direction and social cohesion.

It further seemed to us that men would have always sought to improve their ability to make such important choices between purposes. If men were as omnipotent as their gods then there would be no need for such strivings. Short of being gods men must seek to improve their choices in ways that would have to show up in changes of one or another of the four parameters of the choice situation. Even in the absence of conscious conceptualisation of these parameters we expected that by sheer trial and error over many millenia there would have emerged a close mapping of common ideals and these parameters.

The next step is a tricky one. It is rather like choosing synonyms. The best matching we could manage in our first effort was the following:

Table 4.1.1. The parameters of choice and related ideals.

Parameters of choice	Related ideals
a. Probability of choice (familiarity, accessibility)	Plenty
b. Probable effectiveness (knowledge)	Truth
c. Probability of outcome $= f(a, b)$ (understanding)	Good
d. Relative value of intention (motivation, needs, affects)	Beauty

(Ackoff and Emery, 1972).

What emerges is a finite, rigorously defined set of ideals that men will always strive after if they are at all ideal seeking. Will they indeed?

Even as we settled on these synonyms I was for other reasons back into the study of Asia, Mo Tzu, Mencius and the like. In the same period I continued to be plagued by doubts. Ackoff and I very deliberately took a plunge in deciding to publish our chapter 14 on 'ideal seeking systems'. We thought that it was far more important to start the debate in the wider circles the book was intended to reach than to wait till we could publish a definitive statement. There were other doubts. In *Towards a Social Ecology* I had a strong feeling that ideals and values represented some important differences even if they were 'essentially of the same nature' (p. 68). They are similar in that they both refer to potentiality, *i.e.* they can exist even though no force on behaviour is present or, under proper conditions, they may evoke wishes or ought forces on behaviour (Heider, 1958). They differ in that ideals refer to people's ultimate strivings for perfect beauty, perfect health, *etc.*, but people do not try to 'reach' the value of fairness; 'fairness' guides their behaviour.

There is an asymmetry in the relations between ideals and values. No amount of dedication to the observance of a particular value converts that into ideal pursuing behaviour. In fact we are inclined to regard dedication to, say, always telling the truth as somewhat pathological. On the other hand, it is hard to see how ideals could be pursued without generating values to guide the pursuit in everyday affairs. Successful collaboration with others in the pursuit of ideals would seem to presuppose some shared values.

These considerations led me to attribute greater significance to the special role of ideals in adapting to turbulence, and hence to turn a very critical eye on them. Our own set of ideals seemed a good place to start. First, these ideals, unlike our two social design criteria, seemed not to indicate what *values* people should follow in their daily life. In fact, the current pursuit of plenty through industry, of truth through science and universities, of good through the churches and of beauty through the arts, all seemed destructive of human values. This did not seem at all like the relation one would expect between the pursuit of ideals and the observance of values. Second, as I tracked the course by which Mao Tse Tung was leading the Third World back to ideals like those of Mo Tzu, I had to ask myself whether our synonyms were not just those that existed in Western christianity.

Reflecting on this I think there is considerable merit in our attempt to define the core set of human ideals. I now think, however, that our synonyms are irrelevant to the problems of turbulence that currently face Western societies, and dangerously divisive in a future where East and West must find a new modus vivendi, a conscious sharing of ideals.

Let us take our initial identification of *probability of choice* with the ideal of *plenty*. Probability of choice is very much a function of familiarity and accessibility. Regardless of all else in a choice situation, people in a choice situation will tend to be guided by the old folk sayings that 'better the devil you know...', 'old ways are best ways', or 'a bird in the hand...'.

Familiarity with courses of action and accessibility of means is not simply a function of plenty of material means as we tend to interpret it in Western societies. Our Western concept of plentitude is well enough represented in our belief that growth in G.N.P. and a nationally guaranteed minimum income would significantly improve probability of choice for everyone. Plenty of love, care and concern has precious little to do with these notions. In fact, the guaranteed minimum income concept is treacherously near the Roman concept of bread and circuses, pay-them-off and forget-them. On the one hand it appears to recognise that even the poor are human, but on the other it says we now have no responsibility

for any particular disability you might have, including any disability
that might effect your ability to use that income to meet your family needs.

I am very much inclined to the view that improvement of probability of
choice is to be found in increasing _homonomy,_ not in material plenty. By
this I mean that it is in more closely relating themselves to their neighbours, workmates, _etc.,_ that people will improve their probability of
choice. The experience of others is a prime source of 'familiarity with'
the world, and 'the others' are usually best able to provide access to a
wider range of courses of action.

The pursuit of homonomy, a sense of relatedness and belongingness
between self and others, seems to be an ideal that is more likely to improve
probability of choice than individual pursuit of plenty. It is an ideal that
simply presupposes the existence of interdependent others. It does not
presuppose growth in G.N.P. It is an ideal that can be pursued at any
level of G.N.P. per capita. It is an ideal that is equally relevant to people
in the East or the West, in subsistence or overdeveloped market economies. In a sentence, the richest gift a person can have is in his friends and
'family' not in his material possessions.

Improving probability of choice means that a person is more likely to
choose the course of action that best fits his real world than he would
otherwise do. I suggest that this improvement is more likely to occur if a
person is richly connected to his fellow men than if he is richly connected
to non-human resources. The re-identification of this ideal would seem to
imply certain redefinitions of _values_ for everyday life. I will mention
just a couple of examples. This ideal implies strong negative evaluation
of all forms of contempt of the other, whether the other is poor, coloured,
female, foreign, young or old. It implies negative evaluation of the
pervasive use of shame that lies at the basis of so-called conscience. It
implies strong positive evaluation of trust and openness.

The formulation of this ideal as a universal trend toward homonomy,
'the need to belong and identify with persons', (Angyal, 1966, p. 114)
denies the validity of the postulations about ideals being 'the super-ego
operating with the Ten Commandments'. As Angyal observes about this
sort of super-ego 'it is not inherent in human nature as such but is an
extraneous result of social development, something required not by the
individual but only by society' (p. 114).

Marcuse discusses the same kind of pseudo-idealseeking individual in modern society as a product of 'surplus repression'. Within our theoretical framework the 'ideals' that stem from such a super-ego ridden individual reflect a system level considerably lower than that of an ideal seeking system. Such an individual would have to be regarded as operating at a lower system level than the institutions instilling his norms. The sense of sacrifice associated with such *norm seeking* 'boils down to fear of punishment or ostracism' (Angyal, 1966, p. 114). The sense of sacrifice associated with the ideal of homonomy is avoidance of 'the betrayal of somebody or something one loves' (Angyal, 1966, p. 115). The ideal, I suggest, is this 'wish to be *in harmony* with a unit one regards as extending beyond his individual self' (Angyal, 1966, p. 15); not in *dependence*.

The second dimension of choice between purposes is *relative effectiveness.* This seems to be almost self explanatory when choice is between goals that can probably be achieved within a time that does not seem to require another choice. Choice between purposes is a different matter. Even in a disturbed-reactive environment the choice of *a* purpose has to be protected from the unexpected by the evolution of operational objectives (to create, hopefully, a closed system between tactics and strategies). If choice between purposes is the problem, then the effort will be towards such omniscience and such a control over resources that interruptions in mid-course will be minimally disruptive. In a type 3, disturbed, reactive, environment this end was pursued by growth in wealth, size, market share etc. In a type 4, turbulent, environment this seems to be self defeating. With so many systems confronted with the same challenges to survival the nature of 'relative plenty' has to be redefined. 'Autonomy', the behavioural trend that should so obviously counterpose the homonomous trend as an ideal, does not appear to be appropriate. If we bear in mind the conditions that contributed to the emergence of turbulent social fields (Emery and Trist, 1965) it becomes clearer that the ideal must define a trend towards plenty of knowledge and of know-how and of efficient means. The ideal is increasingly difficult to approach as one cannot determine what means are going to be required to make the pursuit of one purpose more effective than another. It was this difficulty that led N.A.S.A. to rule that special 'project type' organisations be specified as part of any contract for a major space system; there was no way of knowing beforehand what, or whose, physical resources and knowledge were going to be critical. The emerging ideal is that resources must be regarded as at all times part of the common pool of society's resources even though at any one time some individual or organisation (public or private) had definite privileges of access to those resources.

In our earlier formulation we referred to this as 'an ideal scientific state of *truth*'. This puts it in a nutshell. But I think the shell is too cramped. When many seek to define ideals within which choices of purposes will not be unduly cramped by inability to choose effective purposes, we think they will be as much concerned with availability of all material means, know-how and skills as with scientific knowledge. It is part of a dying worldview to imagine that advance of pure scientific knowledge is the sole key to this progress, or the paradigm of it.

I flinch from putting to this ideal the first name that comes to mind. In searching around I am aware of the extent to which previous assumptions about resource availability (or non-availability) have been undermined by overriding concerns of national defence, 'Naderism', consumer and conservation movements.

One thing emerges clearly; the name of the ideal we are seeking is not that of 'Truth'. It must be an ideal that in some real way subsumes the concept of truth. The best that I can manage at this stage is the notion of nurturance. This seems like a profound divergence from the original concept we used, namely 'truth'. Not, however, if we accept that truth, scientifically established knowledge, must be truth about the 'other' and the self as well as of the physical world in which we both exist. In this context we are implying that the emergent ideal cannot be just a contribution to an impersonal growth of scientific activity nor an openness to sharing the results of such activity. What I am implying is that in a turbulent environment the need for survival is going to press people towards nurturance of others (although not by any means all others), not simply Welfare State type succorance, and certainly not a simple survival goal of proving one's self, or one's organisation a charitable giver on all possible occasions.

Pursuit of this ideal of *NURTURANCE* would, I infer, mean that people will choose those purposes that contribute most to the cultivation and growth of their own competence and the competence of others to better pursue their ends. The culture-free ideal is best conceived of as the probable effectiveness of cultivating, not of making.

Margaret Mead's interpretation of Arapesh culture exemplifies this concept:

'To the Arapesh, the world is a garden that must be tilled, not for one's self, not in pride and boasting, not for hoarding and usury, but that the yams and the dogs and the pigs and most of all the children may grow. From this whole attitude flow many of the other Arapesh traits, the lack of conflict between the old and young, the lack of any expectation of jealousy or envy, the emphasis upon co-operation' (1952, p. 100).

That is, pursuit of this ideal implies a 'fundamentally different experience of the world: nature is taken, not as an object of domination and exploitation, but as a 'garden' which can grow while making human beings grow' (Marcuse, 1956, p. 216).

The third parameter, _probability of outcome,_ is a derivative of the first two. The individual system that is doing the choosing will be affected by the interaction between the first two parameters. (*e.g.* between two sources of action that both look reasonably effective 'but this one is really the only one that *we* would consider taking'.) The course of action that will appear to provide the most probable outcome will be some amalgam of what is effective and what is fitting or appropriate to the choosing system. As an ideal I think this is best described as an ideal of *HUMANITY*. Given that at any time we know of many different purposes that we might pursue and our tendency will be to choose not the 'best' but the one that best fits our nature. In a sense the issue is expressed in Norbert Weiner's title *Towards the Human Use of Human Beings*. Historically it has been expressed in the notion that 'man is the measure'.

Originally this was referred to as the ideal of 'Good'. I am now just being more specific about the question of 'good for whom?' We would simply note at this point that the ultimate reference for humaneness is how individuals are affected, not organisations. Thus a judicial decision cannot be judged as humane or inhumane unless we know how it affects the individual(s) concerned.

I do not suggest a change in the label for the fourth dimension of choice *relative intention.* As an ideal 'Beauty' does not seem 'culture bound'. The meta ideal of omnipotence becomes vacuous if all desire, all relative value and intention is eliminated; that is, if a state of Nirvana is attained. Therefore, omnipotence presupposes desire, and this, in turn, requires that more desirable goals and objectives replace old ones once they have been obtained. Thus an ideal seeking system would enlarge its desires, and the succeeding objectives that it sought would be more desirable to it. In an ideal state, all purposeful individuals would be ideal-seeking. Such a state can be referred to as the ideal *aesthetic* state of *BEAUTY*.

What this means in terms of choosing between purposes is fairly clear. 'Relative intention' expresses the liking for and desire for certain outcomes, as distinct from recognising that certain outcomes may, objectively, be more probable. The ideal that men pursue is not that they simply prefer what others prefer, but that they actually desire and affectively react in ways that are not necessarily the same as are those of others, but are not contradictory.

This has been put very well by Caudwell:

'whenever the affective elements in socially known things show social ordering, *there we have beauty, there alone we have beauty.* The business of such ordering is art, and this applies to all socially known things, to houses, gestures, narratives, descriptions, lessons, songs and labour' (1949, 106).

I am suggesting that men will increasingly choose and more consciously strive to choose those purposes that manifest intentions calculated to stimulate both themselves and others to expand their horizons of desire, and to rationalise conflict. By rationalising conflict we mean the demonstration that the conflicts are containable within a higher order of ends, a higher rationality.

One implication of what I am postulating as an ideal is that men will increasingly reject the pursuit of purposes that are likely to be ugly, deforming, degrading or divisive, *i.e.* the kinds of purposes intrinsic to the maladaptive strategies.

Other important properties certainly attach to my efforts at defining a constellation of ideals that men will pursue as they become increasingly free to do so; and increasingly unable to adapt unless they so do.

However, a summary of my postulations may be helpful. This summary may stimulate more critical thought if I juxtapose my set of ideals with those proposed by Trist (Emery and Trist, 1972).

Table 4.2.1. Human ideals: past, present and future.

Trist		Our's	
Under industrialism	Post-industrial	Transition	Post-industrial [1]
Achievement	Selfactualization	Truth	Nurturance
Independence	Interdependence	Plenty	Homonomy
Selfcontrol	Selfexpression	Good	Humanity
Endurance of distress	Capacity for joy	Beauty	Beauty

At no point did I strive for comparability with Trist's list; my concern was with rethinking the original Ackoff-Emery formulations. Nevertheless the comparison is of interest. The two points of disparity are with Trist's self-actualization and self-expression. These disparities help me reaffirm my intended meanings. I do not think that self-actualization in a turbulent environment can be adaptive if it is not also an active concern to nurture the 'self-actualization' of others. I do not think that self-expression, 'doing one's own thing', is an adaptive ideal unless it is concerned with expressing that which is human, and concerned with inducing a human response.

It will be noted that these difficulties in translation are of the same kind as we experienced in moving from the ideal of 'plenty' to that of 'homonomy', from 'truth' to 'nurturance' and from 'good' to 'humanity'.

1. If the ideals put forward here are meaningful then they would have to, at least, pass the test that their opposites are in general abhorrent to people. (I cannot assure the reader that this is a fair test because it is I who have picked out the labels for the opposites):

homonomy	selfishness
nurturance	exploitation
humanity	inhumanity (c.f. Nuremburg trials)
beauty	ugliness

I think that these alternatives are universally abhorrent. These alternatives could at best constitute goals or purposes of man. They are obviously goals and purposes that have frequently overridden pursuit of ideals. That is not the problem to which we have been addressing ourselves, here.

I suspect that this diversion relates to an increasing concern on our part, that the values and countervalues of previous societies (and not just industrial society) have been premissed on man as a subordinate part of his enduring social institutions. I believe that the social forces that are introducing the modern turbulent social field make it possible and necessary to state a different set of assumptions about the ideals that will move people and, also, about the way people pursue ideals.

Specifically I postulate that:

1. _Only individuals can be ideal seeking systems._ By implication, the institutions or organisations that men have created can be, at best, purposeful systems, no matter how old and sacrosanct they may be. They can purposefully act to create conditions under which more of their members can, on more issues, be ideal seeking systems. They cannot, except as a deciet for dominance, even claim that they are the ideal seeking system. Ackoff and Emery put this forward almost as an axiom (1972, Chapter 13).

As an axiom its proof could lie only in the resultant organisational geometry. The movement towards participative management would seem to be some such proof. At the level of ideals and values Tomkins puts a clear viewpoint. Analysing what an individual can do, and what an 'organised individual' can will to do, he observes that:

'Indeed all normative theories of value derogate not only positive affect but human beings as such, insofar as they fail to embody in their behaviour those norms which are postulated to be prior to, more real than and more valuable than the human being, who, it is asserted, must be governed by such norms if he is to become good' (1963, vol. 2, p. 265).

2. _Individuals can sustain the ideal seeking state only temporarily._ As I have defined it the pursuit of the ideal is a pursuit of the infinite, and unattainable. For the individual this could produce only informational overload and nervous breakdown if he remained focussed on ideals, the choice of purposes. What does seem to be empirically established is that men can support each other to be ideal seeking. Thus the ideal of nurturance seems to be central to individuals being able to sustain the pursuit of ideals.

3. *It is only within group life that ideals emerge.* It seems inconceivable to me that ideals could be relevant, much less emerge in a true Robinson Crusoe setting. Our proposition does enable us to explicate the relation between individuals as ideal seekers and organisations. The 'relevant uncertainties' of the social fields created by interlocking purposes and goals is the prod to the emergence of values and ideals. There is no way in which the turbulence produced for man by *nature* can be mitigated by evolving ideals shared by man and nature alone. Man's only response to naturally induced turbulence is to look to his own defences and perhaps practice magic. However, group life not only prods man in the search for ideals but provides more or less fertile soil for the sustained pursuit of ideals. Some historical 'soils' have clearly been sterile. Dodds in his study *The Greeks and the Irrational,* notes how the third century B.C. Greek society so closely approached 'open society' in which conscious and deliberate choices were being made between alternative purposes (p. 237). And yet, 'when the masses were seized with fears of turbulent 'astral determination' ' (p. 252) the retreat began. Writing in 1950 Dodds thought that the same prospect now confronted the emerging hopes of Western society. His final reflection was 'that once before a civilized people rode to this jump: rode to it and refused it' (p. 254).

He expressed his belief that it was the horse, the irrational, that refused the jump, not the rider. Like me he feels that this time we may better understand the horse.

4. *No ideal can be pursued singlemindedly without sacrifice of the others.* This is obvious, if considered simply as a matter of allocating resources. But I deliberately use the term sacrifice, not 'hindrance' or 'neglect'. I am trying to make a much stronger point, namely that singleminded pursuit of the ideal of nurturance (not breast feeding but nurturance of one's own and others' ability to choose between purposes) is likely to lead in other choices to inhumanity, autonomy (in the sense of man against or over man) and ugliness. Similarly with singleminded pursuit of any other ideal. Hence the need for and the relevance of the meta-ideal omnipotence, or what Marx called '*man's historic struggle for freedom*'. The need to harmonise in the pursuit of ideals seems inherent in the active adaption to turbulent social fields.

5. *Deciding on what sacrifices of other ideals should be made in any particular choice between purposes is of the essence of wisdom.* In other words
wisdom is a function of the totality of an ideal seeking system. It is not
simply a more elevated form of 'understanding'. It is not simply a matter
of seeing further into the future, like a soothsayer. It cannot be a special
property of some ideal seeking system concerned primarily with one
ideal; nor can one expect it to be easier to find in any organisation concerned with supporting the pursuit of a single ideal, *e.g.* amongst Nobel
Prize winners or the Academy of Arts. This last point is not irrelevant as
people do seek new leadership to accomplish new tasks.

I have tried to identify the ideas that men are likely to pursue as they
seek to strugle through current turbulence to something that might be
termed the 'open society' (Dodds, Popper). In doing this I have noted
that the ideals are most probably something beyond the self-referring
ideals postulated by Trist or the traditional Western ideals postulated by
Ackoff and myself. Lastly, I have predicted that in actively adapting to
current social turbulence men will overcome the myth of organisations
and institutions being themselves ideal seeking systems, value givers
(ceteris paribus re physical turbulence). They will increasingly treat their
organisations as special environments, habitats, whose purposes are no
more than to support, nurture and protect the efforts of individuals to
imagine and aspire to the unattainable. They will reject the kind of organizational arrogance that Koestler dissected in *Darkness at Noon*. In
freeing themselves of guilt laden organisational norms, men will not be
moving simply to 'the permissive society' or 'the Sensate Society' (Kahn's
prediction). While they will not be preoccupied with the sinfulness of
pleasure there is still, as Angyal shows, a conscience associated with the
ideal of homonomy.

It has taken me some time to come to the final point but I think that, in
our present social turbulence, institutions like the universities, the courts
and the churches deceive themselves if they insist that they are the true
bearers of ideals. They may or may not be institutions that offer particularly favourable habitats for ideal seeking individuals. However, so long
as they insist on this deceit they denigrate the status of man. In practical
terms they offer their institutional rewards to those who are most dedi-

cated to serving the institution, not to the ideal seeking. Traditional sets of institutional values are given much lip service but their function is to mould institutional conformity; they are not organically rooted in the ideals the institutions purport to carry. The institutions themselves reveal this deceit by demonstrating repeatedly in their histories that there is no ideal for which they would sacrifice their survival. It seems almost too much to expect them to do other than treat as heresies the sort of transformation of ideals that I have outlined above.

4.2. A theoretical note on the parameters of choice (and hence decision making)

This note starts from a development in the theory of decision making advanced by Ackoff and myself in 1972. The effect of the development is to close the circle between the work we did on organised systems and the work that had been done on systems of environments. The latter part of this note traces through some of the consequences of these for the theory of ideal seeking systems.

Observation of choice behaviour has given a great deal of credence to the four parameters of choice outlined in *On purposeful systems* (Ackoff and Emery, 1972). A disturbing feature about this postulation has been the absence of a reason as why there are just these four parameters. Could we not, on the past history of studies of choice behaviour, expect yet another necessary parameter to be identified? Or two, or three others? (*e.g.* Jordan's 'law of minimum certainty', 1968, p. 133).

This possibility becomes even more disturbing when we derive a limited set of human ideals from the earlier postulation of a limited set of parameters of choice. The derived set of ideals could be disarrayed if an additional parameter of choice subsequently appeared to be necessary.

However, there does seem to be a theoretical justification for four parameters of choice; and just these four. This justification lies in the proposition discussed in chapter I:

'a comprehensive understanding of organizational behaviour requires some general knowledge of each member of the following set, where L indicates some potentially lawful connexion, and the suffix 1 refers to the organization and the suffix 2 to the environment:

$$L_{11}, \quad L_{12}$$
$$L_{21}, \quad L_{22}$$

L_{11} here refers to processes within the organization – the area of internal interdependencies; L_{12} and L_{21} to exchanges between the organization and its environment – the area of transactional interdependencies, from either direction; and L_{22} to processes through which parts of the environment become related to each other (*i.e.* its causal texture) the area of interdependencies that belong within the environment itself' (1969, pp. 242-243).

Choosing is a form of behaviour of an organised system. In fact, it appears to be the distinguishing characteristic of a purposeful system. This being the case, the set L_{11}, L_{12}, L_{21} and L_{22}, represent a complete set of the parameters (conditions) of choice behaviour.

A comprehensive understanding of the choice behaviour of any organised system thus requires some general knowledge of the L_{11} relation. This we have referred to as probability of choice, familiarity (1972). The choice behaviour of a system will depend to some degree on how the parts of the system pull together. There will be an inevitable tendency for the parts to pull together in ways with which they are familiar; certainly to favour ways that preserve the integrity of the system even if they are not the most effective possible ways. In folk terms this is well expressed as 'better the devil one knows'. Instead of interpreting *probability of choice* as 'familiarity' we could have used the stricter but stodgier phrase '*system conservation*'. The influence of this parameter is heightened when the environment is seen as familiar, unchanged.

The L_{12} relation concerns what the system can do in its environment. It refers to what changes it *can effect* in its environment. In our terms (modified after the 1972 publication) this is the parameter of *probable effectiveness*. We used the label '*knowledge*'. This was too narrow. The *can* effect includes *power* to do so, and as Heider points out

'... the power factor is often represented by ability; there are other characteristics of a person that affect his power, temperament for example, but ability is commonly felt to head the list' (1958, p. 83).

There is more to 'can' than this:

'...can refers to the relation between the power or ability of the person and the strength of the environmental forces. The relationship might be further specified as:
   can $= f$ (power, ability, difficulty of environmental factors)' (*ibid*, p. 86).

That is, the reference is clearly to an L_{12} relation.

Probability of outcome, I suggest, is that parameter of choice which encompasses the L_{21} relation. It does not, however, encompass only the L_{21}. In 1972 we postulated that it was a derived member, not a prime member of the set, *i.e.*

   probability of outcome $= f$ (probability of choice, probable effectiveness).

Nevertheless, we stressed that the multiplicative relation generates a qualitatively distinct feature of choice behaviour, namely the level of understanding reflected in that behaviour. When we speak of an intelligent choice or a stupid choice we are referring to this parameter. Now we are able to identify what it is that particularly distinguishes this parameter:

$$\text{probability of outcome} = f \; (\text{probability of choice, } L_{11}, \text{ and probable effectiveness, } L_{12})$$
$$= f \; (L_{21})$$

Thus the parameter of probability of outcome is not just a derived member of the set. It qualifies as a prime member because it, and it alone, draws in the L_{21} relation. It stands in a unique position in the total set because it also *generates* and not just derives from the two parameters of probability of choice and probable effectiveness. Elsewhere I have argued that the L_{21} relation encompasses what we call learning *i.e.* learning about the L_{22}. This learning is at the base of the generative influence of the effect of changes in probability of outcome on the other two parameters.

   The interpretation I am placing on the parameter, probability of outcome, is explicated by Heider's analysis of 'conditions of outcome':

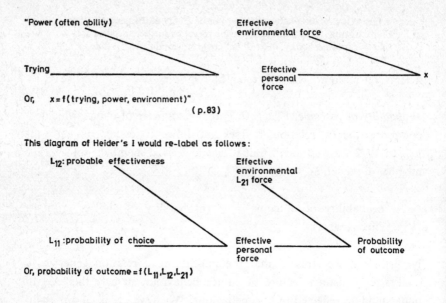

"Power (often ability)   Effective
                                                   environmental force

Trying_____   Effective_____x
                                                   personal
                                                   force

Or,   x = f (trying, power, environment)"
                                      (p.83)

This diagram of Heider's I would re-label as follows:

L_{12}: probable effectiveness   Effective
                                                   environmental
                                                   L_{21} force

L_{11} : probability of choice_____   Effective_____Probability
                                                   personal   of outcome
                                                   force

Or, probability of outcome = f (L_{11}, L_{12}, L_{21})

It should be noted that the environment as it enters into the determination of L_{12} (probable effectiveness) is a body of barriers and frustrations. It is a view of the environment through a tunnel. In L_{22} we are dealing with a panoramic view of the environment; a view of the environment as a source of valences, positive or negative.

The parameter of *relative intention* appears to be that which maps the L_{22} relation. It reflects, first and foremost, the array of valences, goals and noxiants, in the environment. The strength of intention with respect to any objective will be relative to the perception of what is possible. What one thinks *can* be achieved, what is worth *trying* to achieve and what one thinks is probably achievable are dependent on what is seen to be possible.

It is easy to assume that the parameter of relative intention simply maps what psychology has designed as 'motivation'. Tomkins has already argued that motivation is not a unitary concept and must include at least 'needs' and 'affects'. It would argue that any identifiable parameter of choice must have implications for the motivation of people to choose, to choose this rather than that course of action.

Summary

What has been written above may be summarized as follows:

Parameters of choice	Interpretative labels	Open system parameters
a. Probability of choice	Familiarity	L_{11}
b. Probable effectiveness	Knowledge	L_{12}
c. Probability of outcome $= f(a, b)$	Understanding	$f(L_{11}, L_{12}, L_{21})$
d. Relative value	Intention	L_{22}

I started off to show that there was a theoretical reason for finding only four parameters of choice behaviour. I think I have demonstrated that the parameters of choice behaviour map the parameters of an open system. There could be neither more nor less parameters. The mapping appears to be accurate. Further light is thrown on probability of outcome.

4.2.1. Ideals and the parameters of choice

From the above it seems clear that there is no prospect of the theory of the ideal set being thrown into disarray by discovery of new parameters of choice behaviour. More than that, the improved theoretical clarity of the postulated parameters may enable me to throw more light on that set of ideals.

The ideal of *humanity* was associated with man's inevitable striving to improve the probability of outcome in his choice behaviour. We have seen that this ideal cannot be interpreted as simply a joint function of man's pursuit of homonomy (probability of choice) and nurturance (probable effectiveness). If that were so, then the ideal of Humanity could be approached by a combination of males bonded in brotherhood and men, women and children bound in nurturance. This sub-set of ideals could find its accomplishment in a Mafia (*e.g.* the novel 'The Godfather'). As now defined, the ideal of humanity introduces an element, the L_{21} relation, which is absent from either of the ideals of homonomy or nurturance. Pursuit of the ideal requires also 'some general knowledge' of what the world is doing to man, the L_{21}. Ability to pursue this ideal is built up from pursuit of purposes that increase learning and understanding; not just the exercise of already attained knowledge as in the L_{12} relation.

If we examine the ideal of *nurturance* we can see how much easier it is to derive this from the concept of the L_{12} relation than from the label of 'knowledge' that we had previously placed on the parameter of probable effectiveness. (As a label 'knowledge', like the other labels of 'familiarity' and 'understanding'; was a best guess at a pointer to the referent of the formal parameters.) L_{12} refers unambiguously to the actions of a purposeful system out into and onto its environment. The environment is a co-producer of the outcomes of behaviour and hence the ideal to which men will strive is to act so as to achieve not only their immediate objectives but to develop, nurture, an environment that is a more beneficial co-producer. The environment to be nurtured is not only that of other human beings but also the wider biological and physical environment.[2]

This is a far cry from the notion of using our accumulated scientific knowledge and know-how to shape the environment to our immediate purposes.

Deriving the ideal of *homonomy* from L_{11} relation also gives us a firmer grip on its referent.[3] The concept of homonomy, which was so central to the published work of Angyal, has been notoriously slippery to grasp. He presented the concept in 1941. For his second book, in 1965, Angyal reworked the chapter on homonomy completely, feeling that his earlier formulations had failed to convey the full meaning of his concept' (Editor's note, p. 15). Even Fritz Heider, for all of his unusual depth of

2. That we should 'do unto others...' is an ideal that has been long espoused. That an ideal of nurturance with respect to the environment is an ideal in the Judeo-Christian tradition has been challenged. However, Jurgen Mollmann, Professor of Dogmatic Theology, University of Tubingen argues that it was part of that tradition until the recent centuries of the capitalist economies. In the earlier tradition true believers were enjoined to nurture the environment as part of God's creation.

3. In the original formulation we labelled this parameter of choice, 'ideal of Plenty'. The pursuit of plenty has certainly been a pervasive and persistent purpose of man but, as he envisages the real possibility of achieving plenty, it becomes obvious that it is no ideal. 'Possession and procurement of the necessities of life are the prerequisite, rather than the content, of a free society' (Marcuse, 1956, p. 195). In this release from repressive labour Freud and Jung saw a threat to the whole structure of a civilisation necessarily based on sublimation. I see instead a transformation from striving after pseudo ideals to striving after ideals that are deeply rooted in the nature of man.

perception of human affairs, could pass homonomy off as 'to be in accord with forces from the outside which impinge upon the person' (p. 239) 'a trend to fuse and be in harmony with superindividual units...' (p. 239) This would hardly distinguish homonomy from conformity and gregariousness. In the same context, however, Heider also tries to convey about the notion of homonomy that 'p (the individual) can be part of superindividual social wholes only if other people participate' (p. 241). I think that the identification of homonomy with the L_{11} relation removes any such ambiguity. In this context homonomy is clearly the *relation of part-to-part within a whole*. Certainly it includes love as the homonomous relation of part-to-part. Certainly it includes some element of conformity as the relation of part-to-part. However, homonomy is not simply the relation of part-to-part nor part-to-whole; it is the relation of part-to-part within a whole. That is, it is an L_{11} relation. Against this background the purposive pursuit of love or conformity are not necessarily ideal seeking. They may be.

It was earlier proposed that the ideal of *beauty* is that ideal which flows on from man's concern with the relative value of his intentions in any choice situation, *i.e.* what does it mean to him whether he makes a better choice or not.

Now I wish to go further and suggest that both 'relative value of intention' and Beauty refer to the L_{22} relation. If we ask what it is about the L_{22} relation that entices an ideal seeking system to enlarge its desires and to finding its succeeding intentions of even greater value, then the most adequate answer lies in man's pursuit of Beauty. As I quoted Caudwell earlier:

'Whenever the affective elements in socially known things show social ordering, *there we have beauty, there alone we have beauty*. The business of such ordering is art, and this applies to all socially known things, to houses, gestures, narratives, descriptions, lessons, songs and labour' (1949, p. 106).

The ordering that people seek as beautiful is not just the degree of ordering that George Birkoff sought in his aesthetic measure. This is necessary to beauty but not sufficient. The ordering must be a tense ordering of articulated shapes that conveys to man not a state of quiescence, but a sense of dynamic equilibrium with the world and a sense that he and his other ideal strivings belong in that world. As Arnheim says of man's art:

'...art is not meant to stop the stream of life. Within a narrow span of duration and space the work of art concentrates a view of the human condition; and sometimes it marks the steps of progression, just as a man climbing the dark stairs of a medieval tower assures himself by the changing sights glimpsed through its narrow windows that he is getting somewhere after all' (1971, p. 56).

It should be clear that this kind of ordering is not just social ordering. Man responds as well to the beauty of nature and, insofar as he is ideal seeking, he seeks to avoid the degradation of that which he sees as beautiful. We would not expect man to pursue ideals that were not deeply rooted in man's nature, and not critical to his evolution. Discussion of beauty is so rarely undertaken in this context that some people might think it strange to find it in bed with such obvious survival oriented values as nurturance, homonomy and humanity. Sommerhoff has suggested a clear answer to such doubts. He suggests that tense orderings of articulated shapes that seem beautiful to us,

'always conveys the immediate impression that it is a whole in which a number of perceived parts occupy purposefully assigned positions and have purposively assigned formal relations' (1950, p. 192).

Arnheim (1969), provides an exhaustive treatment of this proposition. In the contemplation of beauty there is purposiveness without any particular purpose (Kant). As to why man should have evolved such an instinctive attraction to beauty, Sommerhoff suggests that:

'...such an instinctive desire is part of a general psychological mechanism whose function is to lead the individual to the most organic part of the environment, or rather to those parts in which there exist the greatest concentration of directive correlations and which offer, therefore, the greatest opportunity for the coming into existence of higher levels of organic integration between him and the environment' (*Ibid*, p. 193).

Coming back to my original postulation I would reaffirm that beauty is the ideal most opposite to man's strivings with respect to the L_{22}, and as such is a necessary member of the set of ideals.

Summary

Providing a theoretical basis for the parameters of choice behaviour has enabled a sharpening of our conception of human ideals. A revision has not been necessary but, by now knowing where to look for answers, it has been possible to put those conceptions on a firmer base and search out further implications. Thus the revision can leave us in no doubt but that 'No ideal can be pursued singlemindedly without sacrifice of the others'. To be obsessed with for instance, the L_{22} at the expense of the L_{12}, *etc.*, would lead to nonadaptive choice of purposes.

The image of closing the conceptual circle can be graphically depicted as follows:

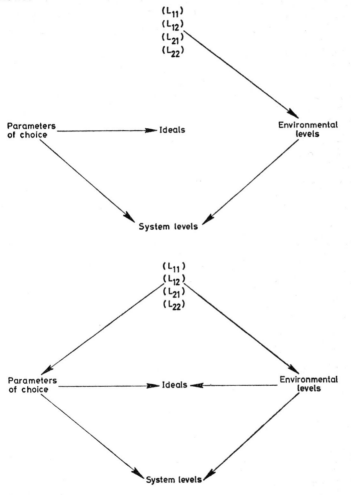

4.2.2. Choice environment and ideals

This seems to be an appropriate point at which to enter into some speculations about where further search might be fruitful.

Whilst the four parameters of choice define the necessary and sufficient conditions of any choice, not all have the same practical relevance or salience in every situation. Thus a government department or an individual may be so cosseted from the outside world that 'some general knowledge about the L_{22}' is pretty irrelevant. Following through on this idea for its implications for the levels of learning and planning required to adapt to different levels of environmental ordering led to the following paradigm (Emery, 1972, 1973):

Table 4.2.2.1. Environmental levels and salience of parameters of choice.

Environmental levels	Salience of parameters of choice	Forms of learning (L_{21})	Forms of planning (L_{12})
1. Randomized	L_{11}	Conditioning	Tactics
2. Clustered	L_{11}, L_{12}	Meaningful	Tactics-strategies
3. Disturbed, reactive	L_{11}, L_{12}, L_{21}	Problem solving	Tactics-operations-strategies
4. Turbulent	$L_{11}, L_{12}, L_{21}, L_{22}$	Puzzle Solving	Adaptive planning

The righthand side of the table shows that we are probably dealing not only with shifts in relative salience (as shown in column 2) but with transformations in the qualities of the relations as they change in salience, and context.

The distinctions in learning and planning have been so useful that it is tempting to ask whether differences in environments has a similar effect on the relative salience and qualitative interpretation of ideals. I am prepared to yield to this temptation. Table 4.2.2.2 is a first guess.

Table 4.2.2.2. Environmental levels and salience of ideals.

Level of environment	Salient parameters of choice	Salient ideals
1 Random	L_{11}	Homonomy
2 Clustered	L_{11}, L_{12}	Homonomy, nurturance
3 Disturbed, reactive	L_{11}, L_{12}, L_{21}	Homonomy, nurturance, humanity
4 Turbulent	$L_{11}, L_{21}, L_{2,1}, L_{22}$	Homonomy, nurturance, humanity, beauty

This is what the theoretical structure suggests. What could it mean? First it should be noted that the type 1, randomized environment is a theoretical limiting state (Toda, 1962). Under rather special circumstances the human condition approximates this, but it is highly doubtful that the course of human evolution started from less than a type 2, clustered environment. However, in the type 1 environment, we would expect from this table that homonomy would be the salient ideal, insofar as ideal seeking was present. This is not to say that the other ideals are completely absent, never pursued.

At the other extreme the type 4 turbulent environment, the implication seems to be that pursuit of beauty must take its place with the other ideals if choice of purposes is to be adaptive. The pursuit of beauty would no longer be the concern of just the social elites. This may be manifested in the current widespread concern for conservation of nature and that 'black is beautiful', 'small is beautiful'.

4.3. The embodiment of ideals

I have tried to identify the values and ideals, that men will most probably pursue. I have assumed that if they desire to pursue these ideals they will find ways of doing so. Now I will drop this assumption and examine 'How do these ideals actually enter into and shape the life of the individual?' and 'How do these ideals enter into and shape the organisations that men create'? If we had to find separate answers to these two questions the task could be rather forbidding. Individuals live their lives in schools, families, communities, work places, associations, *etc.* Organisations operate in public and private sectors, banking, mining, education, fabrication, *etc.* In other words a large number of disparate worlds each of which might seem to require a different set of answers. Given the nature of ideals I have formulated, I do not think this is the case. The two questions can be answered, for the interim, by a single strategy.

4.3.1. Two basic organisational designs

In choosing their organisational designs people do not confront an infinite range of choice. Far from it. If their organisations are to be purposive they have to be adaptive over a wide range of evolving circumstances. The alternative is some sort of servomechanism with a fixed repertoire of responses and capable of surviving only within a very narrow range of foreseeable conditions. To achieve this adaptiveness redundancy has to be built into the system. This is an important property as with each arithmetic increase in redundancy the reliability of the system tends to increase exponentially (Pierce, 1974).

There are two basic ways that redundancy can be built in:

1. by adding redundant parts to the system; each part is replaceable; as and when one part fails another takes over;
2. by adding redundant functions to the parts; at any one time some of the functions of any part will be redundant to the role it is playing at the time; as and when a part fails in the function it is performing, other parts can assume the function; so long as a part retains any of its functional capabilities (*i.e.* functional relative to system requirements), it is of some value to the system.

The first design of redundant parts has been described by Mumford as the *Megamachine* and he has traced its long Asian history and more recent Western debut (Mumford, 1967). Feibleman and Friend characterized the logical properties of the first design as *subjective seriality*, in which 'The governing relation is *asymmetrical* dependence. The sharing of parts is necessary to one of the parts but not to both' (1945, p. 36). The second design is characterized by them as *complementary seriality*, in which 'The governing relation is *symmetrical* dependence. The sharing of parts is necessary to both of the parts. Neither part can survive separation' (p. 36), '...parts are on a parity with respect to their relations with other parts, and each is dependent upon the other' (p. 38). It is of interest that their analysis of *The structure and function of organisation* revealed no more than just these two basic designs at the level of purposeful systems.

If redundancy is sought by having redundant parts then there must be special control mechanisms (specialised parts) to determine which parts are failing and have to be rendered redundant, and which have to be activated for any particular response to be adaptive. If the control is to be reliable it too must have redundant parts and hence the question of a yet another level of control emerges. The more difficult it becomes to determine the failure of dependent parts in time to make adaptive replacements the more the levels of control tend to proliferate (compare the many levels of control to be found in an army or an oil refinery with the few that are found necessary in a car assembly plant).

One can expect a bias toward choosing the first design if:

1. the costs of the individual parts are cheap; and
2. there are long lead times available for the organization to learn new modes of response.

Certainly, once this first basic design is chosen, efforts will be made to keep down the cost of the individual part by sustaining a pool of unemployed, obtaining access to, pools of poor and preferably dispossessed peasantry (*e.g.* the 'Gastarbeiter' of Germany and Australia's post-war migration scheme), or specializing and standardizing the function of the individual parts to minimise costs of training and retraining (Taylorism).

Regarding the second source of bias toward the Megamachine it is worth starting our considerations from the often made observation that this is a great way to run a railway or an army:

'There are irrefutable advantages to this kind of organisation. Discipline is good, errors in routine procedures rarely go unchecked, and if the very top man is an exceedingly able executive he can usually make the whole organisation jump to his command very quickly. It usually takes a long time to build, and it is at its most successful when the function of the organisation is to control a very large number of people all doing more or less the same thing. It is the way most armies are organised – platoon, company, battalion, brigade, division, corps, army – and if you want to make a million men advance or retreat at a few hours notice it is hard to think of a better system' (Jay, 1967, p. 73).

Armies fight for short periods of their life under conditions of great uncertainty, great turbulence. Hence it is hard to reconcile Jay's enthusiasm for organising armies in this way with the contention that they are only adaptive when allowed 'long lead times for learning'. It is also hard to reconcile with the organisational logic that underlies this contention, that *this type of system is inherently error-amplifying*. The governing principle of asymmetrical dependence means that errors will leak in from the environment like water from a sieve. It is in no one's interest to have himself rendered redundant because an error, of failure, can be associated with him. Even without that psychological weakness the relation of asymmetrical dependence will ensure that the flow upwards of information from one level of control to the next will take the form of

$$T = (1\text{-}F)^n.$$

If a manager had five good people reporting to him, people who were truthful (T) eight times out of ten, *i.e.*

$$T = (1.0\text{-}0.2)^5,$$

then there would be, on average, only one in three occasions that he could say to himself that this must be sound advice because they are unanimous. However, the same principle applies at all levels. If he and four others at the same level as himself have been well chosen, and hence are right nine times out of ten, then the chances of their superior getting such a good straight message coming up through them from the level below are, on the same arithmetic, 0.002, twice in a thousand such communications! (Stafford Beer, 1972). This very disturbing property of error-amplification arises in a system based on asymmetrical dependence because each manager must seek to maintain the asymmetrical dependence of his subordinates on him. Hence he will seek to ensure that each of his subordinates gives him their *independent* judgement and that they cannot go into collusion to influence his decision. But the mathematics of this are inexorable. The more he achieves this aim of controlling his subordinates the deeper he gets into error; even if the subordinates are not psychologically motivated to protect themselves by hiding their errors.

Given this inherent weakness a major part of the effort of utilising cheap dependent labour by this first design has gone into control systems that will minimise the weakness. Thus Jay, in the above quote, says that in these types of organisations discipline is usually good. I suggest that in these types of organisations one usually finds good discipline, not because they naturally create good discipline, but because they cannot function without imposing good discipline. That they cannot function unless their individual parts are not only replaceable, but are also so threatened by punishment or withdrawal of rewards; that they will be-have in a preprogrammed manner regardless of the evidence of their senses or their common sense. Lewis Mumford has documented the vicious practices of torture and maiming that were introduced with the earliest emergence of the Megamachine. Poet-laureate Masefield has documented the inhuman disciplinary practices of the Royal Navy up till the age of steam. Taylor and his contemporaries simply devised new sticks and carrots so that this organisational design could function within societies like the U.S.A., where the Constitution forebade 'cruel and in-human punishment'. There was no change in the aim. The aim remained that of blocking the holes of the sieve, preventing error getting into the system. By elaborate pre-programming of the parts at the work face, and of the control systems, expected contingencies could be met and failure of a part quickly identified. As Jay observed, such an organisation 'usually takes a long time to build'. Standard operating procedures, rules, and regulations and training manuals have to be multiplied to meet the ever newly emerging contingencies. They can rarely be wiped off the book because there can rarely be agreement in the control agencies that those contingencies might not occur again. New contingencies are slow to be recognized in S.O.P.'s because it is never too certain whether they are inventions of subordinates trying to cover up mistakes that might lead to their redundancy.

I can now summarise the learning properties of an organisational design based on redundant parts. There is an optimal amount of error that is necessary for learning by any type of system. The error amplifying characteristic of this type of system threatens to swamp it with so much error that it is reduced to the response strategy of an addictive gambler (or a cat in a Thorndike puzzle box), *i.e.* stick rigidly to a system, right or wrong. The major active response to error is to prevent it getting into the system, even those errors that are necessary for learning; and to eliminate or send to limbo any part that appears to be associated with the intake of error or its perpetuation. With this sort of learning where is the adaptive-ness?

Jay is undoubtedly correct in stating that with this sort of system it is hard to think of a better one 'if you want to make a million men advance or retreat at a few hours notice'. It is possible, with months of work, to pre-programme so many to start to advance or to start to retreat within hours of the starter's gun. Adaptive control, however, more or less finishes after that point, unless one has pre-programmed reserve forces to be fed into the subsequent action. Field Marshal Haig released a vast pre-programmed army across the front at the Somme at 7.30 a.m., July 1st, 1916. At 3.00 p.m. that day he had precious little idea of where his many divisions were or what they were doing, although none of them had gone more than a mile or so from where they were at dawn. They had disappeared into the fog of war. This sort of information flow hardly augures well for adaptability. When the Passchendaele offensive opened on July 31st, 1917 there was little evidence that learning had occurred in the previous year. As I said earlier this type of organisation needs a long lead time for learning. So long, indeed, that Liddell-Hart said that armies normally prepare themselves to fight their last war.

The criterion of survival can be somewhat misleading in circumstances where the competing parties are all organised on the first design principle. The big battalions win the wars but lose the peace, because of the price they pay for victory.

It should be clear by now that choice of the design principle of redundant parts predetermines the ideals that such a society will pursue. Man will be set against man in the asymmetrical master-servant relation to ensure that their collectivised labour will produce *Plenty* in the form of pyramids, skyscrapers or other such indicators of the greatness of their masters. Better ways to ensure increased productivity will evolve and when evolved, be widely adopted. But increasingly people will doubt whether these means of increasing plenty are reconcilable with the quality of human life.[4] *Truth* will be a precious commodity in an environment where it decays so quickly in transmission up to the key decision makers. Every effort will be made to arrive at better ways to establish the truth and to disseminate such methods when they emerge. The good will be an ideal of high standing, as befits an ideal. Science becomes the new fountain of wisdom and becomes increasingly mistrusted in societies based on

4. These three criteria for identifying an ideal are taken from Churchman and Ackoff, (1947).

this first design principle. The concept of the 'good samaritan' evolves into the Welfare State. Good deeds are increasingly done by numbers, and the poor, deserving or not, wonder whether they are not just replaceable ciphers in a code that they cannot break.

The ideal of *Beauty*, an ideal that should move all people, suffers a particularly cruel fate in systems designed on this principle. The ideal becomes embodied in that which is biggest, whitest and most durable, and capable of demolition tomorrow. The criteria of beauty, and that which attracts patronage, are grandeur and being esoteric. Both place beauty beyond what might be aspired to by a servant in a system based on master servant relations, *i.e.* subjective seriality. The alternative design based on redundant functions (multi-functional parts) has been the favoured design in the Western cultural tradition, if not always in practice. It also appears to have been the general preference in human societies up to the point where swidden agricultural gave way to societies based primarily on sedentary cultivation and the use of metals.

The basic conditions favouring the alternative design are, to rephrase the earlier statement (p. 93):

1. the individual parts are costly (*e.g.* well educated or skilled) or highly valued;
2. adaptation has to be to a highly variable, complexly intercorrelated environment, *i.e.* one in which a great deal of potential error is present and it is not randomised.

In contrast to the first design this one is essentially *error attenuating*. The system by its own functioning tends to suppress errors that come into the system. The formula given by Beer is

$$T = (1\text{-}F^n)$$

Thus, if as in the first example a manager has five people reporting to him who are each usually right in their judgement eight times out of ten, then

$$T = (1.0\text{-}(0.2)^5)$$

Only about three times in 10,000 will they unamimously give him the wrong advice. The relation of symmetrical dependence means that they will check with each other as to the quality of the advice they were thinking of giving. We have assumed that they are no better as individual managers than those in the first example, and no better than each other. Each is assumed falable in two occasions out of ten. They will not, however, be falable in the same ways, and hence, working to this second design, they assist to suppress each others tendency to err.

With this quality a great deal of error can be accepted into the system and learnt from. Rigid barriers of standing operating procedures and manuals do not have to be defensively manned as in the first design. Error is coped with by continuous learning and rearrangement of functions; not by prescription and rearrangement of parts. In this system advantage can be taken of the principle that the total sum of error in the system is equivalent to the square root of the sum of the square of the errors of each part. Attention can be directed to the weakest link, as this principle requires, and not to the specialised controlling parts as required in the first system. A further distinction between the two designs arises when the sources of error in the environment are to some extent correlated, *i.e.* 'it never rains but it pours'. The first design is at its best when the sources of error are independent, and only randomly occur together. Where this is not naturally the case, special efforts are devoted to approximate this condition, *e.g.* keeping external relations in special compartments, and being very secretive about what is going on in those compartments. The second design learns better to adapt by exposing itself to the difficulties that arise for itself from these external interdependencies.

A striking difference between the two systems occurs in the switching mechanisms. In the first design the critical decision is switching some parts to redundancy and activating others. The individual parts are probably not keen to be rendered redundant and not even very enthusiastic about being activated. These decisions are for the special control parts, and it is pretty irrelevant to their function whether the parts know *why* they are switched. In fact, anything that psychologically separates the special control parts off from the others would help to ensure that proper decision rules are followed, and are not obfuscated by *merely* human considerations. In the second design, with its governing principle of symmetrical dependency, the switching is governed by the conditions of mutual help. The problem is that all parts, or enough parts, need to be alert and willing to bring their unused capabilities into action when the shared task demands it. *Without considerable sharing of values and objectives, the potential of this design may not be realised*, which may be one reason why Taylor turned to revamping the first design for the utilisation of the multi-national work force pouring into U.S. industry in his days.

One other property of these systems was noted by Feibleman and Friend, and has frequently been observed. Organisations based on redundancy of parts constantly strive to accumulate a superfluity of parts; to ensure that at any one time they have more parts than they actually need for what they are doing. These reserves of duplicated parts are essential to ordinary day-to-day operation, and the major insurance against the unexpected. This superfluity of manning is sought at all levels except the very top. By contrast organisations based on redundancy of functions (capabilities) find their optimal level at a point where undermanning stretches their joint resources, and challenges them to frequently reallocate functions.

In choosing this second design for their organisations, people are implicitly making choices amongst ideals. For homonomy rather than self-seeking, self-serving autonomous strivings; for mutual help and nurturance rather than own survival in the system; for inclusion of the criteria of humaneness along with the usual decision rules of effectiveness and efficiency. It may be difficult to grasp, but the emergence of a rich complex field of directive correlations within such organisations would even make them seem to be more beautiful settings to be in.[5]

I do not think that man can hope to actively adapt to turbulent environments without restructuring his major institutions along the lines of the second design principle, redundancy of the functions of individual parts. As noted above, bureaucracies are based on the first principle and the

5. In *Logic of the living brain* (1972), Sommerhoff tried to identify models that would explain the uniquely adaptive characteristics of that organ, and still do justice to the knowledge we have of its structure and functioning. He was led to reject the design based on redundant parts and to postulate two variants based on redundant functions. These two variants closely parallel the two discussed by Emery and Emery (1973).

individual is an instrument of the system. *An instrument functions as a lower order of system than the system that uses it* (Ackoff and Emery, 1972, pp. 31-32). Quite simply, using an analogy from mathematical statistics, an instrument is always going to operate with one degree of freedom less than the system using it. Thus, although a social system is a purposeful system whose members are purposeful, there is a constant tendency towards *increasing* or *decreasing variety* in the range and level of the behaviour of the individual members. In systems based on the first principle the tendency will be towards *variety decreasing*; the range of purposeful behaviour will be restricted and increasingly behaviour will be at a lower level of multi-goal seeking or goal seeking behaviour. The assembly line has been the epitome of this process but the same phenomenon appears in the bureaucratic organisation of even scientific and engineering work (Burns and Stalker, 1961).

Systems designed on the second principle will tend to be *variety increasing*: to maintain and extend the multi-functionality of their members they will seek to extend the range of their purposeful behaviour and increase the opportunities and support for ideal seeking behaviour. That is, such systems will be founded on the assumption that they are best served by serving as an instrument to the potentially higher system capabilities of their individual members.

4.3.2. Democratisation of work

As put forward in the previous section the choice of organisational design is simply two-fold. In a turbulent environment only the choice of the second principle is potentially adaptive. Only organisations based on this principle can be expected to develop and nurture ideal seeking individuals. Only a sufficiency of ideal seeking individuals can offer people the choice of bringing turbulent social fields under control (Winnicott, 1950).

Work, and the organisation of people about work, is the 'leading part' of Western societies. What happens at work tends to determine what can and does happen in the areas of family life, education, leisure, *etc.* This is not to deny that these other areas of living have their own history and their own self-determining characteristics.

Bureaucratisation of work in Western society has been a major contribution to the present social turbulence; both in negating Western values and in creating great monolithic organisations whose decisions could set off autochthonous processes in their environments.

It might seem that people could meet part of their present needs by simply debureaucratising their organisations. This is not a viable solution, as is well enough demonstrated by the anemic failure of such movements to change the nature of industrial life as the Human Relations movement of the 40's and 50's and job enrichment of the 60's. The efficiency of an organisation can be only reduced if its various parts or aspects are designed according to contradictory design principles. There must be interfaces between such aspects or parts, and at these interfaces the conflict in principles would undermine coordination. In discussing how the U.S. aerospace industry was forced by environmental pressures toward the second design principle in their R & D work but were, overall, hung-up on the first principle, Kingdon observes:

'Of course these two principles, or organizational purposes, may not always be in accord with each other. In fact, it is more nearly the case that the two are in conflict with one another and that conflict resolution is a necessary part of the matrix organizational form' (1973, p. 18) (see also Burns and Stalker, 1961).

The target that men will increasingly set for themselves is not just debureaucratisation but the positive target of redesigning their work organisations on the second principle, *i.e.* a target of democratising work.

The movement to do just this can be clearly traced from the first experiment in the Bolsover coal mine in 1952 (Trist *et al.*, 1960; Emery, 1973; Davis, 1972) to the publication of the U.S. Department of Health, Education and Welfare report on *Work in America* (O'Toole *et al.*, 1973).

Before examining in detail what is entailed in the notion of democratisation of work let us note two general features.

First, the essential change in the design of work organisations is that the 'building block' is changed from the unit of one man, one job under direct supervisory control, to the semi-autonomous group of peopel carrying responsibility for a unitary task. In this latter type of organisation the interface between the individual and the organisation, no matter how large that is, is the face-to-face group.

The success that has arisen from reorganising work around small, relatively autonomous groups would seem to follow from the shift in instrumentality. When the small social system becomes an instrument for its members there is a tendency for it to become *variety increasing*; they are able to pursue not only production goals but also purposes and even ideals that pertain to themselves; the ideals of homonomy, nurturance, humanity and beauty. This possiblity emerges only when they have the responsibility for managing how they will relate to each other, what responsibilities they will assume to each other.

Second, the starting points of this movement gives some explanation of why I think this will become the dominant trend in Western industry. The first moves wcre in the science based industries, particularly the process industries. The very nature of their technologies challenged the rationality of bureaucratic organisation. Only in the seventies did the assembly line become a key focus. This time it came as a revulsion against the tool-like use of human beings. This general revulsion has already spread to challenge most forms of bureaucratised work, mental as well as manual, professional as well as nonprofessional. The other aspect is that the first and deepest commitments to change came from Scandinavia. I believe that this was easier to start there not only because of the socially advanced nature of Norwegian and Swedish society, but also because they were smallish, culturally homogeneous societies. Their industrialisation had started late and had neither created deep divisive class hatreds nor far removed them from their pre-industrial culture. It is probably only by the example that they have been given, that the other larger countries have felt able to grasp the nettle.

4.3.3. The assembly line: its logic and our future

Nowhere do the issues involved in the democratisation of work come so sharply into focus than in discussion of the future of the assembly line.

The principles of the assembly line seem to be the basis on which Western affluence is built and yet it creates a multitude of inhumane, degrading jobs: jobs that increasingly have to be filled by second-class citizens. The challenge is to achieve the low cost of mass produced goods without creating the human cost. Two facts have led me to choose the automobile assembly line as an example within which to spell out the general principles.

First, Henry Ford's introduction of the continuous flow conveyor to the assembly of automobiles was the epigee of a modern mode of human management. A mode that started to emerge with Frederick Taylor and Gilbreth in the late 19th century. General Motors much publicised fiasco with their Lordstown plant in 1972 seemed to mark the end of that era. Volvo's announcement, within the following months, of their radically new concept for their Kalmar assembly plant seemed to announce the beginning of a new era of human management.

The second set of facts that support the notion of a direct approach is that the logic of human management that was enshrined by the car makers became the logic that was worshipped by practically all other large scale manufacturers. It came to be seen by the forties and fifties as the only *sure* way of manufacturing increasingly complex products at a cost price that could serve a mass market. As the real cost of labour has increased through the 20th century it has been seen as the only *possible* way of creating mass markets, or of meeting the demands these mass markets make for industrial inputs. So, it was not too surprising to find a process industry like I.C.I. (U.K.) as the leading proponent in Britain, in the post war years, of the philosophy of Henry Ford.

What I am suggesting is that the logic of the car assembly line is a keystone, probably *the* keystone, to prevailing 20th century concepts of human management. The logic of production by a continuous flow line was well understood in the early phases of industrialisation. Both Charles Babbage and Karl Marx spelt out this logic. The logic was an 'if X then Y' logic. If a complex production task was broken down into a set of constituent tasks then the level of craft skills required was lowered and hence the cost of labour was lowered. At the extreme a class of unskilled labour emerged to perform the very elementary tasks that practically always remained after a complex task has been broken down to its minimum skill requirements. Such unskilled labourers would have had no part to play in craft production. There is another valuable side of this penny that was not obvious till a much later date. That is, that if one lowers the level of craft skill needed for a product it becomes much easier to swing to production of major variations of that product, *e.g.* from swords to ploughshares. Massive reskilling of craftsmen is not needed.

Once the partition of a task had been successful in reducing the necessary level of craft skills it was only natural that men should seek further partitions leading them into even broader and cheaper labour markets. World War II recently gave a further great stimulus to this approach. The military demanded large scale production of very complex machines when often the only available labour force was that conscripted from outside the traditional industrial work force, *e.g.* women, pensioners and peasants. The lessons flowed over from blue collar work to the organisation of offices. Insurance offices, taxation *etc.*, organised for mass flow production of documents.

However, to realise the economic advantages of task segmentation it was necessary to cope with several sources of cost *inherent* in the method;

1. transfer costs; 2. standardisation; 3. 'balancing'; 4. external coordination and 'pacing'.

1. *Transfer costs.* Individual craft production requires a minimal movement of the object under production. Partitioning of production requires transport of the object between each of the work stations at which someone is performing a different subtask. The costs are those of sheer physical movement and repositioning so that the next operation can be proceeded with, and, also, the costs of 'waiting time' when valuable semi-products are as it were simply in storage. Henry Ford's introduction of conveyor belts to car assembly seemed to be the natural outcome of the attempt to reduce these transport costs. Conveyor chains had already transformed the Chicago slaughter houses. Palletisation and fork lift trucks continue to reduce these costs in assembly areas where continuous belts or chains are not justifiable.

2. *Standardisation.* Partitioning of a production process was simply not an economic proposition unless there was a fair probability that the separately produced parts could be reconstituted to yield a workable version of the final product (it would not have to be as good as the craft produced product if its cost was sufficiently lower). This was obvious enough with the 18th century flow line production of pulley blocks at the Woolwich Naval Arsenal and the early 19th century production of Whitney's muskets. Reduction of this inherent cost has a long history. From Mauds-

ley's slide rest onwards there has been a continuous evolution in specialised tools, machines, jigs and fixtures to enable relatively unskilled labour
to continuously replicate relatively skilled operations to a higher degree of
standardisation. The aim throughout was that expressed by Whitney:

'to form the tools so that the tools themselves shall fashion the work and give to every
part its just proportion – which when once accomplished, will give expedition, uni-
formity and exactness to the whole'.

The most radical developments emerged in the second quarter of this
century with metrology, the sophisticated concept of tolerance levels expressed in statistical quality control, and national standards authorities.
The difficult emergence of this latter revolution in Australian industry is
well documented in Chapter 7 of Mellor's volume of the World War II
History.

3. '*Balancing the line*'. This is a problem that does not arise with the
individual craftsman. Whatever the problems with a given phase of production on a particular lot of raw materials, he can proceed immediately
to the next phase as soon as he is satisfied with what he has done. He
does not have to wait to catch up with himself. When the task is parti-
tioned that is not possible. Each set of workers is skilled, or rather, semi-
skilled, in only its subtask. They are not skilled to help clear any bott-
leneck or make up any shortfall in other parts of the line: they can simply
stand idle and wait. Theoretically there is in a flow line an '*iron law of
proportionality*' such as Marx writes about. Theoretically it should be
like the recipe of a cake; so many hours of this kind of labour, so many
of that kind of labour, *etc.* and hey presto the final product. Unfortunately for the application of the theory it is not as simple as making
cakes.

Balancing the line, to reduce downtime, was an on-the-line art of observation until Taylor and Gilbreth came on to the scene. Their contribution was M.T.M. At last the balancing of a line seemed to be a science.
Controlled observation and measurements seemed to offer a way of
balancing not just the labour requirements of the major segments of a
line but of scientifically planning the work load and skill level of each and
every individual work station. Planning and measuring costs money, but

there has seemed no other way to reduce the downtime losses inherent in the original fractionation of production.

Let us now look briefly at the fourth major source of costs inherent in line assembly. Then we can ask what all this means.

4. *External supervision and 'pacing'*. So long as the individual craftsman produced the whole product, control and coordination of his work on the various sub-tasks was no problem. He managed that himself. With the fractionation of production a special class of work emerged, the work of supervision. Each person on the assembly line has to attend to his own piece of the work and hence someone else must coordinate what is happening at the different work stations, to reallocate work when the line becomes unbalanced, to re-enforce work standards when individual performance drifts away from them. A major headache has been the near universal tendency of workers on fractionated tasks to drift away from planned work times. The selfpacing that enables the craftsman-producer to vary his work pace and yet maintain good targets for overall production times appears to be absent from small fractionated tasks that are repeated endlessly. Tighter supervision and incentive payment schemes seemed appropriate forms of the carrot and stick to replace this element of selfpacing. However the moving line emerged as the major innovation. Once properly manned for a given speed it seemed that this speed had only to be maintained by the supervisors to ensure that planned work times would be maintained. Dawdling at any work station would quickly reveal itself in persons moving off station to try and finish their parts. It is not quite as simple as that as it is possible on some work stations to let unfinished work go down the line with a chance of it not being detected until the product is in the consumers hands. Anyway, the main point was readily learnt. The conveyor was not just a means of lowering transfer costs but also of reducing supervisory costs. At certain tempos the line even gave operators a satisfactory sense of work rhythm; a feeling of being drawn along by the work. Davis' 1966 study even suggests that the contribution to control may often be the main justification of the conveyor.

What I have spelt out is old hat to any production engineer. Nevertheless it prepares the ground for the point of this part.

We have heard a great deal lately about the demise of the automobile assembly line. The new Volvo plant at Kalmar does not even have conveyor belts. The E.E.C. pronounced in 1973 that the assembly line would have to be abolished from the European car industry.

I suggest that the new Kalmar plant does not represent any departure from the basic principles of mass flow line production. In the first place they are still seeking the maximum economic advantages to be gained from fractionation of the overall task. In the second place the plant and its organisation have been designed to reduce the same inherent costs of mass flow production, *i.e.* costs of transfer, standardisation, balancing coordination and pacing. Kalmar is designed as a mass production flow line to produce an economically competitive product. There is no radical departure from the principles of flow line production, only from its practice.

Note, however, that I previously stressed that their aim was 'maximum economic advantage from fractionation' *not* maximum fractionation.

What they have done is to recognise that the costs we have discussed are inherent in production based on fractionated tasks. The further one pushes fractionation the greater these costs become, particularly the costs other than transfer because they are more related to human responsiveness. *The objective of gaining maximum economic advantage from fractionation cannot be the objective of maximum fractionation.* There is some *optimal* level to be sought at a point before the gains are whittled away by rising costs.

Why has this logic been so obvious to the Kalmar designer's and yet appeared to escape other car plant designers? I do not think it is just because M.T.M., quality control, production supervision, designers, *etc.*, operate in separate boxes with their own departmental goals. After all, at the plant design phase there are usually opportunities for the various specialities to come together. I think the reason lies deeper. If we look at the traditional practices in designing a mass flow line we find a critical assumption has slipped in and been re-inforced by the widespread reliance on M.T.M., as a planning tool and as a control tool. This assumption is that it must be possible for each individual worker to be held responsible by an external supervisor for his individual performance. On this assumption M.T.M. goes beyond being a planning tool to determine or re-determine the probable labour requirements of sections of the line. It becomes part of the detailed day-to-day supervisory control over production. Under this impetus fractionation heads down to the L.C.D. (Lowest Common Denominator) of the labour on the line.

The same assumption that a line must be built up from the individually supervised one man-shift unit has gone into the design of algorithms to determine line balance. Ingall (1965) has reviewed ten or so of the major algorithms. They all embody the same assumption. They go further along with M.T.M. to assert that this is a firm organisational building block by assuming that, on average different operators work at the same pace, on average an individual operator works at the same pace throughout a shift, on average cycle time of the operation is irrelevant, on average learning on the job can be ignored, on average variations in parts and equipment can be ignored.

An average is just that, an average. It represents the mean value of a set of different observed states of a system parameter. It does not even tell us whether the exact average state has ever occurred. One thing is pretty sure; at any one time on a line it is most improbable that all aspects are operating at their average value. Typically something is always non-average, wrong, and when one thing is wrong so are half a dozen other things.

The practical problems of balancing a line simply cannot be solved by abstracting this aspect from the total system of potential gains and inherent costs of flow production. As Ingall concludes in his review of assembly line balancing:

'Knowing whether these problems occur together is important because analysing them separately is not sufficient if they do. Using the 'sum' of the results obtained by analysing each problem separately as the procedure for the combined problem can be a dangerous pastime' (1965).

The practical significance of the balancing problem may be gauged from the finding of Kilbridge and Wester (1963) that the U.S. automobile industry wasted about 25 per cent of assembly workers' time through uneven work assignment. No doubt this figure had been reduced at Lordstown, 1972.

I have wandered a little afield because I wished to stress how far this assumption about the individual building block has unquestionably grown into the professional ways of looking at the assembly line. It is this, I suggest, which has prevented others from seeing the obvious logic of the line as did the Kalmar designers. This hidden assumption has, I think, had a further distorting effect on thinking about the line.

Some people in the car industry during the fifties and the sixties became sensitive to the fact that pursuit of maximum fractionation was self-defeating; and they realised it was not at all like the engineering problem of pursuing maximum aircraft speed by reducing friction and drag. They realised it was not a problem to be solved by the grease of yet higher relative pay, by featherbedding or by any of those things that Walter Reuther of the U.S. Automobile Workers' Union bitterly referred to as 'gold plating the sweat-shop'.

The response of these people to these critical insights was to look again at the building block, the one man-shift unit, to see what could be done about that. They did not question whether the individual was the appropriate block for building on.

One proposal to arise from this was to employ on the line only people who were at or very close to the L.C.D. used by M.T.M. and the planners, *i.e.* donkeys for donkey work. This proposal does not look so good now that the international pool of cheap migrant labour dries up. In any case there was little future in this proposal. Provided the line designers pursue the same twisted logic of maximum fractionalisation they would inevitably design around an even lower cheaper common denominator and the other costs would rise again.

The other proposal was to discard the concept of an L.C.D. and accept job enlargement or enrichment up to a point which would come closest to optimal fractionation for a majority of the people on the line. Imposing such enrichment on the minority whose optimal was below this level was an immediately obvious practical flow. A more deep seated flaw was that this job enrichment approach argued from consideration of only one aspect of the system: task fractionation. It did not simultaneously confront the other parameters of the system: balancing, pacing, *etc.*

As I have stressed these parameters constitute a *system* of production. If some people on the line are responsible for only one parameter and someone else has the problem of looking after the other parameters then you have designed in inefficiency and trouble (Ackoff and Emery, 1972, pp. 222-227). No designer in his right senses would design a purely technical system in that way, unless there were a very considerable lagtime between changes on that parameter and changes on the other system parameters. I think I am safe in saying that no such protective time lag exists for the parameter of degree of task fractionation in a mass flow line. If something goes wrong with, for instance, the line balance or pace the operator can very quickly find himself frustrated by a stoppage and consequent break in his rhythm of work, or find himself temporarily slotted into some other strange station on the line.

An organisation like this is basically unstable and rendered even more so when the other party (or parties) looking after the other parameters live in the other more powerful world of management, *i.e.* when communications are subject to the constant distortion of messages going between 'them' and 'us'. Inevitably the supervisors, M.T.M., work programmers, *etc.*, respond to the predictable system problems by pushing for more fractionation and tighter controls.

The instability I am referring to is not that of the technical system of mass flow production. The instability is that of a superimposed organisation which has very different roots in history. This organisational instability has very serious practical consequences. Firstly, it makes it pretty well impossible to enrich individual jobs whether this is done as a programme or slipped in by supervisors who have taken to heart their exposure to courses on human relations in industry. As the pressures build up the screws are back on again. Second, it is not just on the line that the pressures are experienced. As the instabilities cumulate to their recurrent crises on the line all levels of staff are sucked down to coping with deficiencies in performance of the levels below them. Even the plant manager can find himself living by the hour to hour performance of the line. Third, the almost universal experience of these phenomena of instability has created a sustained history, almost an addiction to technical solutions that would design people out of the system, or at least create 'fool-proof' technologies.

It is in looking at the mass-flow production line as a *socio-technical system* that we come to what is really radical about the Kalmar design.

The designers' approached their task with an awareness that the problems of flow line production could be theoretically approached in different organisational designs. At one extreme they literally examined the old cottage industry. More seriously they compared the Norwegian experiences (Thorsrud and Emery, 1969) with the semi-autonomous work group as the building unit as against the traditional individual-shift-work station unit.

The most striking outcome was the discovery that in an appropriately skilled and sized work group, all of the key parameters of mass flow production could come together and be controlled vis-a-vis each other at that level. Picturesquely this was labelled as 'a lot of little factories within a factory'. In terms of how we picture a factory, this the groups are not. Walk around Kalmar and you see nothing that even looks like a lot of little workshops producing their own cars. In system terms, however, it is a very apt description; a very valid design criterion.

This becomes more apparent if we look at the production groups formed at Kalmar. The first effects are rather like those some farmers have gained from cooperation. Individually their resources gave them little or no freedom of movement and they had to ride with a market that was basically out of their control. Collectively they have found new degrees of freedom and they have started to shape their markets to allow even more freedom.

Formation of semi-autonomous groups on the Kalmar assembly line has given them a cycle time and buffers that would be negligible if split up for individual work stations. Split up into individual work stations no one could take an untimed coffee break; grouped up everyone can without increasing overall downtime. On individual work stations everyone has to meet the standard work on that particular job minute by minute. In the group setting variations in individual levels of optimal performance can be met with hour by hour. Those that prefer repetitious simple tasks can get them: those that need to be told what to do will be told by others in the group. Within the range of their task the group can balance their work, without outside assistance. If quality control is amongst the group's responsibilities, and they are given time allowance for this, then it can be within their capabilities. Now we come to the fundamental matter: coordination, control and pacing.[6]

6. Volvo engineers came up with an ingenious technical solution to the transfer problems: the individual self-propelled carriage. This allows the groups to vary the times put into each car whilst maintaining average flow onto the next groups.

If a semi-autonomous work group is not willing to exercise control and coordination over its members then the design of flow lines must go back to the traditional model.

At this point I must rely on experience not theory. The experience, over twenty odd years with a wide range of technologies and societies is simply this: *if reasonably sized groups have accepted a set of production targets and have the resources to pursue it at reasonable reward to themselves they will better achieve those targets than they would if each person was under external supervisory control.* If a theory is required then I think it need be no more than that that is spelt out in the six psychological requirements defined in 1963 (Thorsrud and Emery). In groups that have sufficient autonomy and are sufficiently small to allow face-to-face learning these criteria can be maximally recognised. It has been the realisation of these individual human requirements that has enabled semi-autonomous group working of mass flow lines to do what could not be done by M.T.M. and algorithms for balancing the lines. There is also no economic way in which the individual psychological requirements could be maximally recognised by psychological testing procedures to fit individuals to the individual-shift slots of the M.T.M.-er.

I have suggested that the revolution at Kalmar has not been that of throwing out the assembly line. The revolutionary change began with the eradication of an organisational principle of one man – one shift – one station. A principle that had no intrinsic relation to the design of assembly lines. Further, I have suggested that the pay off in the change began with selecting as the building block a socio-technical unit, an appropriately skilled and sized semi-autonomous group, that had the potential of simultaneously controlling from their own immediate experience the basic set of parameters of gain and cost in the total system.

It might be excusable to expand a little on this last point. Just as in scientific fields one of the most critical strategic break-throughs is discovery of the appropriate 'unit of analysis' so in production systems engineering it is the identification of the basic 'unit of design'. Identifying 'unit operations' was such a classic breakthrough in the tremendously complex problems of chemical engineering. With this in mind the British Social Science Research Council funded an international, interdisciplinary team 'to devise a conceptual scheme for the analysis of men-machine-equipment relations with the more common unit operations' (Emery, 1966). The conclusion of this study was that *the basic unit for design of socio-technical systems must itself be a socio-technical unit*, and, *have the characteristics of an open system*.

'In design terms this represents the lowest level at which it is possible to jointly op- timise the human and technical system with respect to environmental requirements (the overall system inputs and outputs). Failure to recognise this may lead to design decisions being made solely on technical and economic cost criteria with consequent inefficiences due to (a) excess operating costs (b) maintenance difficulties (c) lack of growth in system performance (d) high overheads for control and supervision, or (e) lack of adaptability to market shifts' (*ibid*, pp. 4-5).

Now after nearly ten years of living with this conclusion, I think I am prepared to argue even more strongly for a further conclusion unani- mously arrived at by the study team: namely that the best designs will be those that make the most use of the highest human potentials one could expect to find in any average group of 8 to 10 human beings. My argu- ment is this: firstly there is a basic fact about systems that is simply ducked by the current plethora of so-called systems theoreticians, *i.e.* that 'It is not simply the fact of linkages but rather the principle accor- ding to which all linkages fall together in *one controlling order* which makes an organisation' (Feibleman and Friend, 1945, in Emery, 1969, p. 34). 'Every system has one and only one construction principle... *unitas multiplex*' (Angyal, 1941 in Emery, 1969, p. 28). The overriding principle of the mass flow production lines we are talking about is 'economically productive'. From this I would say that any designer who creates a section which was itself unconcerned about being an 'economic productive' part of the total system would have created a 'tool', not a genuine part of the system. As a tool it may be good or bad, sharp or blunt, but it is still a dull nonadapting thing; it does not respond to changes in circumstances, it does not learn, it simply wears in and wears out. A genuine part of a system embodies in its own *modus operandi* the same governing principle as the overall system. In adapting it hews closer to the principle of the system.

The second aspect of systems design goes one significant step further to note that 'Systems are specific forms of the distribution of members in a dimensional domain. ... In aggregates it is significant that parts are added; in systems it is significant that parts are arranged' (Angyal, *ibid*, pp. 25-26).

The usual design of an assembly line does nothing to create system properties in any section of the line. It simply adds more of this or that quanta of labour to the section. In practice in sets up an inexorable demand for labour once the designed line comes into operation. When reality inevitably departs from theory there is a build up of pressure on some individual work stations. Everyone else insists that their work station is a full house and hence additional work stations have to be squeezed in to cope with the peak points. That is, the original design predicates a creep to overmanning; adaptive rearrangement which would be the first response of a system design, comes a very poor second in these designs. It is easy to fob off responsibility for this trend to trade union pressures. It is not primarily due to this. It is primarily a result of the original engineering design. There is sufficient evidence that unions would agree to different designs that offer real advantages to their members. If what the unions are offered are aggregative designs from which the employers hope to maximise their economic gains from maximising fractionation then the unions must exploit this game to the maximum of their ability. Until recently the unions have not had the alternative possiblity of sending the employers back to the drawing board. They have not had this possibility because they have not had that knowledge of alternatives that enabled Gyllenhamer of Volvo to send his designers back and back again to the drawing boards until they got a really new concept of the Kalmar plant. The Kalmar design finished up as a genuine systems design. By the first criteria the groups were enabled to confront and take responsibility for the basic parameters that determined whether they were an economically productive section. By the second criteria the groups were enabled and encouraged to meet variance in their circumstances by rearrangement of their own efforts. Adding further permanent members was very much a last resort, after making-do with rearrangement of themselves or working out arrangements for temporary borrowing of labour from neighbouring groups. As we had seen from the earliest coal mining studies there was a marked reluctance of groups to accept any change of group membership until they had done their own best to cope with their work problem.

There is a third and last step in systems thinking that is, I think, important to the design of productive systems. In the statement of the first two principles of system design I may have appeared to play down the characteristics of the human beings that are the indisposable elements of socio-technical systems.

I have spoken simply of 'overriding system principles' and the priority of 'positions of parts and the arrangement and rearrangement of the parts'. The third principle is, however, that 'the more the inherent properties of parts are utilised as co-determinants of positional values ... the greater the organisation of the whole' (Angyal, *ibid*, p. 27). What this principle means is, quite simply, that the best design for any productive system will be that which not only allows that the goals of any sub system, any part, embody in some manner the overall system goals (Principle I), and allows that any such part is self managing to the point that they will seek to cope with external variances by firstly rearranging their own use of recources (Principle II); the best design will be that which also recruits or develops its constituent parts so that they have the intrinsic properties suited to the demands on the position they occupy. At the simplest level this third principle would indicate designing in a degree of multi-skilling which would meet the probable rearrangements of the section about its tasks. At a more sophisticated level of design, account would be taken of the human potentialities for reasoning, creativity and leadership that might be expected in any group of 8 to 10 human beings. This would mean designing the social system of the small group so that it becomes an instrument for its members: something they largely manage themselves, not vice versa. Then it would become *variety increasing* for them and they are enabled to pursue not only production goals but also purposes and even ideals that pertain to themselves.

4.3.4. The historical significance of democratisation of work

This trend is so central to my view of the future that I will try to spell out some of the assumptions. I can best do this by confronting some of the opposing lines of thought.

From the radical students of Scandinavia in the late sixties came the criticism that the project for democratisation of work was too late and in any case had been too limited in its aims. Because of these faults it drew attention from the need for a total social transformation and beguiled the work people into hoping for gradual reform when only a violent break with the past could possibly be liberating. This appears to differ from the traditional Marxist critique only in its insistence on total transformation. The Marxists believe that transformation of the *class* relations in the productive process had to precede transformation of society at large. My own position would seem to differ from both in:

1. Assuming that the class relations in the productive process have evolved to such a stage of socialisation (in the separation of ownership and management, the definition of the social character of capital, and the professionalisation of management) that it is possible to strive realistically for a revolutionary improvement in the *concrete productive relations* of workers and management. I note, in passing, that the Bolshevik revolution of 1917 left this problem untouched and for the next 50 years the conditions for tackling it apparently did not exist. Similarly, the piecemeal transformations in class relations in the advanced Western societies produced by nationalisation of coal mining, *etc.*, appeared to have no radical effect on the concrete day-to-day relations of managers and workers.

Furthermore I believe that:

2. The transformation of these concrete productive relations does not necessarily involve a conflict in class interests (given the 'socialisation of industry' mentioned above and the current level of technological development).
3. The transformation of the concrete day-to-day relations in production is the key to transforming, or restoring, the other personal, social and institutional relations into which men enter.

These three basic assumptions are all subject to historical validation.

To my mind the Scandinavian experience already validates our first two assumptions that the Marxist contradiction is *depasse*. Of course it is reassuring to see the way the other nations are following the Scandinavian example, but the essential point is that the class structure of Scandinavian industry did not constitute a major obstacle to the realisation of the project. The major obstacle to its acceptance has been the cultural and personality syndrome that Fromm called 'the fear of freedom'. The major obstacles to its spread to other larger capitalist countries would appear to be their complexity and cultural heterogeneity and their difficulties in finding a basis for mutual trust.

This should not surprise us. The fantastic growth in our productive capabilities has confronted us with the elimination of the domination of man over man, not simply a change in the form of domination. To confront successfully the cultures that have emerged over the past centuries as men sought to live with slavery, feudalism and capitalism, it is necessary for men to find common ground in deeper cultural roots. In some societies this will be harder to do than in others and in some, such as the U.S.A., it may well be that it is impossible to confront this task without the guidance of some contemporary examples.

My last assumption was that the concrete relations of production are the keystone to modern societies. This is becoming our most central concern, and yet it is the assumption for which we have the least direct evidence of what it means to a community when its working people are generally engaged in meaningful and challenging tasks.

There is, however, a lot of indirect evidence for selecting this assumption. Consider first the main contemporary arguments against it:

1. The student radicals have on occasion argued that it is the struggle against the universities which is the leading force for social transformation; that it is they who will lead the workers out of industrial bondage. The facts suggest that they are simply reacting to the industrialisation of the universities. Admittedly their reaction is informed with a perspective of the future which was inconceivable to earlier generations, but it is still only a reaction; a riot, not a revolutionary movement. The students suffer from the existing productive relations and may drop out in large numbers, but are in no position to transform them from without. Their experience to date only confirms my assumption.

2. McLuhan appears to be arguing that it is the direct effects of the technology of electronic communication which are currently trans-

forming all social relations including the productive relations. He sees little choice for men in all of this, except perhaps that by gaining conscious insight they might lessen the pain of accepting the changes. Active determination of man's future is, according to him, precluded by the numbness, the 'Narcissus narcosis', that characterises current social relations in general. Marcuse on balance agrees with this pessimistic doctrine, since he refers to it as the general replacement of psychological identification by primitive mimesis (Marcuse, *One Dimensional Man*, p. 25). Contrary to this, I think there is still a point of leverage for change. I maintain that it is by creating meaningful and challenging productive relations that men will be able and willing to put new content into the web of electronic communication. Insofar as man's daily work gives him a sense of personal worth, identity and growth he will enter into the web of general social relations as a conscious individual.

Against these alternative perspectives I am arguing that while they correctly perceive the demise of the old dynamic of the class relation in production, they fail to see that this has laid bare the more fundamental and pernicious contradiction within the concrete relations of production. Labour and the technological progress that is meant to liberate men from poverty and drudgery is still being carried out in a stultifying and degrading mode of domination and subordination. If anything, the scientific rationalisation of the traditional mode is intensifying the contradiction between the possibilities for free development of human potentialities and the actualities of daily life in the work force.

The revolutionary content of the project rests on the realisation that this contradiction can be resolved only by changes in the techniques of production and that the techniques of production include not only the tools but the concepts for their use; thus a lathe with the concept of tolerance limits is a different technology to one without the concept. Techniques of production that include concepts of personal interest, learning, innovation and decision making have been successfully evolved for a number of branches of industry. These efforts are in line with Marcuse's observation that 'as all freedom depends on the conquest of alien necessity, the realization of freedom depends on the *techniques* of this conquest' (Marcuse, *op. cit.*, p. 31). These efforts are contrary to the ideological movement of the human relations schools (MacGregor, Likert, Blake *et al.*). The human relations approach sees the techniques of management as something distinct from the techniques of production and hence readily lend themselves to the manipulation of men and the eventual masking of the contradiction to which we have drawn attention.

Let me now speculate about the third assumption, namely that the concrete relations in production are the leading part, the key link in the transformation of society.

What is likely to happen in other areas of social life as the industrial democracy project takes root?

The effects on education are perhaps easiest to surmise because we are already involved in education of managers and others for roles in the new socio-technical systems. Education for production by autonomous groups clearly requires an educational process in which autonomous groups are a basic element; the ability to use experts as resources presupposes experience with using academic staff as resource people; a naturally curious and creative response to the work situation presupposes that these potentialities are not stultified in educational processes; technical and social innovation and creativity presupposes a genuine polytechnical education and a grounding in the basic facts of man-task dynamics and of group dynamics. If such education is required in the re-education of today's managers, foremen and workers, can we avoid making similar changes in tertiary, secondary and even primary education, *i.e.* in the education of those who will be tomorrow's workers and managers?

Similar considerations arise when I later consider the quality of community life, leisure, the fate of the Welfare State and, hopefully, the quality of family life.

I have so far dwelt on the comparison of my projection with some current alternatives. Marcuse has gone beyond this to postulate criteria for testing the historical validity of any project that seeks to transcend the status quo (Marcuse, 1964, p. 175). The project should be examined against these criteria:

1. *The transcendent project must be in accordance with the real possibilities open at the attained level of the material and intellectual culture.*

As argued in discussion of my assumptions (a) and (b), the democratisation of work appears to meet this criterion.

2. *The transcendent project, in order to falsify the established totality,
   must demonstrate its own higher rationality in the threefold sense that*

   a. *it offers the project of preserving and improving the productive
      achievements of civilisation:*
      Experiments to date show that we have every reason to expect that
      the democratization of work will do just this.

   b. *it defines the established totality in its very structure, basic tendencies
      and relations;*
      As Marcuse himself points out, '*the need for stupefying work where
      it is no longer a real necessity is the tap root of the established
      totality*' (Marcuse, *op. cit.*, p. 23). The tendencies and relations
      that arise from this have been partly spelt out in the early sections
      on maladaptive strategies; the tendencies and relations that arise
      from democratization of work will be spelt out later.

   c. *its realisation offers a greater chance for the pacification of existence,
      within the framework of institutions which offer a greater chance for
      the free development of human needs and faculties.*

The democratisation of work should very materially contribute to the
'pacification of existence' and, as argued above, be a major force in the
remoulding of the 'framework of institutions' to better aid the release and
development of human potentialities. Nor is this effect waiting upon most
work being redesigned. People will almost certainly wish to tackle these
other tasks as soon as they are convinced that accomplishment of the
industrial phase is only a matter of time.

Marcuse's analysis is so similar to mine that it is necessary to ask how
he came to the pessimistic conclusion that the only possibility for change,
and that dubious, lay with those social fragments that lie outside of the
productive process.

The answer to this is that he came right up to the door we are forcing,
e.g. in writing of the Soviet experiment he stated that 'if it could lead to
self-determination at the very base of human existence, namely in the
dimension of necessary labour, it would be the most radical and most
complete revolution in history' (Marcuse, *op. cit.*, p. 49). Having come

this far he had no key to the door. The thin red thread that runs from the early Lewinian experiments on the dynamics of man-task relations (*e.g.* satiation, Zeigarnick effect, substitution, level of aspiration to the 'social climates' experiments), and hence to the socio-technical experiments; this thread was outside his vision (Lewin, 1936).

4.3.5. Matrix organisations

The vertically and horizontally monopolistic organization is an adaptive product of the disturbed reactive environment. I do not believe that there is any way in which such structures can adapt as individuals to turbulent environments (despite Terrebury, 1968). They cannot themselves be ideal seeking and hence their chances for survival are dependent upon creating organisational environments within which enough of their members will be ideal seeking. These organisational environments cannot be created by the individual organisations.

I see two organisational tendencies emerging as potentially effective responses to turbulence: one with regard to relations between organisations, including between national parts of the so-called multinationals; the other with regard to 'corporate planning'.

Whereas disturbed, reactive environments require one or other form of accommodation between like but competitive organisations (whose fates are to a degree negatively correlated), the turbulent environments require some relationship between dissimilar organisations whose fates are basically positively correlated; that is, relationships that will maximise cooperation while still recognising that no one organisation could take over the role of the other. I am inclined to speak of this type of relationship as an organisational matrix; it delimits the shape of things within the field it covers, but at the same time, because it delimits, it enables some definable shape to be achieved. While one aspect of the matrix provides for evolution of ground rules, another independent but related aspect must provide for the broader social sanctioning. Insofar as the sanctioning processes can be concretised in an institutional form, it should be possible for the component organisations to retain an effective degree of autonomy *and* to engage in effective joint search for the ground rules. Within the domain covered by such a matrix there needs to be further sanctioning processes to control the diffusion of values throughout the member organisations.

Outstanding examples of such organisational matrices are those that have emerged to cover international communication.

It should be noted that, in referring to the matrix type of organisations as one possible way of coping with turbulent fields, we are not suggesting that the higher level of sanctioning can be done by state controlled bodies, nor are we suggesting that the functioning of these matrices would eliminate the need for other measures to achieve stability. Matrix organisations, even if successful, would only help stability. Matrix organisations, even if successful, would only help to transform turbulent environments into the kinds of environments that I have discussed as clustered and disturbed, reactive. Within the environments thus created, an organisation could hope to achieve stability through its strategies and tactics. However, the transformed environments can no longer be stated in terms of optimal location (as in type 2) or capabilities (as in type 3). The strategic objective has to be formulated in terms of institutionalisation. As Selznick states in his analysis of the leadership of modern American corporations:

'the default of leadership shows itself in an acute form when organisational achievement or survival is confounded with institutional success'. '...the executive becomes a statesman as he makes the transition from administrative management to institutional leadership'.

This transition will probably be rendered easier as the current attempts to redefine property rights clarify the relations between the technologically productive area and the total social system. Private property rights are being increasingly treated as simply rights of privileged access to resources that still remain the resources of the total society. To that extent, the social values concerning the protection and development of those resources become an intrinsic part of the framework of management objectives and a basis for matrix organisations (Hill, 1972).

It is of interest that May's mathematical modelling of large complex systems suggested a similar strategy for avoiding instability. Referring to the Ashby-Gardner computations he notes,

that 12-species communities with 15% connectance have probability essentially zero of being stable, whereas if the interactions be organized into three separate 4 × 4 blocks of 4-species communities, each with a consequent 45% connectance, the 'organized' 12-species models will be stable with probability 34%... Such examples suggest that our model multi-species communities, for given average interaction strength and web connectance, will do better if the interactions tend to be arranged in 'blocks' – again a feature observed in many natural ecosystems' (1972, p. 414).

For passively adaptive systems this would mean no more than the strategy of segmentation discussed earlier. For actively adaptive systems we are suggesting that matrix type organisations will, like the logic of cluster sampling, maximise the variance within their particular matrix organisations and hence lessen the variance and difficulties of the ends they agree upon, being related to other such matrices. This is opposed to the logic of strata sampling, and the strategy of segmentation, which seems to minimise the variance within strata and consequently maximises that between them. When one considers the interpenetration of sources of variance in a turbulent social field it is not surprising that the logic of matrix organisation so closely approximates that of cluster sampling.

4.3.6. Adaptive planning

The processes of strategic planning are also modified. In so far as institutionalisation becomes a prerequisite for stability, then the setting of subordinate goals will necessitate a bias toward those goals that are in character with the organisation, and a selection of the goal paths that offer a maximum convergence about ideals held in common with other parties (Simmonds, 1975).

I have already referred to the technology of planning that emerged in the disturbed reactive environment. I think that this style of planning for optimisation will be not just ineffective but maladaptive: the pattern of active maladaptation response we discussed earlier as 'synoptic idealism'. Ackoff has identified the emerging pattern of 'adaptive planning' (1970).

This notion of active adaptive planning may be compared with Lindblom and Hirschman's 'disjointed incrementalism'. The convergence is not surprising as disjointed incrementalism was identified as the type of planning required in the face of gross complexity, future uncertainty and the difficulty in mobilising human potential for implementation. At the same time, active adaptive planning lays a stress on the conscious identification of shared values or shared perspectives, past or present, that is absent from disjointed incrementalism. Of the ten characteristics associated with disjointed incrementalism (Hirschman and Lindblom, 1969, pp. 358-359) at least four, 1, 2, 3 and 8, are essentially in the satisficing mode. As a result this way runs the risk of degenerating into the passive adaptation of parish pump politics. Active adaptation requires some sense of desirable futures as a deliberate step to avoid entrapment in the past.

Notions of planning are so central to current concepts of how society will deal with its futures that I think the whole concept needs to be rethought. It is not simply a matter of 'corporate planning' but of planning for cities, leisure, social welfare, economic growth, *etc.* As I have indicated the extended treatment by Hirschman and Lindblom seems faulty; that of Ackoff's was only meant to suggest what is needed.

The decision to plan implies some commitment to bring into being a state of affairs that does not presently exist and is not expected to occur naturally within the desired time. The kind of planning we expect to emerge is that which will produce plans that will *probably* come to pass. It is not enough to have one of the optimiser's *feasible* plans. We need planning which will probably come to pass because the people involved in or served by their implementation want them to succeed. The hard won agreements that the optimiser has for the initial, hard-nosed definition of objectives are no guarantee of active support when it comes to implementation. On the contrary, I think that these agreements carry within them the seed of subsequent subversion (as insistence on doctrinal purity in other fields of human endeavour carry the seeds of deviationism and heresy). Nor can the optimiser carry the day with his arrays of facts, statistical forecasts and impartial, objective calculations of the cost-effectiveness of alternative paths. These things do carry weight and may silence overt opposition, but, where there is a feeling that justice is not being done facts will not convince otherwise. One has only to recall the instances where the nagging doubts of one individual have eventually led to a murder case being reopened. The apparent dilemma in 'modern' planning is '*how does the expert make his contribution to planning without alienating people?*' This almost has the makings of a paradox for social planners: the more knowledge the expert accumulates the greater the gap in understanding between him and the people, and the less likely they are to go along with his plans for implementation or, to put it otherwise, the more we know the less we can do. In his own context Mao posed it as the problem of 'red or expert'.

I do not think we can suggest any way to resolve this dilemma unless we confront simultaneously another dilemma. Planning to produce a new state of affairs seems to presuppose that we know where we want to go, we know where we are now, we know what paths will take us from here to there and we know what means we have for traversing those paths. For turbulent social environments this presumes an awful lot of knowledge. When the social setting and the human instruments of change are both changing the knowledge we have today is increasingly less relevant. The dilemma is '*how can we expect to improve our planning in the face of relatively decreasing knowledge?*' Again we come close to a paradox: the more society changes the more we need to be able to plan but the less we have the knowledge with which to plan.

The common element in the two dilemmas is the notion of 'expert knowledge'. If we are to resolve these dilemmas we will have to ask whether what we understand to be 'expert knowledge' is the kind of knowledge required for planning social changes in a changing society. I think there is room for doubt on at least three scores.

First, decision makers mistake the nature of the situations for which they are seeking a planning solution. Even the optimisers seem to think they are engaged in problem solving. They think they know the problem and simply have to search through existing knowledge in order to come up with a range of probable solutions which they can then compare. Social planning has, however, come to be more like puzzle solving than problem solving. Each situation is so complex and unpredictable that one has to learn each unique set of steps that lead to a solution. In problem solving it is typical to have the insightful 'Eureka' experience when a solution suddenly becomes apparent, and after that it is just a matter of work to put the pieces together. In a puzzle one does not get this. The relation between the pieces is very much a matter of local determination. One can determine what is required for the piece to fit but, until that piece is found one has very little idea of what is going to be required of the piece after that. Previous experience or training cannot enrich the repertoire of solutions; at best they may help a person 'learn how to learn'. This does not sound like our expert. The expert is usually chock-a-block full of knowledge about what solutions will solve a given class of problems.

Not suprisingly the Oxford English Dictionary helps to clarify the distinction I have tried to make. A problem is literally 'a thing thrown or put forward'. The implication is that when faced with a problem we are also given a knowledge of from whence it arose, was thrown from or put forward by. This implication is enhanced when the O.E.D. states that in logic a problem can be that of arriving at the conclusion in a syllogism; in geometry 'a proposition in which something (further) is required to be done'; in physics and mathematics, 'a question or inquiry which *starting from some given conditions* (my italics) investigates some fact, result or law'. Chess 'problems' are similarly defined by the O.E.D. as deriving from a given arrangement of pieces and set of rules. Beyond this the O.E.D. does indicate that the word was once upon a time used to indicate that something was puzzling, enigmatic, a riddle; their last quote for this useage was dated 1602 AD.

A puzzle is not defined by the O.E.D. in terms of what is out there that indicates and may assist what the person does by way of producing a solution. A puzzle is defined as simply a state of mind – 'the state of being puzzled or bewildered; bewilderment; confusion; perplexity how to act or decide'. What is 'out there' in the case of a puzzle is indicated by a discussion of Chinese puzzles. Essentially it is a matter of a person being expected to achieve a result that seems impossible to achieve, *e.g.*' to remove a piece of string from an object without untying it'. Interestingly, the word puzzle (unlike 'problem') has also readily assumed the form of a verb, *e.g.* 'to search in a bewildered or perplexed way; to fumble, grope for something; to get through by perplexed searching', 'to puzzle out: to make out by the exercise of ingenuity and patience'.

Second, the experts in this field have tended to act on a faulty model of so-called rational decision making. They theorise and write as if decision making was explicable in terms of only two dimensions. Probable efficiency of different paths and relative value of the outcomes. Another dimension is necessary (Heider, 1946; Jordan, 1967; Ackoff and Emery, 1972). This other dimension is the probability of choice and reflects the *intrinsic* value of a course of action to the chooser (as distinct from its *extrinsic* or means-end value). This human dimension is reflected in the old folk wisdom of 'better the devil you know', 'furthest hills are greenest', 'a bird in hand...'. The persistent and pervasive role of these non rational factors has been explicated by Heider (1946, 1959), and unwittingly demonstrated in the 'uncooperativeness' of humans in the recent rash of experimental studies of decision making. Similarly, established organisations show their own style in non rational preference for ways of acting, particularly those that have had a special significance in their past, *e.g.* Rolls-Royce.

Third, people have tended to assume that what we need to know are more and more facts when what is needed is knowledge of human ideals. This had come up very strongly with so-called enlightened operations researchers. Faced with the sorts of difficulties outlined above they have sought for yet more knowledge: knowledge about people's motivations and how they can be managed to bring about predictable changes. I suggest that they are not about to get this knowledge from the social sciences (despite the pretensions of some social scientists) and that even if they did they would still be in a puzzle situation. The situational features to which the people respond would still be emerging in unpredictable ways. Where people are expected to go from *A* to *B* in ways that can be determined only as they proceed it becomes more important that *they* have a bit more knowledge about some of the paths. They must themselves be able to learn so that they can evaluate.

If one were to take seriously these strictures then the role of the planners would be no longer that of the experts riding with the powers that be. Instead the planning functions would be seen to involve

1. conduncting some search process whereby the main parties to the proposed change can clearly identify and agree about the *ideals* the change is supposed to serve and the kinds of paths most in character with them;
2. designing a change process which will enable relevant learning to take place at rates appropriate to the demands of time. This being the time within which change must occur to avoid intolerable costs of not changing and the time by which decisions need to be made if adequate resources are to be mobilised;
3. devising social mechanisms for participation whereby the choice of paths will reflect the instrinsic value of these paths for those who will have to traverse them.

There are many considerations that lead one to regard identification of ideals as the first requirement for planning social change. Only ideals seem to have the necessary breadth and stretch in social space and time. Motivations, attitudes and social objectives may well change as planning and implementation proceed, but human ideals do not appear to change so readily. This is not to say that the relative weightings of the ideals may not change* but even here we tend to have storm warnings well before the shifts become socially relevant (*e.g.* the shifts in 'the Protestant ethic' which have only now become broadly relevant but which were heralded many years ago by the Beat generation of Kerouac). Similarly, only ideals seem to have the breadth of influence to encompass the range of contesting interests that can be expected in an area ripe for planned change. Ideals do not ordinarily have the same urgency in human affairs as motivations but what they lack in this respect may be more than compensated for if their identification recentres a zero-sum conflict to pursuit of common interests.

Ideals have the further advantage that they are not esoteric. Certainly social scientists can lay no claims to expertise in deciding these matters. If a planned change is supposed to serve certain ideals then the layman can and will understand the criteria for judging the planning process before being confronted by the final and possibly irreversible outcome. The layman's judgement may not extend to a learned appraisal of why things are going wrong or what action should be taken but at least he may sound the alarm in time for something useful to be done.

One special property of ideals needs to be noted because of the damage it does to the optimiser's claim to 'planning excellence'. The ideals that influence the behaviour of people cannot be subsumed under a single ideal. Omnipotence which is the one ideal that if achieved would permit the achievement of all other ideals is only directly and singlemindedly pursued by infants and some sick dependent people. Identification of the ideals involved in planned social change is almost certain to identify more than one non-comparable ideal, *e.g.* homonomy, nurturance, humanity and beauty. In such a context of multiple ideals the skills of

* In my experience differences in relative weighting have not been a serious obstacle to co-operation; providing valuation has been uniformly positive or negative.

the optimizer cannot yield *the* plan. Hopefully his skills may still be utilized for tactical problems.

The other direction in which it was suggested that planning might change was toward designing ways of 'learning to learn'. Clearly this cannot be just a matter of pushing people in at the deep end. There must be some way of using accumulated experience and expertise to advantage.

In this mode of planning the main cognitive searching shifts from search for means to search for ends. The search for means becomes less of a cognitive activity and more that of field experimentation. By such intervention one may get some sense of emerging possibilities and difficulties; for what resources are actually needed; what resources, including human commitments and innovations, can be generated in the process of change; what shifts in emphases or changes in time-taken are needed. In a situation of social change this kind of intervention can give us information for the choice of paths that we cannot expect to get from the massive cross sectional surveys favoured by the engineers-cum-urban planners. These surveys give us little more than history. By intervention, by pushing, tugging and tearing at the causal strands, we start to get some idea of the changing texture of the social field in which change is planned.

It will be noted that in this mode of planning the 'logical' order of planning activities becomes somewhat confused. Implementation and the selection of courses of action become inextricably involved with each other. Similarly, the allocation of resources becomes a means of encouraging the finding and selection of the best path(s). Resources do not automatically flow to those courses of action that on previous cognitive analysis have been determined to be 'the best'. Instead resources flow toward those areas of implementation that show the most promise. Nor can one expect clear decision rules to decide what shows the most promise. The very notion of 'showing promise' involves what is hoped for but not really expected. An initially disastrous experiment may be regarded as a place to channel resources if it shows that a lesson has been learnt and local commitment created.

Planning in this mode must upset the optimiser. Where, he will ask, is the control that will ensure that each part of the plan is enacted in a way and at a time that will ensure optimal use of resources? Where are the objective, impartial decision rules (and protective departmentalisation of *the* planning function) that will ensure that politically and personally motivated choices do not subvert the planned ends? These features are in fact absent and their absence could be critical, to the optimiser's plans and planning: our point is that in a rapidly changing society the optimising mode of planning for social change is about as adaptive as a pig in water: the harder the pig tries to swim the more it slashes its own throat.

The optimiser tends to assume that he is preparing plans for a uninodal organisation that will have the authority and power to command, through their existing channels of coordination and control, that the plan be translated into reality. The new mode of planning assumes that there will be a multiplicity of nodes of power and only a measure of cooperation between them will produce change in the desired direction. Consequently, in this new mode, the planners create the basis for control that emerges from a shared sense of ideals and present requirements and creates channels of communication and irritation appropriate to the shared needs for coordination.

In a very real sense the most important product of this style of active adaptive planning is not the plan but the *community-in-planning*. The process creates the conditions for learning to learn; affirms the overriding significance of shared ideals and reduces the need for planning as a separate organisational activity. We can expect that this style of planning will generate an institutional form that will be as much part of our emerging societies as the campfire was to the aborigines, namely 'the search conference'. When new 'matrix' formations seem necessary, or old need to be discarded we can expect those with potentially relevant *operational* responsibilities to come together for a brief span of days and nights to jointly search for the implications of sensed changes in their shared environments. Thus, for instance, union leaders and leaders of productive enterprises will seek such opportunities to share their understanding of how the 'rules of the game' are changing. They will not relegate this task to 'research officers'; they will not risk waiting to infer it from changes in each other's tactics and strategies; they will not attempt to deal with such matters in committee. In committee it is necessary to stick with that which is *significantly* probable and trade from unchangeable corners. In 'search' even the improbable must be considered as a possible key to the future. Existing bodies of data and current notions of what is relevant can be no substitute for people's own sense of what is coming over the horizon. The reason for this great openness is simply that today's probabilities are not a sure guide to the future but the future is likely to emerge from some of the possibilities that now exist. However, most people abhor such a degree of openness and are not likely to put up with it unless given ample time in which to search, freedom from the compulsion to arrive at explicit decisions and freedom from the outside interruptions of work and family.

It is this latter point which has led to the use of 'social islands'. The participants are brought together to form an isolated community for as many days and nights as seem necessary for their work. This temporary community not only reifies the overriding purposes but provides psychological support to the individual. It represents a return to the older wisdom of the Persian tribes, reported by Herodotus, that no group decision reached at night was binding unless reaffirmed by daylight, and vice versa.

It may seem that an undue conservatism is built in by the stress on participants including 'the persons with the highest operational responsibilities'. However, if the search process is to issue forth into a wide range of experimental interventions it must have the sanctioning of the existing powers and it must have the active support of those who control the operational units. If this support is not forthcoming the matter is one for a power solution, not a planning solution. One further matter offsets the conservative bias. In a rapidly changing social setting the greatest resistances to planned change are likely to arise from fear of change rather than from vested interests. Vested interests can be identified, calculated and negotiated as part of the price of change. Fear of change cannot; hence the great value of winning the hard core of professional leadership.

To identify the ideal goals that will be relevant to the planning process the participants will tend to build up a shared picture of where the system has come from, as well as a shared picture of its likely futures. Beyond this they will evolve guiding strategies for change that will bring others into the planning process and win their commitment to the ideal goals. As is stressed by Ackoff and Schon, this means the emergence of broadly participative social systems that will 'learn to learn'; not just create mechanisms whereby they are fed knowledge accumulated by experts.

5. The most probable future for Western societies

I will first consider Western societies in isolation from the rest of the world. Later I will drop this assumption but, for the moment, I wish to identify those changes that are most likely to occur if Western societies develop in their own ways.

These changes can possibly be best handled under the headings of:

1. work;
2. education;
3. family;
4. leisure.[1]

With respect to changes in these areas I will try to be quite specific. My concern is primarily with the changes that are likely to take place in existing institutional arrangements and social mores. I shall try to sustain consistency between these predictions and the general scenario for Western societies that I have outlined. I could not hope to cope with the variations on these themes that occur between individual Western nations. Each of these has preserved in various ways significant aspects of its pre-industrial past. Our primary focus is on U.K., U.S., Australia, New Zealand and Scandinavia. The matters referred to seem generally relevant to Western societies, as they come up to meet them, or even if they have not already solved them.

5.1. Probable futures in work

1. As spelt out at length, the major change predicted is a change in the

1. I have taken government and religion to be back-up systems. They will necessarily tend to take on the characteristics demanded by changes in the unavoidable activities of men. If we accepted that they were, or could be, genuinely ideal seeking systems, then a different treatment would be necessary.

quality of work. It seems *almost* inevitable that Western industries will de-bureaucratise and move toward democratic forms of work organisation. This means the end of 'the job'. Individuals will enter into work roles within semi-autonomous groups that offer a chance of working in a humanised environment and pursuing ideals, not just turning out work to some impersonal standards.

The changes in this direction are unlikely to abstract people from involvement in non-work activities. Where it has been possible to study the effects of change in quality of work over a period (*e.g.* Hunsfoss, Norway, since 1965) the evidence is quite to the contrary. The observed effect is that men whose work has been so changed are *more* active in union and professional organisations, *more* active in the local community affairs, *more* constructive in the use of their leisure time. This makes sense. Compensatory use of leisure does occur in some cases but generally the less one does the less one feels up to doing. Arousing of awareness in real possibilities for self-development does the opposite. The potentialities for self-development are not just those that are best met in the workplace. We already see this phenomena in the life of young professional managers in the Western societies.

Beyond this general change in the content of work I wish to look at the likely changes in the forms of working. These changes in the form often imply corresponding changes in other institutional arrangements, *e.g.* in education, family. For simplicity of treatment I will try to look at each institution in turn whilst recognising that this becomes increasingly difficult.

2. People will once again start entering the work force, fulltime, at about 15 years of age. Physical maturation is occurring earlier and fewer tasks will require the physical strength and endurance of an adult. From the society's point of view there will be significant advantages in the children having the experience of working in semi-autonomous groups of all ages and working with a technology. This will not be a difficult move as society will undoubtedly devise ways for most to re-enter education. More significantly it undermines one of the relatively new and socially harmful divisions between generations (the return of women to work is a process already well under way).

3. The concept of a life time career is unlikely to survive past 1980. This will be so with respect to practically all the old variations on this theme, as being a carpenter or lawyer for life, being a dirt pusher, being a railwayman. The expectation will be that a person will branch out in different directions at different stages of his life. This may happen from choice or from obsolescence of plant, product or skills. In any case one can expect a combination of state and enterprise retraining resources to facilitate this sort of mobility. What Rehn introduced into Sweden twenty years ago will, in more sophisticated forms, become common place in Western societies trying to cope with turbulence and more purposeful people.

4. The contractual form of employment will increasingly shift to the salaried staff form of contract and away from the hourly labour form. This is already happening in the process industries. As workers are brought into more responsible involvement in their work the hourly wage contract will be seen as increasingly archaic, and discarded. The newer forms of contract will go beyond even those currently enjoyed by salaried workers. They will include corporate assurances of retraining where the deskilling has resulted from employment.

5. The working week will in the leading Western countries move toward the four day, 35 or 36 hour week. Once this is achieved it will probably, within a decade, be levered into a thirty two hour week, 4×8. There is now much variation between Western societies at the moment, and much variation within and between public, private, salaries, hourly, *etc*. The four day week, once it has gained a certain level of acceptance, will generate pressures toward it which will override old differences. It will simply be too attractive to employees; will generate a host of 'leisure oriented' markets and offer too many opportunities for reducing investment in the infra-structures of cities. The 'work day' seems to be unpredictable. My guess is that with a four day work week the weekend will no longer be so sacrosanct and shift work (for the continuous process industries) no longer such a felt burden. We cannot expect that actual 'average hours worked' will decrease to the same extent. People will be more able and willing to 'moonlight' for extra income; for family requirements, educa-

tion or the like. This should be particularly helpful to the growth of the services sector. It also increases work choices for the individual. He or she is better enabled to match income requirements to labour market needs and hence manage his or her fluctuating requirements arising from changes in family cycle, *etc.*

6. Annual leave will move to a four week pattern but this will be temporary. The pattern Western societies will be pushed toward is the 5 week leave that allows both a winter and summer holiday. This will be needed as work becomes increasingly the task of information processing and more personally involving. People will voluntarily expend more of themselves in their work, as already tends to happen in professional work. We can expect that these extended holidays will be accompanied by additional holiday pay to ensure that employees take a proper holiday away from home, with their families.

This change will further support the growth of leisure oriented industry and help mend the sex and age divisions of current society.

7. Western societies are likely to come much closer to McLuhan's suggestion that work will be learning. In every technology we find that instrumentation, automation and computerisation are transforming the interface between people and machine or plant. And the interface becomes increasingly similar regardless of the technology. Production becomes critically dependent upon people effectively dealing with information yielded by the technical system and contributing the most appropriate information to the control and guidance of that system. Some of these informational flows are confined to individuals who take information from the technical system and feed back guidance directly into it. Other informational flows must be carried at any one time by a network of many people at many different organisational levels.

Each step in this direction undermines the significance of the old craft skills and the power of the trade unions built on them. It further undermines the distinction between white and blue collar work, and that between 'men's work' and 'women's work'. It also erodes the distinction between adult work and children's work.

These new technologies are constantly changing and particularly are their interfaces. Hence the notion of an apprenticeship or education that can be done once for all is inappropriate. Operators and managers are mainly concerned with problem solving and continuous learning. When a new automated plant is brought into production it is now possible and economically desirable to design the tasks of operators and managers so that the performance of the plant will reflect a learning curve over its entire operating life. This is only possible where the chosen task structure places a premium on learning, experimenting (*e.g.* George Box's Evolutionary Operating Procedures) and problem solving. The pressure toward greater productivity will hasten these changes and merge with the social pressures toward 'democratisation of work'.

8. The recent upsurge in the return of married women to work will almost certainly continue. Their labour is needed for economic growth, they can be used for any increasingly wide range of work and there appears to be an increasingly rapid spread amongst women of the belief that their liberation requires no less than this. The big difference in the occupational level of women's work and men's work that we currently observe will be eroded. In the past work was assumed to be done on the basis of early educational achievements, and paid accordingly. Time out of the work force was assumed to result in deterioration of those educational attainments and hence women could not expect to come back into the work force at the levels achieved by males who had stayed at work. As stated above I believe these assumptions are becoming increasingly erroneous. Existing traditions will hamper the emergence of the new trends but once these start to go they should go quickly.

9. The distinction between work and leisure will become increasingly hazy, in people's behaviour, not just in their minds. For people whose education stopped when they 'left school', 'graduated' or got their apprenticeship, the distinction is clear; leisure, of a sort, begins when they 'knock-off work'. With the emerging knowledge centred industries, as we currently observe with much professional work, the distinction will not be so clear. Work problems in which they are involved will not be dropped at the factory gate, or the office door. They will find their way into the home lounge, to the fishing spot, *etc.* Upgrading of know-

ledge to meet perceived classes of emerging problems will find those people voluntarily and eagerly involved in various forms of continuous education, whether organised by their organisation, outside bodies or amongst their peers. Insofar as knowledge is a growth in social capital this is more than likely to offset reduction in formal working hours due to reduction in the hours of the working week or longer holidays and institutionalisation of long-service leave.

10. The concept of a fixed retiring age about 60 or 65 will very likely be scrapped. Life expectancy has moved well beyond these years and, with the emerging redistribution between work, education and leisure, the idea of a few last years in glorious idleness or travel is turning sour. We believe that this anachronism has persisted this far only because within the bureaucratic type structure there could not be enough room at the top to allow talent in without scrapping the old. Japanese industry and Western political organisations have managed to avoid this problem. With the debureaucratisation of industry, it is probable that final retirement will be a matter decided between the individual and his doctor. The wisdom he may have accrued as manager or operator will be treated as an asset by the organisation.

5.2. Education

1. The basic change will be the shift from the notion that education is rather like a ballistic missile, *i.e.* once powered and pointed it will follow a more or less predictable trajectory for the rest of its useful life, dependent of course on the weather it happens to meet on the way to its end. The emerging concept is closer to the concept of the guided missile, with a built in capability of some selfguidance. The need for the latter properties are obvious in a turbulent environment. *A 'controlled turbulent environment' will not necessarily be changing at a lesser rate, only changing less unpredictably.* A great deal of what we called education is capable of being programmed for computer handling, and is being programmed so that at a multitude of interfaces with real life the Western citizens find that the calculations, the print-outs and the reading-in have already been

done, by machine. The credit card and the Giro system already demonstrate this. We are not suggesting that basic skilling in the three 'R's' will become irrelevant. What I am strongly suggesting is that it is nonadaptive to cling to the notion of a person being filled up with just so much knowledge that he can, with the amendments slowly gained from practical experience, make his way through the rest of life. The alternatives to the technologically outmodel educational technologies of 'drilling' and 'cramming' are not those of the so-called progressive schools (*e.g.* Summerhill). We can see what the minimal requirements are for a guided – missile type system so it should not be too difficult to work out what we need of an education that must serve an industry that is increasingly a knowledge oriented system. Initial education, even if it goes to at least 27 years of age for a psychiatrist or Ph.D., cannot remain what it is. The only viable form for the future is that which enables a person to program, or reprogram, his learning requirements in the face of new and unprogrammed needs for knowledge. We are not expecting that he will have to do this on his own, or that initial education would give an adequate capability in this respect. Institutes of Continuing Education will obobviously have to cope with the invevitable shortfall. However, the pattern of initial education seems clear. Its concern will increasingly be with cultivating the ability of 'learning to learn'. This phrase has become hackneyed but we think it is necessary to be more specific. We clearly do not think that it has anything to do with absorbing the contents of textbooks, written usually by persons with second hand experience of the research process and second hand knowledge of how knowledge is transmitted. Nor does it have to do with cultivating the sort of 'brightness' that shows up so well on current tests of I.Q. Learning to learn is first and foremost learning to cultivate in oneself an interest in what it is that one needs to know. Study techniques, *etc.* are secondary.

The kind of intelligence that is relevant is not simply increase in degree of knowledge of efficiency of different courses of action, but increase in understanding, of 'apprehension of the relevant structure of the total behavioural field, relevance being defined in terms of the immediate and presumptive future purposes of the actor(s)' (Chein, 1943; Quoted, Ackoff and Emery, 1972). This will rarely be achieved by students working in isolation. The minimum conditions for a learning group moving toward a deeper apprehension of the relevant structure of its total behavioral field would seem to be:

a. that the group has room to engage with the different parts of its behavioral field in different ways;
b. that it can participate in setting goals so that they constitute a challenge to the group (goals set by others are likely to miss the mark and, by being too easy or too difficult, fail to motivate),
c. that it has a feedback of performance against targets that will make it possible to learn from mistakes.

In practice the first condition implies that the group can operate only in areas where it has protected territorial rights and adequate social sanctions for the kinds of changes it would like to experiment with. If there is inadequate room for experimentation, learning is unlikely to be sustained, as has been well demonstrated by studies of the effect of institutional settings on intellectual development. The second condition is vital in large heterogeneous systems, *e.g.* universities, seeking to do many things. It will usually not be practical to involve everyone in the process of initially identifying the overriding values and objectives. However, even when these are clearly understood and accepted they are unlikely to invoke commitment unless they can withstand the acid test of translation by the 'students' into goals that they think can be achieved in their area in an acceptable time period. Fortunately at this level the learning process is engaged in by smaller social groups who probably have some knowledge of each other and even some existing mechanisms for democratic participation. (Note: In industrial settings it has often been found best to avoid existing mechanisms such as joint works councils because they are steeped in negotiating from separate interests; but relatively easy to create new mechanisms when the parties recognized common interests in their shared environment. Universities, *etc.* should avoid the illusion of student participation by elected representation.) The third condition is above all what is likely to require that some educational expertise is available, and hence facilities for monitoring emerging systems are likely to require analytical skills not commonly available in the early stages of the planning process.

2. It is in the changes in the nature of this 'educational expertise' that we will see the greatest move away from the present. The present structure of our educational institutions is essentially bureaucratic. Its basic module being the teacher (supervisor) with his subordinate class of students each directly responsible to him for their performance. The gross inefficiency of this method of teaching has brought education in the Western societies to a crisis. The rate of growth in educational expenditures and in the numbers engaged in teaching cannot be sustained. At the same time Coleman's massive survey of U.S. education has shown no correlation between the educational results achieved and expenditures whether they be on teachers, equipment or educational facilities. 'De-schooling' has become the most likely outcome. I do not believe that in Western societies it will be as drastic as Illich recommends for the underdeveloped areas. We do think it will, however, be radical. The educational institutions will, like the new university of Roskilde (Denmark), be built on the basic module of the 'learning group', not the class. The small selfregulating group of peers have as their group task the education of themselves, making such use of the resources of expertise, *etc.* that are available to them. Practically all of the education that we need can be done in these settings. And practically all of student's time will be spent in them, or in preparing individual contributions to the group work. There appears to be no other way of ensuring that the individual student will find a meaningful place in educational institutions and get the support he needs to sustain him through the inevitable bad patches of boredom, confusion, anxiety and despair. These groups can provide conditions for learning as good as the best teacher can under ideal conditions of small classes and frequent contact. They can certainly provide better conditions than are provided by mediocre teachers with very large classes and infrequent contact. Insofar as a great deal of the teaching load is taken over by the students teaching each other, the need for teachers is radically reduced. Insofar as the teacher's role is then simply that of having some expertise or experience that the learning groups may use, the whole extensive apparatus of Teachers Colleges and the like becomes moribund. It was the classroom that created the need for semi-professional skills of the teachers as disciplinarian, blackboard demonstrator, subject specialist. It is the disappearance of the classroom that will make them as irrelevant

as the old metal craftsman. The expertise that the learning groups will want to call on is not that sort of expertise but more likely the expertise that is to be found currently in one or other of the knowledge based industries. Thus, 'teachers' are likely to cease to be an isolated, certificated body of persons seen as specially qualified to teach. They are more likely to be people who simultaneously work somewhere other than an educational institution, or who are in-between working in noneducational institutions.

3. With this basic change in perception of education and its current institutionalisation we can expect that there will be less pressure to 'grab them as young as possible and keep them as long as possible'. When Dutch and Norwegian universities wish to keep their psychology students at their studies until age 25, there is something obviously going wrong. Quite a different pattern will emerge. Quite simply my prediction is that within the years immediately ahead we will see a significant movement toward an educational pattern more closely designed around the developmental patterns of human beings, not employment requirements. As already suggested educational requirements have already slipped out of gear with what industry requires. The emerging requirements will, I believe lead to the following changes in educational institutions:

a. schooling being delayed to the age of seven. The Norwegians, for instance, have always retained this despite the industrial revolution. The Anglo-Saxon countries have tried to preserve this with the notion of the 'infant grades' at school. I believe that this pretence will be dropped. Children of this age are not 'infant graders' of the normal primary school system. They cannot be counted on to maintain even ten minutes of attention to an imposed task. Their requirements are psychologically different, and cannot be anywhere near adequately coped with in a normal primary school system. With women wishing, and being wished, back into the work force the concept that will best describe the under seven age group is 'child-care' not 'pre-schooling'.

b. leaving school about fifteen to enter work for a couple of years. Even before that age we expect that childreen will be allowed and expected to have some parttime experience of work. The Labour Laws that were introduced to protect children from the dreadful conditions of the early industrial revolution, and subsequently to keep them in school will be a hindrance and be treated as such.

c. having the opportunity of entering junior colleges after about seventeen. We can expect that these would cater for those who wish to pursue part-time studies as well as fulltime; and allow for a mixture of people of all ages regardless of any educational certification. For many, this institution will provide something like a broadly based first degree; for others the means of meeting a special interest in mathematics, Asian Studies or the like. I am implying that the High School, the Lycee, the Gymnasia will die with the death of their era.

d. there will be, generally speaking, no way of going directly from these junior colleges to universities. Further experience in work, travel or home-studies are likely to be required. The universities are in a crisis as deep as any part of the educational systems of the west. The contrast in development is markedly conveyed by the contrast between M.I.T. and the new Danish university of Roskilde. Both aim to turn out engineers and scientists, but not just those. M.I.T. is based on the traditional bureaucratic model with something like the craft-apprenticeship for the fortunate; Roskilde is based on the small learning group and small sets of learning groups housed together. M.I.T. is a vastly expensive architectural setting, particularly the colossus of the Earth Sciences Building; Roskilde is, and is planned to remain, small in numbers and cheaply housed in one and two storied buildings. Whereas M.I.T. is the glaring expression of the ideal of knowledge and plenty; Roskilde embodies in its design and organisation the ideals of nurturance and homonomy. As with the junior colleges we can expect that at any one time the universities will be catering for part and full-time students, for young and old. We can also expect, although more slowly, that the traditional departmental design will give way to 'project type' organisation. The tenured academic will become as archaic as the professional teacher.

e. some sort of cross between the technical colleges and the Danish Folk colleges is likely to proliferate. As people who have learned how to learn are challenged by the work of knowledge-based industries, and their own expanding range of purposes, they will seek ways of bringing themselves to master new, relevant techniques. Much of this will of course be provided by the employing organisations but a lot of the demand will go beyond what organisations recognize as relevant or economically justifiable. The source of the rising demand for skill training facilities of this kind is that people will be concerned with wanting to be able to do more things but accept that there is little point in using their time in general education developing skills that they may never need or that may be rendered obsolete by change.

f. 'continuing education' as we know it should undergo a revolution. Education will in fact tend to become continuous, an on-off thing throughout life. The sorts of changes in educational institutions outlined above suggest that they will cater for most of the sort of coursework run by current centres for adult or continuing education. Thus it should no longer be necessary to take university members of an Asian Studies Department out of their academic roles and settings just so that they can impart their knowledge to people who are not formally enrolled as students of that department. However, a major requirement will exist for supportive educational resources that can be rapidly and flexibly deployed to meet the needs for new knowledge and understanding at the interfaces of differently purposed organisations; and where these needs are sensed to be emerging from people without, as yet, any organisational expression. The key tool for such bodies would be the 'search conference' (as discussed above in relation to adaptive social planning); their main aim to institutionalise the education, that is identified as needed, in the structures discussed above or in some new forms that do not involve themselves as an ongoing part; their main competence as an educational body derives from their own sensitivity with being continuously involved at such interfaces and concerned with the emergence of genuine novelty in educational requirements.

4. The subject matter of education is also likely to change both in content and shifts in relative significance. Several of these changes seem to be identifiable:

a. the major shift will reflect society's shift in concern from the man-nature relation to the man-man, or more correctly the man-woman relation. This was heralded in the late sixties when the top graded students of Sweden reversed the old tradition of opting in the majority for the social sciences courses in the universities instead of the old plum professions of engineering and medicine. At first thought to be a statistical freak it has become a widespread phenomena in the Western societies, and unlikely to change. There was irony in this. They moved to subject fields such as psychology, sociology and even economics where they thought they would be concerned with the ideal of humanity. They found that these were subjects that had desperately moved toward a mechanistic model of man at the same time as physics was moving away from its earlier mechanistic models, *i.e.* in the first decade of the century. We do not therefore predict that this shift will be reflected, except for a brief transitory period in widespread introduction of social sciences courses into all levels of education. This could be only retrogressive. *The humanisation of the processes of education and work will, themselves, be the main educational tool for learning about human beings.* What we do think is that where the relation of man-man and man-woman becomes the central concern of society the central concern of education will for many decades to come be the rethinking of old concepts of the man-nature relation in the sense of the revolution of thought Rachel Carson projected into ecology, the concept of Area Studies that the U.S. Army found necessary to introduce to meet its massive educational requirements in World War II, and the realities of genuine polytechnical education that emerge when people find themselves an active force at the actual interface of people and technology, not mere cogs.

b. the bedrock of education, the 3 R's, will undergo major transformation. The teaching profession, not of course the academics, cling to these as the core of their claim to professionalism. (Academics only arrange for sub-academics to cope with the increasing failures of the teachers to instil the 3 R's.) There is nothing about the 3 R's that cannot be more effectively learnt within multi-aged learning groups of children, with reference persons, than in our typical class rooms. I think that this will emerge. The 3 R's will at all educational levels be transmitted by pupil, as is spoken language, children's games, children's folklore. This will be easier as it seems that the esoteric 'new maths' will soon be displaced by the more natural introduction to maths of the ordinal concepts of 'bigger than', 'more than' that children know before they even come to school. Reading and writing cannot be expected to remain a stranglehold of one generation on the next. If the children move to writing 'Tolkien' fashion or to reading texts like a newspaper it is better that the adults see this emerging, and try to understand why, than to try a tighter strait-jacket.

c. with more adult people we see that they will be increasingly concerned with more direct confrontation with the man-man and man-woman relation. Not in the form of courses in the known psychology or sociology of these relations but with exposure to specially protected changes to search out these relations themselves. We can already see the remarkable growth of involvement in encounter groups of one kind and another. This current movement may be just a response to the transition phase of entering turbulent environments. Nevertheless I think that a part of this must remain relevant for a long time to come, if adaptive strategies prevail. Within adaptive strategies is the assumption that human problems are the most critical for organisations, educational or noneducational. The dilemma for education is that this function offers not more knowledge than the productive organisations can stop to give but more experience than those experience giving bodies can risk providing. The need is so obvious and pressing that I think ways will be found to ensure that this type of education will be widely available.

5.3. The family

1. Perhaps the most significant change foreseeable in the institution of the family is that, in being expected to cope with less it may actually contribute more to society. As work and education become humanised the family will no longer be just a setting where compensation is sought for the shortcomings of those places. As human ideals start to be realised in daily work and education there should be correspondingly less pressure

on families to produce the guilt ridden superego's studied by the Freudians. However, even this understates the change. Modern, bureaucratically organised society seems already to have undermined the families' role in character formation. As Marcuse put it:

'Now ... the formulation of the mature super ego seems to skip the stage of individualisation: the generic atom becomes directly a social atom. The repressive organisation of the instincts seems to be *collective*, and the ego seems to be prematurely socialised by a whole system of extra-familial agents or agencies' (1956, p. 97).

I suggest that families will be expected and will be able to do more than that. That they will be able to recognise that as an institution they are potentially less than their members. Their function is nurturance of individuals as ideal seekers. I do not think this function can be performed by the *isolated* nuclear family. In isolation the nuclear family structure imposes such mutual compression of the space of free movement of husband and wife that it is unstable, and prone 'to go critical' (Lewin, 1948). The solution which realises the potentiality of the nuclear family whilst lessening this danger is the move toward the small neighbourhood group of dwellings to permit the overlapping and sharing of *personal* resources. It is unlikely that Western societies will move towards the imposed organisational forms that have made present-day Shanghai more a great collection of villages than a metropolis of 10-12 millions. However, in building and rebuilding their towns and cities we can expect people to create the environmental designs that best support the family in its new tasks.

2. Parallel with the family regaining it's social significance families will be formed earlier but make less use of legal forms. This will occur simply because the laws will be so slow in evolving to encompass the new roles that people will wish to take as husband – wife, mother-father, child. The significance of the family will remain such that eventually adequate redefinition of the laws must occur. But a great deal of experimentation can be expected as people try to find appropriate degrees and forms of openness. It would not be surprising if various forms are eventually recognized as viable alternatives for different stages of the family life cycle.

3. The size of the average family is likely to fall below two children whilst

people find themselves still confronted with turbulent social environments. Within a decade it should move closer to an average of two. This is the smallest number that conveys genuine group properties on the family (Ackoff and Emery, 1972). More are not needed to cope with current child mortality rates and more are not needed 'for company'. The small neighbourhood, child-care centres and the more open school provide for that need.

4. More people are likely to be married more than once in their lifetime. Even granted that many of the current divorces reflect the inordinate burdens placed upon the family, I feel that the opportunities for continued growth for the adult individual and the 'means-character' attributed to the family (*i.e.* not a sacred end in itself) will lead to more changes in marriage partners. This may lead to further population pressure if the remarried people feel the urge to have another child or two in the new marriage; but hardly a serious pressure.

5.4. Life patterns: security, mobility and leisure

1. Anxiety about financial security will not readily be shaken off by the older generations but even their behaviours have been deeply affected by the post-war growth in real incomes and continuing high levels of employment. For the native born citizens of Western countries this improvement in their lot has been even more striking than shown by national statistics. Migrant labour forces from rural economies have increasingly been allotted the unskilled labouring jobs of low income and low security. One effect has been that the pattern of long term accumulation of small and regular savings for old age, or for 'a rainy day' has given way to a pattern of 'saving in order to spend'. In the latter the aim is to save enough, so as to borrow the extra which will enable one to enjoy the product of the spending as soon as possible. It certainly does not generate less saving. With short term attractive goals, saving can be more intense than in the old system. Growth in leisure, and leisure related durables and services, will continue to stimulate this saving pattern, and change in traditional banking practices.

This pattern of saving and spending by the affluent sections of Western societies has highlighted the dilemma of the minorities locked into poverty. Nevertheless I do not think that solution of this problem will push Western societies back away from this pattern and toward the high taxation Welfare State that was formed to handle the poverty of earlier industiialism and, in particular, the mass poverty of the Great Depression. That model emerged as a compassionate, charitable support for those unable to sell their labour power. In its determination to stop such support going to those defined as 'able but unwilling' the Welfare State developed a markedly bureaucratic tendency to tie the individual up in rules and to decide what was best for the individual. Not only is this incompatible with debureaucratising other areas of social life but its underlying concept of the haves and have-nots is being undermined by changes in thinking that promise to be at the very least as radical as the impact of Keynesian economics on concepts of employment and sound economics. The challenges are two-fold but convergent. McHale represents those confronting the technological interdependencies of modern society:

'The new wealth generated by industrial technologies is no longer dependent on the old forms of land, materials, and property.
    Physical materials are now increasingly interconvertible. They are not 'used-up' but increasingly recycled and re-issued in the industrial process. With decreasing input of human and machine energies, physical products have no intrinsic wealth in themselves – other than their human use value. Material property is no longer a major source of economic power and ownership, no longer a necessary use-relation between people and material goods and services.
    Within the new socio-economic realities of this emergent system the older conceptual models of scarcity and competitive marginal survival are not only obsolete but counter-productive and inimical to society's forward development. The new wealth generators, information, knowledge and organization do not lose in value by any range of distributive sharing – as did the older wealth forms of material resource, land, property – they can only gain' (McHale, 1970, p. 264).

We believe that it is this sort of technical change that has led to early recognition in science-based industry that property rights only give privileges of access to resources that are still inalienable parts of a society's total resources (Hill, 1971).

The other challenge is abstruse, publicly unobstrusive and yet potentially more deadly. This is the challenge of the so-called New Cambridge economics (Harcourt and Laing, 1971). Basically they demonstrate that a sound economy is not dependent on allowing real wages and the rate of profit to find their respective levels in the market place, 'the value of either the real wage or the rate of profits is provided from outside the production system (but not via relative demands)' (Harcourt and Laing, *ibid.*, p. 18). Why this challenge is so deadly is that if proposals come forward for negative income taxes, or other forms of income redistribution, they cannot be automatically ruled out as *economically* disastrous, as in past days were ruled out, on theoretical grounds, proposals to limit unemployment, child labour and to shorten the working hours.

The above circumstances will very likely lead to a significant change in 'one of the most extraordinary and little-noticed features of 20th century societies ... In all the Western nations – the United States, Sweden, the United Kingdom, France, Germany – despite the varieties of social and economic policies of their governments, the distribution of income is strikingly similar' (Kristol, 1972, p. 79).

This change is likely to come from re-thinking a whole range of matters from negative income tax and the burdens of indirect taxes on lower income earners to the re-allocation of charges for economic 'externalities' such as pollution, travel to work and replacement of the work force.

2. *Personal mobility* has the aspects of mobility between work-places, between occupations, between communities and mobility for leisure. We will leave comment on the latter till the next section. The mass migration between Western societies that has voluntarily occurred in the post-war years seems to have about run its course. The pool of ablebodied men from the agricultural countries of southern Europe is drying up and there is less and less push on labour in the North to seek better opportunities for themselves and their families in Canada, Australia, *etc.* This would also seem to be true of mass movement within societies from the country to urban areas. The remaining large country groups in France and Germany do not seem about to leave their way of life whilst they have the political power to command economic protection. There is not much room left for change in the other Western societies as they have either completed their agricultural revolution or depleted the supply of 'guest workers'.

Movements between communities within the same society are likely to increase. The newer science-based industries tend to be amortised more rapidly in the expectation of their being rendered obsolete more rapidly by scientific and technical advances. Thus new decisions about location have to be made more often, and under changed conditions. As economic externalities are increasingly taken into account, we can expect some radical changes in location of industries and offices. The costs to the individual of such relocations are likely to be shared by the organisations and the society. All told, fewer people can expect to spend their whole life in the same community.

The pattern of movements in and out of organisations is likely to change significantly. As work is humanised, we can expect marked reductions not only in the minority who contribute, out of all proportions, to labour turnover rates but also in the large body who hang on to their security, with one organisation, for a lifetime. This latter phenomena is no longer appropriate to large organisations who need the flexibility to adjust their numbers to medium term changes in the demands made on them; it becomes less necessary as transportability of pensions and free retraining becomes more generally available; it becomes less desirable as new conditions of work and back-up security make it possible for people, at all ages, to consider new vistas of employment.

Changes in occupation are harder to predict because of the change in the nature of occupations as they become increasingly based on knowledge and less on specialised craft/professional skills or specialised experience. That is, occupations will inevitably become more generalised and diffuse and it will be more difficult to determine whether there is a change of occupation or just an extension of occupational capabilities, or simply a shift in emphasis in what one is doing because of external exigencies. However, whatever the difficulty that census takers might have with labelling the changes, we will see persons being occupied with more different kinds of work in their life than at any stage since bureaucratisation became a general phenomena.

The one major type of personal mobility that has not been referred to is class mobility. This has been the focus of many scenarios of the future. In the more modern scenarios associated with maladaptive strategies the view has usually been taken that societies will find it in their interest to reduce mobility between social classes e.g., Huxley's alpha-beta-, etc. and the 'meritocracies' of Orwell and Young. There has been an older tradition of Utopia's in which all men are equal. I believe the modern scenarios to be based on the false assumption that bureaucracies are here to stay. With the changes discussed above, about work, education, family and security, I think that the issue will become as diffuse as occupational distinctions (they are usually closely related to much fewer distinctions than required by bureaucratic organisation; because coordination is more necessary than supervision and domination). Distinctions in educational level will be less relevant because of both the greater relevance attached to experience in learning-type work and the difficulty of deciding when a person has finished his education. Distinctions in terms of location of residence are likely to be less relevant as people seek to maximise the growth opportunities of their children by seeking to live in small neighbourhoods of high heterogeneity. This latter pattern is of course quite contrary to the present pattern. Those that have a choice today typically choose to live where there is minimal variation from the slot in society for which they are targeting their children or their own occupational future. That is, company directors seek to live where other company directors live. By default, those with little power of choice must live together.

An overview of the predicted changes in personal and family, mobility does not yield a picture like Toffler's transient California. It does not suggest such a regression to superficiality in human relations because it assumes that these patterns of mobility will proceed from debureaucratisation of our major social institutions. I have tried to identify the patterns of mobility that will emerge as individuals, and their families, increasingly shape where and when they move. The Californian type patterns occurred at a peak of bureaucratisation in the society. Masses of highly specialised engineers, scientists, managers and craftsmen chasing an employment boom to capitalize on their special training. The situations are so different that I feel there is little future in Toffler's 'future shock absorbers' (1970, p. 339). These are obviously conceived as tactical ways of better confronting the stresses of turbulent environments; not as adaptive strategies. Nor do the range of tactics refer to the much larger numbers in Western societies, whose growth potentialities are frozen in a life as unchanging as their work, but who watch the rest of their world parade past on the T.V. screen.

3. It may seem strange that I seek to deal with the future of *leisure* in a subsection, unlike the prominence given to work, education and family. I did, however, do the same for the topic of economic security/affluence, for the same reason. The significance of leisure, per se, in future Western societies seems to have been grossly overestimated because the people specialising in studying leisure have made simple assumptions about the evolution of the rest of the society. The most gross assumption, that had considerable airing, was that automation would render redundant the great mass of unskilled and semi-skilled workers. Western societies would then be faced with the circuses and bread problem of later Rome. By the end of the sixties this scenario seemed strikingly irrelevant. There was no sign of a relentlessly increasing mass of unrequired labour. It was obvious that the great majority of people would be continuing to work.

A new scenario emerged that recognised that the mass of unskilled and semi-skilled work was not going to go away, in either manual or mental work. It predicted that we could and would use our growing affluence to automate out those tasks which were especially dangerous or brutalising, reduce the hours of work, raise incomes and seek to enhance the quality of individuals compensatory areas of choice in their lives: to choose between a wide range of leisure oriented products. This is a pretty good prediction of the present. Hours worked per lifetime are declining, incomes are increasing and the 'leisure market – from electronic gear to second homes – is probably the fastest growing market in Western economies. To organise this market there is an emerging profession of 'recreationalists', displacing in significance the older skills of the physical educationalist. In line with this way of thinking the question is being asked whether education will not have to become 'education for leisure'. A great deal of this new leisure is organised about the increased mobility offered by car, jet aircraft and cruise ships (Patmore, 1972). Working on trend lines from 1955 it would seem an easy matter to project the future of leisure. More and more of the same, only increasingly sophisticated and more capital intensive. The main cloud on the horizon of this scenario is the emerging paradox that the more people are free to choose their leisure the more they spoil it for each other. We are not here referring to the modern gladiatorial spectacles of football because these are increasingly for the viewer, not the spectator. We refer to the more affluent forms of leisure that require access to, and use of outdoor areas. However, well planned and developed and managed these outside resources are it seems inevitable that leisure choices would become more and more restricted, and hence less compensatory.

This will not be the future of leisure and we should not expect to see, except for the next few years, local elections fought between those representing the day-trippers, trail-bikies, hunters, *etc.* and the conservationists. That is, between those concerned with exploiting the environment in pursuit of individual pleasure and those concerned with the continuing potential of the environment to give pleasure.

Whilst the current scenario sees an end to inhumane and brutalising work and to unendurable hours (playing with 'flexible hours', for 4 day weeks) it still takes for granted the persistence of bureaucratised work as the norm. The problem for us is to try to see what people do with their leisure as worklife and schooling are increasingly democratized and the family changes to exploit the new possibilities. Leisure is in its nature free, relative to the other roles in work, family and education which always retain some core of commitments. To that extent if is even harder to predict what might happen. The amount of genuine novelty is likely to be too great. What is not likely to happen is easier to predict because of what we know about how current and past forms of leisure are embedded in their social contexts. Thus, there seems little reason to believe that we are moving to the classic utopian situation; to the Big Rock Candy Mountain. Commitments remain too many. Similarly, I do not see a real possibility of the second leisure scenario working its way by bureaucratising leisure. What the 'surfies' did to undermine the almost paramilitary Surf Life Saving Clubs of Australia is evidence of the hopelessness of this solution even before debureaucratisation has hardly begun. Technological solutions, such as colour television, are not viable solutions. People who feel themselves to be growing by way of meaningful involvement in work, family and education are not likely to be seduced even by a technological opiate as rich as that envisaged by the science fiction writer Ray Bradbury in *The Illustrated Man* (1967).

Thus it does not seem possible to make the more specific predictions that I made in other areas because there is so little that must necessarily carry over to the future. There is, however, a clue as to what may well be the overriding ideal that will tend to guide men in the choice of their leisure purposes. This clue is given, in pretty obvious form, by De Grazia in trying to predict 'Leisure's Future' at the end of his classic study *Of Time, Work and Leisure*:

'Leisure, given its proper political setting, benefits, gladdens and *beautifies* the lives of all. It lifts up all heads from practical workaday life to look at the whole high work with refreshened wonder. The urge to celebrate is there.

Felicity, happiness, blessedness. Certainly the life of leisure is the life for thinkers, artists, and musicians' (1962, 415).

The conclusion to draw from De Grazia's clue is this: the pursuit of the ideals of homonomy, nurturance and humanity are unavoidably those that will engage men in their involvement in work, education and family. It is only in leisure that men will be able to wholeheartedly pursue the ideal of beauty, without which harmonious social and personal development is unlikely.

In the earlier discussion of the ideal of beauty I identified it as that dimension of choosing between purposes that concerned relative value of intention. What I am now saying is, that, in his leisure, man has a chance to lift his eyes above the level of better fulfilment of his commitments to ponder on whether there may not be a more harmonious, more beautiful order in his pursuits. I am predicting more, namely, that no matter how much men may shape their leisure to allow of pursuit of other ideals, they will be increasingly concerned in their leisure with the pursuit of beauty. Their concern with this will be enhanced as they are able in work, *etc.* to pursue the other ideals and hence realise that approach to the overriding ideal, the meta ideal of omnipotence is not possible without some concurrent ability to pursue the ideal of beauty (as a side comment I feel that those engaged in higher intellectual pursuits will probably be able to reach the same conclusion and hence be desirous of making a place in their lives for leisure despite the dire predictions of these people being headed for a seventy-two week whilst the ordinary folk head for the twenty-seven hour week).

6. A Scenario for Asia and the West

In composing the scenario for the Western societies I assumed that those societies were the leading part of the world's societies; where they went the other societies were bound to follow, sooner or later.

This appears to be the commonly held assumption. Even Kahn, in his study of Japan as *The Emerging Superstate*, gave a picture of Japan as if it were just another competing Western-type nation and would remain so. Admittedly, in the second last paragraph of the book, he reveals that his contact with Japanese culture had created a small doubt in his mind:

'It does appear that the Showa generation (post-war) will carry forward – with added confidence – essentially those policies that made Japan the world's third economic power; *but* it is not unreasonable to think that the 1970's may also produce a reassertion of nationalism and an attempt to redefine Japanese national and cultural identity, rather than pursuing the adoption of foreign models that has characterized the twenty-five years since the end of the war '(p. 183; our italics).

We shall come back to this doubt even though Kahn does not elaborate on it. For the moment, however, let us turn to Drucker who has given a very clear and unambiguous statement of the common assumptions. The chapter in which he does this is entitled 'The Vanishing East' and it sums up his belief that:

'Every single one of the new countries in the world today sees its goal in its transformation into a Western state, economy and society, and sees the means to achieve this goal in the theories, institutions, sciences, technologies and tools the West has developed' (1957, p. 235).

He stresses that

'This is not speculation. It is experience. In the three oldest and most advanced and richest non-Western cultures – Japan, China and India – the attempt has been made to base a viable society on inherited, non-Western foundations – and in all three it has failed' (*ibid.*, p. 238).

That was in 1957, now, in 1973, one can no longer assume that the West is *the* leading part, if only because China is not following. I believe that the picture may be changing even more radically and that China may be emerging as the leading part amongst the Asia nations. Whether this is a world polarising around different and potentially conflicting centres is a question I will leave until I have examined the apparent about-face in China.

6.1. China as the leading part in Asia

Despite the great economic strength of Japan there would still be some general grounds for considering China as at least the potentially leading part. The whole history of mankind knows of no phenomena comparable to that of China. On any objective criteria of cultural homogeneity they are by far the largest group of people sharing the same culture, language and territory in the world. This has been so throughout written history (which in any case probably begins with their 'Bamboo Annals') and the Chinese themselves seem to have been aware of this, hence their description of China as 'the Middle Kingdom', the middle of the world. Not only this but their culture extends back beyond the early mists of time without any significant breaks.

However, there are more compelling grounds at the present time to consider China as actually emerging as the leading part in Asia. The scenario for this future has been written by none other than Chairman Mao. When, at the end of 1958, Chairman Mao Tse Tung stepped down from Headship of the State, it was not hard for outside observers to accept that he had done so in order to devote his attention to formulating a general plan for China's future. Chinese society has such a past history of the wise man retiring to the hills to contemplate that this was not a strange turn of events. However, when Mao returned to the forefront in September 1962 there was still no sign of the expected blueprint. Our belief is that the document *On the Ten Major Relationships* is the document we were looking for. It was not produced in the period we were watching, 1959-62, but had already been produced, as one might have expected, before the change of course in 1956.

We consider that the document in question has generally been overlooked, although Franz Schurmann working only from Liu Shao-ch'i's brief mention of it in one page of his fifty page report to the 1958 Congress session, manages to discern much from the relation the speech bore to the Great Leap Forward. (Schurmann, 1965, 74ff.) He quite correctly views the 1956 speech in conjunction with the 27 February 1957 speech *On the Correct Handling of Contradictions Among the People*, the first being seen primarily in terms of economic contradictions and 'relationships' and the second in terms of political and societal contradictions. This is important in erecting what he presents as his 'dialectical conception of Chinese society' (*ibid.*). The creative employment of these various contradictions was part of the rationale of the Great Leap, which, Schurmann maintains, was more the product of a vision than of a plan. We would suggest that an examination of the full text of the 1956 document shows that it is much closer to a plan than Schurmann believed, although it most certainly is not a plan in the sense of providing a blueprint for the future, complete with targets and figures on projected development.

It is important if we are to trace the viscissitudes of Mao's model building through the maze of official actions and policies to try to interpret the historical course of this particular document. A comparison of this paper with Mao's speech of 31 July 1955 on *The Question of Agricultural Cooperation* reveals a qualitative leap. In his 1955 speech there are some opening generalisations that in retrospect read like premonitions of the great rush to the communes in 1958 but the details of the speech spell out with apparent approval all of the critical features of the Soviet model. First, it is *the* model, next, the priority of industry and within that of heavy industry, the step-by-step development of the economy through successive five year plans, the step-by-step development of relations of production in agriculture in lock-step with the development of the means of production and, lastly, 'to raise steadily the socialist consciousness of the peasants ... and so minimise any feeling that their mode of life is being changed all of a sudden' (Schram, *ibid.*, A 346). Bearing in mind the contradictory tone of Mao's opening speech and the fact that Mao, not much earlier had had to fight a twelve month's political campaign before he annihilated Kao's Manchurian group (1953-1954), it seems more likely that 'the voice is the voice of Jacob but the words are the words of Esau'. The reaffirmation of collective leadership after the Kao Jao could as well

have been to contain Mao as to prevent the emergence of new Kao Kangs.
It did coincide with the anti 'stalinistic cult of the individual' phase
abroad and was to be followed in September 1956 with the removal of
the reference to *The Thought of Mao Tse Tung* in the Party Constitution.
The alternative hypothesis, that Mao underwent a major disillusion and
formulated his model, all within the nine months between the delivery of
these two documents seems humanly improbable. After all, he was, unlike
Saul (Paul), not picking up a readymade model of man's future relation
with the heavens.

The political climate within which Mao was to further develop his
model of the future is well indicated by the fact that is *On the Ten Major
Relationships* was not distributed by the Central Committee, even to its
own bureau, until 27 December 1965, although the 'poor but blank' notion was released by Mao in April 1958 (Schram, p. 351). That is,
throughout the nine years from 1956-1965, Mao's alternative scenario for
the future was denied to the Chinese people and even to the party cadres
who were charged with the responsibility of carrying out the critical
social experiments to test the new model in the Commune Movement and
the Great Leap Forward. Under these conditions, where the experiments
were carried out by a centralized party bureaucracy who did not even
know the rationale for the experiments, it was little wonder that Mao
should remark bitterly that those experiments only failed because some
people did not try hard enough.

The circumstances of the release of this document provide a clue, also,
to the opening period of the Cultural Revolution. Its release in December
1965 just preceeded this critical phase. We suggest that the other Central
Committee members were aware that Mao was determined to get a decision to launch a Cultural Revolution (*cf*. attacks on Wu Han in November
1965). The model that the majority of the C.C. decided to release to the
cadres represented Mao's thoughts *before* the experience of the Communes and the Great Leap. It did not reflect any development in Mao's
thoughts that might have occurred in his second 'Yenan period' the
three and one-half years (1959-1963) that the C.C. originally announced
as an opportunity for Mao to contemplate future course of China. It
begins to look as though Mao's colleagues, confronted with the shambles
produced by their handling of his 1956 model had suggested that he go

away and think again. There has been some suggestion that Mao himself
was unhappy at being sent to vegetate. In particular, the 1956 document
could not reflect any of Mao's thoughts on the negative role of the party
bureaucracy in those first experiments (Schram, p. 353). The C.C. noted
that:

'This document is a recorded copy of the speech made at that time (*i.e.* not something
that Mao had had a chance to touch up). Recently Comrade Mao Tsetung found it not
very satisfactory after going through it, but he agreed (note: not 'he decided') to send
it to the lower level to solicit opinion'.

So, with the opening of the Cultural Revolution, Mao once again found
himself in the position of having his ideas tested out in practice without
his ideas being communicated to the cadres responsible for the field
testing.

By looking at the historical viscissitudes of the document *On the Ten
Major Relationships* we may have gotten a valid sense of the climate of
the struggle and counter-struggle that must have greeted the presentation
of the document. More important are the facts of the contrast between the
1955 document and the 1956 one, the long delay in releasing the 1956
document and the C.C. refusal to allow Mao to amend it, or even add
postscripts. These facts warn us that when Mao has spoken he has not
necessarily spoken what *he* thinks (presumably Liu Shao Chi had to
suffer similarly). One must be prepared to look for the post 1956 developments in Mao's thoughts in the Aesopian language of the combative
leader forced to conform to 'collective leadership' but determined that
'one must divide into two'.

Having roamed so far afield let us now return to *On the Ten Major Relationships*. If analysis of this gives us a clear map of Mao's model for the
future it should be a lot easier to identify subsequent emendations.

To help us appreciate the content we wish to draw attention to two
aspects of the immediate context within which Mao presented the paper.

1. 'This policy (Mao's Mass Line Policy) should be carried out both
   in the course of the revolution and in the course of construction'.
   (The *Current Background* version (*CB*) 892, p. 21). This is a straightout
   declaration of war by Mao on the Soviet Model. The proponents of

the Soviet model had to insist that Mao's path that led to 1949 was simply an historical peculiarity and that the leadership had to fight for the qualitative break onto the Soviet path.

2. It seems on internal evidence that the meeting to which Mao delivered this paper was called specifically to enable a confrontation of the two models of the future (*i.e.* it was not just Mao who expected a fight). Thus as Mao said in coming to the final point 'The meeting of today is convened not for other purposes but for summing up the two points of experience: merits and demerits' (pp. 32-33). What two points of experience? The merits and demerits of what two points of experience? He says this in the second paragraph dealing with the tenth relationship, the relationship between China and other countries. We know with what other country China and its future planning was most imbricated. For a man who founded the rebirth of his nation with the promise that 'it will never again be an insulted nation', it is fairly obvious that when he starts on this relationship by urging his colleagues to 'have the courage to discard state pretentiousness' he is asking them to see through the screen of pretensions put up by the Soviet state.

He followed this introduction with the statement that 'Each nation has its strong points and that is why they can exist and develop. The acknowledgment that each nation has its strong points does not mean there are no shortcomings and weak points' (p. 32). This seems to be saying that just because the Soviet model survives and develops in the Soviet Union, it is not necessarily China's model.

The other thing to bear in mind is that this meeting took place only after two months within which the Political Bureau had separately heard *and* exchanged views (presumably in meetings by themselves) on the work reports of 34 Departments of Economics and Finance. The mind begins to boggle at the sustained intensity of effort involved in that exercise. One could be forgiven for assuming that something serious was afoot, something that was number one item on the agenda of the Political Bureau, not, mind you, the State Planning Committee. It does suggest that Mao had moved from spoiling tactics to wholesale offensive against the Soviet model. It was not just 'the meeting of today' which was called to consider the relative merits and demerits of different countries but what must have been a nearly total absorption of the Political Bureau of the Chinese Communist Party for two months. By the criteria of any political system this would count as a particularly significant event.

Turning from the immediate context in which Mao presented his document we can now examine the context of the Ten Relationships.

The first eight relationships essentially present Mao's model; the ninth relationship deals with how this model can be realised and the tenth with the implications that taking such a road would have for China's relations with Russia.

The model is presented in three parts:

1. Relationships 1 to 3 cover the principles that should guide the future allocation of China's resources.
2. Relationship 4 covers the principles that should guide the social organisation of production.
3. Relationships 5 to 8 deal with what in Mao's military terminology would be 'the Rear Area'.

What strikes one straight away is the peculiar dialectical formulation that is used for the principles concerning allocation, and only for those. This takes the form 'If you are genuine in saying you strongly desire *A* then you should give the more preference to *B*, although at any one time choice of *B* excludes *A*'.

More specifically, Mao undermines the three great pillars of the Soviet model for economic development.

'If you truly have a strong desire for heavy industry, then you should sink more capital in light industry, otherwise your desire is not 100 per cent genuine but only 90 per cent genuine'.
'If you have a stronger desire, then you must pay attention to the development of light industry and agriculture ... After a number of years the capital sunk in heavy industry will also be greater' (p. 23).

He thus challenges the Soviet dogma of industry before agriculture, heavy industry before light. He even explicitly states that the Soviet model of putting the price-scissors on agriculture has harmed the development of some socialist countries.

In discussing the third relationship, Mao challenges a third principle that has been inherent in the Soviet model, the priority of defense construction over economic construction:

'to become stronger militarily the most reliable method is to keep military and government expenditure at a proper proportion and to reduce it in a number of stages to about 30 per cent of the state budget, so that the expenditure in economic construction can be increased ... in this way, *in not too long a time*, we would own many airplanes and big guns...' (p. 25).

However, it seems that Mao's main objection is to the build up of modern conventional military technology: 'But we also had no airplanes and big guns in the past. We depended on millet plus rifles to defeat the Japanese aggressors and Chiang Kai Shek' (A 25). He makes an exception of nuclear weapons and poses the matter as a strategic choice: either nuclear weapons *or* 'airplanes and big guns'. Note that he does not allow that they could reject both.

'Do you genuinely want atomic bombs? You must lower the proportion of military and government expenditure and carry out more economic construction. If your desire for atomic bombs is a spurious one then you don't have to lower the proportion of military and government expenditure and you can carry out less economic construction. Which is after all the better course? All of you are requested to study the issue. This is a question of strategic policy'.

It is not made explicit what strategy is served by nuclear weapons that is not served by guns, tanks and planes. It can be noted in passing that:

1. the peculiar conditions that give China a high degree of invulnerability to nuclear weapons, *i.e.* geographical extensity, enormous population and primitiveness, do not protect Russia and U.S.A. to anywhere near the same degree;
2. to the extent that China based her defence on a modern military technology it would lose some of this invulnerability as its defense capabilities would rest on such prime targets as the industrial complex of Anshan;
3. a sufficient build-up of modern weapons might enable China to carry the war into Soviet territory but would not allow her to annihilate U.S.A. or Japan. Possession of nuclear warheads and even primitive delivery systems automatically 'annihilates' Japan and it does not matter whether or not Japan chooses to develop nuclear warfare

capabilities. For Mao's war game, as in *wei-ch'i*, annihilated the moment you 'deprive him of his power of resistance'. So much for Herman Kahn's prediction that Japan not China would be the giant of Asia by the year 2000.

Let us, however, look at the remaining problem of resources allocation that Mao discusses as the second relationship. This is an amazing statement for 1956:

'All of us want to develop inland industry. The question is whether your desire is genuine or false. If your desire is genuine and not false, then you must make greater utilisation of coastal industry and promote more coastal industry – especially light industry' (p. 14).

In this matter Mao stresses an urgency that does not appear in his discussion of the other problems of allocation: 'We should make maximum use of the time which can be utilised to develop coastal industry' (p. 23) (*i.e.* maximum not optimal; but within what time limits: why any time limits?). 'It will cost us dearly if we pay no attention to coastal industry' (p. 24).

It could be argued that all of this is strictly within an economic perspective. That the time limit is something like catching up with Western living standards and that 'cost us dearly' simply refers to potential economic loss.

Mao is not discussing the principles of future allocation in a strictly economist perspective. We have already noted his concern that a choice be made between a 'Yenan army and nuclear weapons' or 'a modern army'. In introducing that part of his discussion Mao stated, 'The enemy is challenging us, and we are still *encircled* by the enemy'. Mao would not be sloppy in formulating a matter as important and dangerous as this. How could China be 'encircled by enemies' if Russia were China's ally? Perhaps by 'we' Mao meant the socialist camp? This seems unlikely. His immediately preceeding questions concerned China's *national* defence not combined armed strength of the socialist bloc. Far more significant is the thrust of Mao's proposal. Mao's strategy in war has been that of the wei-ch'i player, that is, to ensure victory one must first seize the edge of the board. Whilst *the* enemy was the U.S.A. the edge of the board was in the northern, western and to a lesser extent the central provinces. Deployment of industry in these provinces was Chinese policy after 1949.

Now in 1956 we have Mao advocating development in the coastal regions within the strike radius of the U.S. Seventh Fleet. This could be the edge of the board only if the enemy were the Soviet Union. If war with the Soviet Union was the most likely eventuality then Mao's proposal was rational. Perhaps Mao was not even thinking about any war as a likely eventuality, only about economic rationality? He explicitly mentions the rationality of spreading industrial development to the inland but 'However, part of the heavy industry must be built and expanded along the coast' (p. 24).

I think we must conclude that Mao had decided by this time that:

1. Russia's Soviet model was contrary to that which constituted an 'integration of the universal truth of Marxist-Leninism with the concrete practice of China' (p. 33);
2. that Russia was not only on a different course but was also an enemy, hence China was encircled by enemies;
3. that Russia was the primary enemy, hence the proposal to develop coastal industry;
4. that conflict was close, hence his sense of urgency about relocation to the coasts.

Mao's desire for an immediate decision about nuclear weapons should therefore be seen in the context of armed conflict with Russia. This could take on a pretty grisly note when we remember that for Mao:

'The annihilation of the enemy is the main objective of war, while the preservation of oneself is the secondary one because it is only by annihilating the enemy in large numbers that one can effectively preserve oneself' (*Selected Works, Vol.* 2, p. 206).

However, a strike at the will-to-fight of the Russian population in the west would meet Mao's notion of annihilation. Nuclear demonstrations would do that.

Just looking at the first three relationships we have found Mao proposing major deviations to three of the fundamental principles of the Soviet model for economic development. We have also found him rejecting the assumption that Russia was a co-producer of China's future, at least in any positive sense. What other aspects, if any, of the Soviet model does Mao revise or reject?

The fourth relationship concerns the social organisation of production in both industry and agriculture. The basic Soviet model was to build these productive organisations on the principal of 'To each according to his contribution', *i.e.* widespread use of economic incentives for individual performance and large skill differentials in wages, salaries and side benefits. Mao challenges this. The problem as he sees it concerns the 'production unit' as much as the individual; the production unit is not simply a transmission belt between the state and the individual:

'We have talked about the need of paying attention to bringing the initiative and enthusiasm of the workers into play. There is also the question of initiative and enthusiasm for the factory as a production unit' (p. 25).

As Mao sees it neither he nor his colleagues on the C.C. have much experience of this (p. 26) but the task is that of 'giving of essential *benefits* to individual producers and certain *initiatives* to production units'.

In thinking this way Mao is in harmony with some of the more recent empirical studies in Western social science (see our earlier discussion of democratisation of work). He is certainly not thinking of the production units as blind agents of a centralised Soviet type planning structure:

'If all things were centralized and even the depreciation funds were taken away from the factory the production unit would have no initiative, and this is disadvantageous' (p. 26).
(Note: Mao did not say 'could be' or 'might be' disadvantageous).

On the other side Mao does not see the 'production unit' as absorbing to itself all 'independent character' and 'differences' to the exclusion of individual independence and differences: 'People would get killed that way' (p. 26). Unfortunately, for anyone seeking strong evidence of convergence with Western thought, Mao's example (p. 26) refers only to allowing individuality between meetings (off the job).

Mao saw the desirable organization of agricultural production in the same light: 'The collective organisation of the peasants is also a production unit' (p. 26). He questions the Soviet model of collectivisation: 'On this question, some socialist countries have probably made mistakes' (p. 26). After demonstrating from the Chinese experience of 1954 and 1955 that the traditional causal relation between peasant welfare and peasant loyalty still existed, Mao pointed out the need in agriculture for the same pattern of *benefits* to the individual and *initiative* to the collective.

Despite the parallelism between Mao's model for the social organisation of production and some recent Western trends it should be noted that his basic notion is at the heart of Asian culture but not of Western culture. For Western culture the dominant ideal has been that reward and achievement should meet and balance with the individual (we are not concerned here with the fact that this ideal is not well represented amongst all that are regarded as Western cultures). For the Asian cultures the rewards of achievement ideally accrue to the family or group, and the individual received benefits as a member, not rewards as an achiever. Not 'rewards' because what he can achieve for the family, or group, he should naturally strive to achieve as a matter of duty to the group.

It is clear that the Soviet model is, and is seen by Mao, as a typical Western reliance upon individual selfishness as the foundation of productive organisation. It is quite likely that Mao sees his shift of emphasis to individual benefits and group initiative as an 'integration of the universal truth of Marxism-Leninism with the concrete practice of China' (p. 33).

The remaining part of Mao's model concerns the organisation of the society. He deals with it in the 5th, 6th, 7th and 8th relationships.

First, Mao rejects the Soviet model of a pyramidal structure whereby an all powerful, all knowing central authority reaches down to plan and control at all levels.

'All ministries issue orders to the provincial departments and municipal bureaux under their jurisdiction every day ... so many returns and reports have to be filed that they assume the proportions of a disaster. All this should be changed': (p. 27). 'In short, local administration must posess appropriate rights, and this is advantageous to our building a strong and powerful socialist society' (p. 28).

Second, whilst emphasizing the need to oppose great Hanism (p. 28) Mao makes a very significant statement which can leave no doubt that the thinks China's future depends on the Han.

'The minority nationalities are extensive in area and rich in resources. There is a big population of the Han nationality and there are plenty of treasures underground. They are essential to the building of socialism'.

Thirdly, Mao sees a marked decline in the historical role of the Communist Party.

'...we must oppose bureaucracy and overexpansion of organizations. I suggest that the Party and government organs be retrenched on a large scale and cut away by *two-thirds*' (p. 29).

Mao could not have arrived at a figure of this magnitude unless he envisaged a qualitative change in China's institutional structure.

Fourthly, on the enforcement of law and order, Mao insists that China should continue to execute 'counter-revolutionary saboteurs and murderers but only if they are not in the government, schools or army'. This is a longstanding deviation from Soviet assumptions about the non re-educability of people but the major deviation is Mao's alternative to the Soviet model of creating a vast labour reserve for the Central Administration:

'The majority of counterrevolutionaries should be handed over to agricultural producer cooperatives so that they may carry out production under surveillance and reform themselves through labour' (p. 31).

Do all these specific deviations give a coherent model?

In order to try and get a picture in our mind of how these different facets of Mao's model come together let us imagine Chinese society as a great wei-ch'i board. On this board the great national institutions and organisations naturally occupy the central position: the heavy industries will be more central than the light industries and the light industries more so than agriculture. Our wei-ch'i player wants to have a determining influence on the future state of the board, many moves ahead. Looking at this board he knows that he cannot control the future state of the board by any degree of power he builds up over the centre of the board. If he wants to 'win' he must move to and control the edges of the board and in particular to find and control the 'corners'.

We suggest that this is basically how Mao has been looking at China and its future. This is what Mao meant when he introduced the document with the statement that 'This policy (*i.e.* Mao's line) should be carried out *both* in the course of revolution and in the course of construction' (p. 21). Just as the typically Chinese strategy of wei-ch'i successfully solved the problems of the revolutionary struggle (see Mao, *On Protracted War* which follows and even explicitly draws upon wei-ch'i) so Mao sees this as the strategy for controlling China's future destiny.

What is important for our understanding is to identify what Mao sees as 'the corners' of the board. This document has suggested two such corners: the 'production unit' not the individual (relationship 4) and the Han people not the minorities or not just anyone (relationship 6).

By moving to the edge of the board and controlling the corners the good wei-ch'i player still cannot predict when or how the board will evolve. The board is far too complex for the forward strategic planning of the Western chess master. However, by further strengthening his grip on the edge of the board and by constant encirclement and counterencirclement the game will start to go his way.

If this then is Mao's model for China's future, how did he propose to achieve it and what would be the international effects of China electing to follow its own peculiarly Chinese path and to 'desert' the Soviet path.

Mao devotes his discussion of the 9th and 10th relationship to these two questions.

In respect to the first, 'The Relationship between Right and Wrong', his answer is clear. Not less than five times he reiterates that 'we should allow the people to make revolution'. That is right. What is wrong is to 'forbid people to make revolution'. To make mistakes (commit excesses?) is not to Mao's mind the main wrong because they and the mistaken people can be corrected. Together with Mao's proposal to dismantle two-thirds of the Party and Government bureaucracy this shows that Mao was thinking of an aroused mass as the main agents of change, not the Party. There is no suggestion in this document that Mao had yet come to see the youth as a 'corner' of the board.

The last of Mao's points has already been dealt with earlier because Mao, in apparent anticipation of a hostile Soviet reaction, had built into his model the about-face on industrialising the coastal areas and the concept of 'a peasant army and nuclear weapons'. What is additional and no doubt critical to Mao's plan is that 'some effort be made to raise the confidence of the Chinese people. We should as Mencius said, 'despise the Lords'' (p. 33). From despising the West to hating the West is a short step, e.g. 'the spirit of despising U.S. imperialism which we (the Chinese) manifested in the resist U.S. and Korea campaign' (p. 33).

So far we have examined the historical circumstances surrounding the release of this document, the context within which it first emerged and lastly its contents.

From the contents of this document it is clear that Mao was proposing for China a new definition of its national and cultural identity and rejecting the Soviet model. Some of the major distinctions between these models are presented in the following paradigm.

Table 6.1.1. Elements of two Models of the future: Soviet and Mao's.

	Soviet (Western)	Mao's
1. Time perspective	Successive five year periods	Fifty + years, 'protracted'
2. Goal selection	Rationally measurable – maximization of individual gain (standard of living and G.N.P.)	Fitting to national character: 'satisfying'
3. Main source of possibilities	In science and technology	In people
4. Emergent social structure	Growing harmony and integration: 'two into one'	Continuing conflict diversification: 'one into two'
5. Where $(5 = f(1, 2, 3, 4))$	Modelled on chess	Modelled on wei-ch'i
6. Extra-model assumption	Soviet as co-producer of the the future	China as producer of her own future

The most striking thing is that Mao is rejecting not just a Soviet model but one that has all the essential ingredients of the Western model: but it is the Western model we identified earlier with adaptation to disturbed, reactive environments and maladaptation to turbulent environments. *The Western model that we saw as emerging to cope with turbulent environ-*

ments appears to have been moving more or less independently toward
something like Mao's planning model.

We may now ask about the effects the document has had and is likely
to have. The Commune Movement and the Great Leap Forward clearly
derive from Mao's model and the fact that they happened shows that the
C.C. had to take serious cognizance of Mao's models. The C.C., however, would not agree to vacate the centre of the board: they wanted it
both ways. Thus they did not release Mao's thoughts to the people, they
did not allow the people to make revolution but preferred to work
through task forces sent out from the centre, they sought to strengthen
party control, not dismantle 'two-thirds'. As these great campaigns
'proved' Mao wrong he withdrew personally toward the edge of the
board to work off-centre with Shanghai and the Peoples' Liberation
Army and evolve his basic model in two important respects:

1. to identify the role that China should play on the wei-ch'i board of the
world and
2. to recognize the youth as a critical corner on the Chinese board.

With the launching of the Cultural Revolution in 1966 China at least took
Mao's recommended path of debureaucratisation on a scale and with a
tempo that was inconceivable and unbelievable to the rest of the world.
Of all the institutions of the society only the armed services stood un-
attacked. Because Mao and Lin Piao had spent the earlier part of the
sixties democratising them and heavily indoctrinating them in 'the
thoughts of Mao'. In fact it was the army paper that officially launched
the revolution on 18 April 1966. Otherwise, the youth of the country
were, with the encouragement of Mao and the army, unleashed against
the Party, the Administration, the trade unions, the educational establishments, the arts.

Looking back it seems that whilst Mao failed in his plan for a Great
Leap Forward in production (using the Soviet type bureaucratic apparatus) he succeeded in his later gamble with the Cultural Revolution.
No one took advantage of their internal turmoil to invade them; the
cultural and social homogeneity kept violence and destruction at sur-
prisingly low levels and allowed central leadership to re-emerge towards

the end of 1968. This time, however, on a basis of more broadly based Revolutionary Committees; their nuclear program seems to have kept to plan despite the disturbances although military observers believe their missile program may have slipped a year or two.

China emerged with what appears to have bettered Mao's target for a 'two-thirds' reduction in bureaucracy. The pattern of semi-autonomous group working appears to be general in industry, agriculture and education. The old 'ballistic' pattern in education seems to have been firmly replaced by a pattern of recurrent education with a close intermeshing of education and work experience.

The small street and production team settings for the family had been in existence before the Cultural Revolution but the widespread revolt of the young against their elders has apparently made it more difficult for the old age and sex subordinations to be reimposed in the privacy of the home. We can conclude that if this is indeed Mao's model for China's future then:

1. after 17 years it is pre-eminent over the Soviet model and, now that it is *the* Chinese model there is no reason why it cannot and will not be grasped and carried on by Mao's successors. Lin Piao's defection was more notable for the ease with which it was coped than for the apparent inability of Piao to accept the 'weight moving to the other foot'; back from heavy reliance on the armed services. Mao has apparently success fully taken the forces of Chinese revolution on this second Long March to the edges of the board;
2. that China will evolve, as far ahead as we can see, by constant revolutions of the people 'to strengthen the grip on the edges' and 'by constant encirclement and counter encirclement' of China's institutions, leading in many cases to their annihilation;
3. internationally there is no end goal in sight for the Chinese, just a protracted relentless struggle to seize the edges of the world board. In this case it seems that they identify the edges with the underdeveloped areas and dissident minorities in Western societies.

There remain several very general questions that are highly pertinent but cannot be answered in the manner we have so far followed. Perhaps it is rash to try to answer them yet.

1. Why the optimism of Mao and the Chinese about China's future when she faced the hostility of the two greatest industrial and military powers in the world, both possessing massive nuclear capability?
2. Why the optimism of Mao and the Chinese that the mistakes, excesses, of the Chinese people in revolution will stay within correctable limits?
3. Why the easy assumption that 'counter revolutionaries' will not corrupt and seduce the producer cooperatives to which they are sent?
4. What was it that Mao wished to write on the 'blank white paper of the peasant mind'?

The simplest answer to the first question is 'remember Engineer Yu'. As the Chinese see it, within their cultural heritage, they have as a people met and survived challenges from ancient natural disasters that surpass anything modern man can conceive.

For the second and third questions the same answer will suffice. If a people are as culturally homogeneous as the Han, and that culture stretches further back before the death of Christ than it does after, then there can be little reason to doubt that, given the right to rebel and make their own future they will make it in line with their past; given the responsibility to correct 'counter revolutionaries' they will bring them in line with China's past heritage. Standing between the Chinese people and their cultural heritage there is only, in Mao's perception, bureaucracy. By elimination of this bureaucracy or, in his 1956 estimate, two-thirds of it, the Chinese people should be able to see and act on their heritage. We cannot believe that Mao has revised this estimate on the basis of the past seventeen years.

To the fourth question we think Mao has given the answer. On the blank white pieces of paper he wanted to write the thoughts of Mao, as once before had been written the thoughts of Confucius. As he was to discover at the end of the 1956 session his model of the future was not going to be released to any others but, in drafting his document Mao seemed well aware that the blank minds of China would be a world-shaping force if imprinted with his uniquely Chinese perception of where they were going, of where they could go.

6.2. China and the leading role of the West

It would seem logically that we should go from considering China to considering China in relation to the rest of Asia, before bringing in the relations with the West.

This had been my intent. However, the dynamics of the situation seem to require a different treatment. China, after her recent internal revolution is clearly leading the rest of Asia on the path they wish to follow; that of overcoming Western influence and defining a social and cultural identity that accords with their people, their history and their economic situation. At the same time China's internal revolution has placed her ahead of the Western societies on some of the key paths that they will need to follow to overcome the turbulence in their environment, *e.g.* debureaucratisation of work, education and administration, liberation of women and children, redesigning city life.

On the international scene China has emerged as the leading part, at least temporarily. Hence we must consider this matter first, as China's relations with Asia will depend to an important degree upon the relation between China and the West.

Most writers have assumed that the West (including perhaps a westernized Japan) would play the leading role for at least the next thirty years. Therefore we need to look closely at our opposing conclusion.

1. With its Cultural Revolution China both shocked the Western world into a realisation that another powerful part of the world was set on a basically different path and confronted it with a set of initiatives to which they could only follow suit.

2. Let us take the first point. Westerners could readily comprehend that foreign invaders might find it convenient to destroy the central institutions of the invaded countries (although even the Nazis were extremely coy of that, *e.g.* the recognition of 'Unoccupied France', and their continued utilisation of the collective farm organisations in occupied Russia). What was shocking was that a politically stable society, for such China was on 5 August 1966, should be incited by its leader to 'Bombard the

Headquarters'; that formal education be stopped for over a year and free transport offered to millions of youths so that institutional leaders in all shapes and forms (except in the Armed Services) could be personally terrorised; that the relevance of all the central institutions could be put to doubt. Production, education, even the Communist Party, were treated as secondary to establishing the universal validity, within China, of Mao's thoughts. The most recent similar event was the emergence of Mohammed and that was in the desert, not in the most populous territory in the world.

3. No Chinese military forces left their territory in 1966 or the following years but, from small beginnings in 1966 the Western world was wracked by student disturbances and, in the U.S.A., racial rioting in 1967 and 1968. Self styled Maoists were prominent in the student disturbances. As the mass demonstrations in Western societies died down, the urban guerrilas and terrorists appeared as a significant and more enduring feature of the relation between Western nations and the 'Third World'. There is no reason for regarding these events in the West as solely a result of conspiratorial planning and provisioning by China. (A special meeting of Western security agencies in Washington, June 1968 even decided by a narrow majority, that it was a Soviet plot!) Meddle they probably did; determine, no. The reason for the reverberations was more likely that Mao, in striking against the massive bureaucratisation that was emerging in his country as his colleagues led it down the Soviet path, was striking against the same phenomenon of bureaucratisation that was felt by students and U.S. urban black ghetto dwellers to be suffocating them. In the underdeveloped countries of the Middle East, Africa and Asia the feelings were probably not much different. The emergent leaderships of these countries would have found it somewhat difficult to get guaranteed agreements from the temporarily relevant no-names of the oil companies and Western governments. It should be noted that until the Cultural Revolution China appeared to be set on a course that was little different to that of Western society, namely economic growth by intensive bureaucratisation. The move from collectivization to communes and the Great Leap Forward were clues that something more was involved but they generally failed to gain Western attention, even though

the first action marked the beginning of the end of ideological identity for China and Russia. It was the Cultural Revolution that produced the shock. A measure of the shock it produced is the degree to which it is now so repressed, so little a part of the consciousness of the West.

4. To this surprise the Chinese added a unilateral withdrawal from the diplomatic world. It is this that leads us to believe that the Chinese have managed to become the 'leading part' in international affairs. They withdrew when they decided to withdraw, they came back when they decided to, and the Western societies almost eagerly followed suit. The U.S. President even placed U.S.-Japan relations as secondary and was prepared to risk U.S.-U.S.S.R. relations. It seems fairly obvious that the Chinese have so established themselves in the international arena (and not just U.N.) that no large international deal can overlook them, their interests and their potential displeasure. This has been achieved in the absence of any ability to project military power beyond those territories on their immediate borders. There is more to this aspect of military power but let us leave this to a later paragraph so as to consider the other aspect of the diplomatic scene.

5. The Chinese did not just establish themselves in the U.N. as one of a group of leading parts. They did, by their initiatives, establish themselves as the leading part. They still seem to retain this initiative. It seems that China is able and likely to do those things that could most change the international scene. The U.S.A., the U.S.S.R., Japan and the E.E.C. could all change their relations in the usual slow foxtrot. China could and probably will emerge with a radical redefinition of her relations with any one of these blocs, at any time. The sheer scale of China and her market potential makes it impossible for the Western powers to ignore her. The land based military potential and historical contradictions make it impossible for the U.S.S.R. to ignore her. The internal security system of China makes it nearly impossible to predict their diplomatic moves. Note, for instance, the years it took for the West to get a copy of Mao's *Ten Major Relationships*, let alone assess it. This is not, however, an adequate explanation. More fundamental seems to be the absence of thinking in Western society that could map the time scale within which

planning is done by the Chinese leadership. For the Chinese the future is a correction of a recent past to a position of international centrality that they think they should always have had. For the West the future is a self-frightening career into the top levels of exponential growth curves. These two concepts of the future are held by major groups in the same world and are pretty sure to produce some unexpected interactions and re-alignments.

The social and political structure of Western societies has allowed little or no room for wisdom. It would be pretty well inconceivable that a Western leader could, like Mao, 'go to the mountain' just in order to think about future possibilities, and expect to be accepted back as a leader. De Gaulle was an exception. There is no tradition in our Western societies that allows a role for the wise man (*e.g.* the treatment of Bertrand Russell, who in any Eastern society would probably have gained some significance as a source of wisdom). Our institutional structures for presidents and prime ministers typically deny them a time perspective less than 10 years. So called 'think tanks' are more likely to be too distant from the exercise of power or too preoccupied with seducing current power holders. The adaptive planning we described earlier is in its infancy.

In the above five points I have tried to indicate the erosion of the West's confidence in its leadership and the increased uncertainty that China has created in the international scene. In earlier periods these changes would have meant increased probability of war being used to restore or exploit the situation. I think that this may not now be the case. As both see each other making progress in *adaptively* coping with their own turbulence, there will be less fear of the Orwellian scenario becoming the future reality, *i.e.* the scenario where East or West have to engage in protracted war in order to justify and maintain regressive bureaucratic societies. In this process of adaptation the West will be increasingly concerned with pursuit of the ideals of homonomy, nurturance and humanity, rather than the restricted ones of plenty, truth as scientific truth and good as absence of conflict (the 'two into one' of table 6.1.1.). These emerging ideals are common to Asian and Western cultures. Hence they provide a basis for common understanding and for joint ventures that go beyond specific contractual deals and treaties.

The Asian and Western societies will continue to approach these ideals from fundamentally different positions. For the Asian cultures the individual is an organic part of his primary group; for the Western cultures the individual is the primary organic being, and the 'primary group' is but a supporting group of other such individuals. Even such an important difference in preferred paths does not offer the same license to misperception, mistrust and conflict as would a perceived difference in desired ends.

It would appear then, that, under the conditions of internal development we expect, rapprochement and active cooperation between China and the West is the most probable course over the next twenty to thirty years. The ties are likely to be basically mediated by France and Germany rather than the U.S.A. The former have a cultural depth into Europe's past and a degree of cultural homogeneity that the U.S.A. does not. This sort of depth is probably critical in this emerging relationship. Together France and Germany have the economic strength and an influence in the E.E.C. to contribute materially to China's requirements.

6.3. China and the U.S.S.R.

The U.S.S.R. was deliberately precluded from the consideration of the Western scenario. From the U.S.S.R. has come little evidence of movement toward adaptive strategies. The emergence of turbulence seems to have been stemmed by a straitjacket of massive bureaucratic controls, even though this has meant the stagnation of agriculture, still engaging about fifty percent of the population, and the disappearance of the once high growth rates.

However, the U.S.S.R. must be brought into the picture at this stage. Those fundamental social changes that offer some convergence of paths between China and the West are enlarging the gulf between the West and the U.S.S.R. The gulf between the West and the U.S.S.R. is not as great because the West still has most of its weight on the foot that remains in the past, with the U.S.S.R. Nor is the West involved in any conflict of national interests with the U.S.S.R. now that the Stalinist threat has been eliminated. For China there is a major conflict of interests with the

U.S.S.R., and one that is probably more deeply rooted and alive than any other current conflict. We have already quoted Mao's promise to his people at the foundation of the Chinese People's Republic, namely, 'China shall not again be an insulted nation'. We know the depth of that sentiment: we know the Chinese reaction to the insult MacArthur threatened in Korea and we know that practically all of the extant insults to Chinese territorial rights have been wiped off by invasion (Tibet), war (India) and politics (Taiwan). At least 1.5 million square kilometres of 'Chinese territory' are still clearly at issue. As Mao said on 11 August 1964 to a group of Japanese socialists:

'There are too many places occupied by the Soviet Union ... About a hundred years ago, the area to the east of Lake Baikal became Russian territory and since then Vladivostock, Khabarovsk, Kamchatika, and other areas have become Soviet territory. *We have not yet presented our account for this list*' (our emphasis).

The original insult has been compounded since 1949 by the arrogant, grasping and perfidious behaviour the Chinese attribute to their erstwhile allies. The build up of USSR armed forces in the East could only be calculated to deepen mutual distrust.

Until the Soviets break out of their own straitjacket there is no more probable outcome than war. The Soviets are confronted with a strong temptation to indulge in a preemptive strike before the Chinese nuclear weapons capabilities develop far; but could no more afford a prolonged conflict than the Czarist empire could afford their failure in the Russian-Japanese war of 1904-1905. This latter led directly to the Russian Revolution of 1905.

For the Chinese this has meant an urgent programme to develop their defenses but there is no apparent urgency to settle the territorial issue. On the defensive side their ubiquitous tunnelling under the cities and in the countryside gives them a chance of absorbing a Soviet first nuclear strike. Their nuclear forces offer a chance of some damaging blows to even the cities of western U.S.S.R., but it is doubtful how much of a deterrent this would be to a Soviet leadership that personally experienced the devastating losses of 1941-1945. They have stepped up the level of modern heavy weapons needed to blunt and slow down a lightning Soviet armoured strike at Peking from southern Mongolia. It is quite possible that Lin Piao's rapid fall from grace arose from his too one sided an adherence to the 'rifle, millet and nuclear' philosophy. Thus leaving it open for a Soviet armoured strike to reach a nuclear shattered Peking within 10-14 days and imposing a puppet Chinese Government. Leaving it open also to Lin Piao, as Mao's constitutional successor, to be the chosen puppet.

The probability of this conflict can be expected to increase until it actually happens, or there is a change in the Soviet system.

In the meantime we can expect the Chinese and Soviet to manoeuvre, as if on an international wei-ch'i board, for encirclement and counter-encirclement.

6.4. China and the rest of Asia

One more factor must be drawn in for this picture. In discussing Mao's model I touched on the implications of China becoming a nuclear power. I referred to it in relation to the U.S.S.R. I wish now to consider it in relation to the rest of Asia.

Throughout the post-war years the Pacific (and the China Seas) were part of a U.S. lake. It was a U.S. lake when the Seventh Fleet could interpose itself between Taiwan and the mainland with the capability of doing to all of China's industrial centres east of the arc Changsha, Shangshow, Peking and Mukden, what the U.S. Navy had done to Japanese cities in 1945. On 27 October 1966 China successfully tested an intermediate range ballistic missile delivery of an atomic warhead (approximately 20 kiloton yield). In 1970 China displayed its capabilities for missile launch and control capabilities by putting a satellite into orbit. This new military capability seriously endangered the in-shore deployment of the U.S. Seventh Fleet as primitive though effective means of target acquisition were available. The Fleet was on notice to vacate the Western Pacific. Nixon proceeded to order withdrawal in 1970 (quite possibly for other reasons but certainly not uninfluenced by the 1967 Report of the Joint Committee on Atomic Energy, 90th U.S. Congress, First Session, which predicted

'On the basis of our present knowledge, we believe that the Chinese probably will achieve an operational ICBM capability before 1972. Conceivably, it could be ready as early as 1970-71' (p. 4).

To judge from the later lag in China's nuclear test program there has been a definite retardation due to the Cultural Revolution. For the seventies, however, it seems clear that off-shore Asia - Japan, Philippines and Indonesia - is under the threat of China's intermediate range ballistic nuclear weapons. To this threat they have no realistic military response of their own. Indonesia and the Philippines could not even attain a nuclear missile capability but Japan could. But to what end?

6.5. Japan

Japan's geographical vulnerability to nuclear assault (let alone her post-Hiroshima sensitivity) contrasts with China's relative invulnerability and her own often repeated insensivity to nuclear scale casualities. There is little reason to believe that Japan will allow herself to be manoeuvred into carrying out a suicidal defence of Western ideals. Under the Chinese nuclear umbrella it seems more likely that Japan will seek a modus vivendi with China. For the Japanese such a modus vivendi is not likely to be acceptable unless it allows them to be thoroughly Japanese. There is no historical reason for them to assume that this might be harder to achieve under Chinese influence. Japan may not be able to survive nuclear war with the Chinese but the Japanese are able to make physical occupation unprofitable.

Given the hard facts of the present, and given selfconfidence in their territorial integrity, the Japanese may find it easy to see a new destiny in a 'younger brother' relation with China. Kahn saw that 'China may play a key role, perhaps *the* key role in the orientation of Japan and of the Pacific Asia area' (1970, p. 170; his emphasis). However, he saw this as a Chinese threat causing a re-emergence of Japanese militarism. I suggest that he overlooked what the Japanese Ambassador reminded his American audience, as recorded in *Japan Report*, 15 March 1965; that:

'Japan is first of all an Asian nation, and although we maintain formal diplomatic relations with Nationalist China, it is impossible for us to cut ourselves off from all contact with mainland China. We cannot erase, after all, our long historical involvement with the Chinese, we cannot obliterate our geographic proximity to the mainland, we cannot ignore our ancient and deep cultural affinity with its people'.

It is to be expected that the death of Hirohito, now in his seventies, will mark the beginning of Japanese public realignment. The realignment does not mean a turning towards communist ideology. It does mean the emergence of a national ideology which will recognise the special cultural and historical relation with China, and, at the same time, mobilise the children of the Showa (post-war) generation about the ideals forming a new Japanese generation. Perhaps it is not too hazardous to guess what those ideals might be. I do not think it will be the past pattern of reaching for heaven (omnipotence) but an all-out pursuit of a subset of the possible ideals. I expect that by invoking a national concern with pursuit of beauty the Japanese will seek to correct the distortions in their pursuit of the other ideals of homonomy (ex-plenty), nurturance (ex-scientific mastery of nature) and humanity. This is not completely guess-work. The Comprehensive National Plan of May 1969 set the goal of returning Japan to its earlier idyllic garden state over the next twenty years. I would agree with Kahn (1970, p. 182) that 'before the twenty-year program is over they will have succeeded in doing so'. To do this they will certainly reduce, very markedly, their current G.N.P. growth rates. This will not be a difficult choice once they renounce the early twentieth century assumption that they had to 'go it alone'. Remembering that then China was bedridden, the 'sick man' of Asia, and the West rapacious.

It is probable that this change of national direction has been already well thought through by the Establishment. In any case, one can expect the Japanese to proceed slowly and coldly in the joint development with the U.S.S.R. of Siberian physical resources. Little discussion has in fact followed the 1968 agreement on a loan-timber-gas deal. On the other hand, they will actively foster relations with China, and in some sort of partnership with China, with the rest of Asia. In this context, a culturally renewed Japan could expect as 'the powerhouse of Asia' to achieve the proper respected role she earlier sought in her Greater Asia Coprosperity plan. The change in image and the mutual restraint between the two giants will make it very probable that they will become the main source of economic and technical aid in Asia. It is also probable that they will actively support the fulfilment of the 'Maphilindo' concept: the concept of a regional bloc in South East Asia composed of at least Malaya, the Philippines and Indonesia. The Japanese were favourably disposed toward this as far back as 1945. The Chinese would have nothing to loose and much to gain from arrangements that would bring political and economic stability to this region. Thus a partnership with a new Japan – a non-aggressive Asian oriented Japan – must seem to the Chinese to be the key to long run peace and stability in Asia (as it did to the then Japanese Prime Minister Sato in 1965, *Japan Report*, 20 January).

Several further developments can be expected from the alliance. Japan's great knowledge in the fields of electronics, microminiaturization and computer technology would become available to China. Up to now the Japanese, out of respect to its U.S. ties, has banned such exports to China. This should lead to a considerable forward leap, in the latter half of the seventies, in China's missile program and the network of sophisticated satellites required for defense against a massive first strike by U.S.S.R. or the U.S.A. By the eighties we can expect China to have a credible nuclear deterrent in the form of a small fleet of nuclear powered missile submarines. As stated, we would expect Japan to welcome the emergence of a nuclear shield over Asia.

6.6. 'Maphilindo'

The British withdrawal of its Strategic Reserve from Singapore and the U.S. withdrawal from Viet Nam and the Asian-Pacific areas meant that for the first time in the modern era South East Asia is freed from Western political domination (except for 1942-1945). Both they and the Japanese know that the situation is not a vacuum into which the latter can agressively assert economic overlordship. And yet both need each other. Japan needs the security of its oil routes from the Middle East, and the products and markets of South East Asia. South East Asia needs political stability and economic and technical aid to pursue a regional identity. The non-Westernized leaders of this region who espouse the concept of Maphilindo see such an identity as based on the racial, cultural and linguistic heritage they share. This heritage marks them off from the other Asian races and offers them a means of overriding the local loyalties that bedevil the archipelago and the divisions imposed by Western conquerors.

It seems likely that a regional trading bloc will emerge in the late seventies. The economies of these countries are, however, likely to be aimed at the predominantly rural model of China. Within this framework rural reform and economic growth are achievable goals.

6.7. India

India is one of the three great Asian nations. However, it stands in marked contrast to Japan and China. Unlike them, it lacks a unity of cultural development. It has typically not absorbed the successive waves of invaders but provided a site for the evolution and refinement of their different civilizations. It is also remarkably diverse in its races and its languages. The largest single block of about forty percent is linked by use of Hindi language and Hinduism.

Economically India has failed to get moving in the way that Japan did. In fact India's agricultural crisis is probably deeper than before the independence and its industrial development is not even comparable with China. In matters of national identity India has made no advance. Gandhi's ideals died with him in 1948. Nehru's nonalignment and democratic socialism had turned by 1970 into alignment against China and a welter of corrupt bureaucracies at all levels; national, state and local. The clashes with China and Pakistan aroused a temporary sense of national purpose but not of identity.

The conditions leading to turbulence in India's social field, like those in China, approximate closely to the general May-Ashby model (rather than to the more specific conditions we listed for Western societies): namely, the sheer number of diverse beings brought into closer communication and greater dependence on each other.

The characteristic Indian response has been described by Nitish De of the Indian Institute of Management as '*a culture of social parasitism*'. He identifies the aspects of this culture:

1. Non-productive phenomena, such as, gold and precious stone smuggling and hoarding, hoarding of essential food grain items, conspicuous consumption, individualised services, sweat-labour based secondary comforts, etc. do receive a premium. Social values in the garb of 'an act of wisdom' as in the case of hoarding and 'a shining example of success in life' as in the case of conspicuous consumption, acquire ligitimacy in our behavioural norms. Such forms of parasitism will have the 'Gres-

ham Law' effect on the productive culture. The 'sanskritisation' effect of parasitism thus takes hold;

2. Black money and corruption will remain a major force in the determination of relevant behaviour including key level decision making roles, thereby weakening such processes of decision making as involve productive parameters;

3. Members of the community involved in production activities will carry on with their responsibilities in the tradition of parasitism manifested in the forms of *competitive economism* and *complementary economism*. In other words, the internalised values of parasitism will gain entry and then ascendancy in the production culture. In this sense, there will be no fundamental distinction between social goods and services and those for private gains;

4. There will develop an yawning chasm between the public posture and the private faith, between the stated objective and the reality, between the creed and the deed generating a climate of mass inauthenticity and abortion of political morality;

5. The reaction against the consequent erosion of national selfesteem and promiscuity in national identity will develop into mass alienation in the young generation. This will occur either in the form of retreatist subculture, or angry backlash, or anguished martyrdom, or docile conformism, or perhaps a combination of some of these, thereby fostering the values of 'lumpenism';

6. As an *apparent* reaction to the economic stagnancy and the hypocrisy of existence that is inherent in the culture of social parasitism, obvious patriotic responses will generate in the cause of production orientation. These indignant votaries of non-parasitic culture will seek the commanding heights of decision making roles for themselves so that the vantage ground of parasitism can be maintained;

7. The 'hard core' of productive culture will get, as a reaction against parasitism, fixated at task-orientation levels with cynical concern for human values and esteem for fellow human beings. Some of them may seek retreat in compensatory activities, such as 'research' and noncollaborative work, and join the 'braindrain' club. Performance orientation may become a caricature of economic progress with an empty moral and ethical shell.

It will be noted that these aspects of 'the culture of social parasitism' are either the maladaptive strategies of superficiality or dissociation. The strategy of segmentalism is documented by him in the same papers with respect to the failure to implement land reform laws and non-discrimination laws for Muslims and untouchables. However, segmentalism is so basic to the Hindu society (with its ancient caste systems) that further manifestations can hardly be expected except in levels of communal violence.

The critical fact is that, despite the efforts of Nitish De and his colleagues, there seems almost no sign of strategies that could cope adaptively with the turbulence in Indian society. It seems most probable that active maladaptive strategies will prevail. Anarchy is not a likely alternative as the armed forces are in a very strong position and overwhelmingly Hindu in their leadership. There is little question of which active maladaptive strategy will emerge. Hinduism is built on segmentation and the right wing Hindu movements (those that assassinated Gandhi) will almost certainly provide the ideology for a 'unique Indian way'; a theocratic version of Orwell's scenario.

The Indo-Soviet Treaty of August 1971 set a seal on the alignment of the two major world powers that are frozen into maladaptive strategies of coping with their futures. They have in common the enemy they both need, China.

Under this strategic nuclear umbrella, we can expect that India will

1. realize the potential of the 'green revolution', at the expense of the mass of small farmers and landless agricultural labourers.
2. Industrialise, with great aid from the U.S.S.R., particularly in those areas relevant to military production and technology.
3. Go nuclear, at least to the extent of tactical nuclear weapons and I.R.B.M.'s. We do not think the arrangements with the U.S.S.R. will permit movement into the nuclear deterrent field.
4. Establish support facilities for the U.S.S.R. Navy to operate permanently in the Indian Ocean. From the Indian viewpoint this would help block the Iranian moves into the Arabian sea.
5. Bring Pakistan to the battlefield once again; this time over Kashmir.
6. Seek to intervene in Burma.

Overall, India in 1973 was clearly moving in an opposite direction to China and Japan. Towards more internal stratification and organised violent repression; towards greater bellicosity to its immediate neighbours. It will be more Asian than Western, but in the mode of old Asia.

6.8. India 1976: a new path ?

It is only in the case of India that I have felt the need to consider a major revision of our views.

I had predicted that India would go nuclear. In some circles in India this forecast was greeted with disbelief. India went nuclear.

I had predicted that India was heading toward organised violent repression. On June 26, 1975 Mrs Gandhi invoked the Emergency Powers residing in Part XVIII of the Constitution. At the Constitutional Convention in the late 1940's one delegate had expressed the concern that these powers might be laying 'the foundations of a totalitarian state'. There is certainly no doubt that the emergency powers have been widely used, and the paramilitary forces greatly expanded. Is this what I had predicted? Certainly many in New Delhi in 1976 appeared to think so. I think not.

What I predicted was '*more internal stratification* and organised violent repression'. I expected that the segmentalist forces of right wing Hindu communalism would get into controlling positions of power through threatening anarchy and thus drawing in the predominantly Hindu led, armed forces. The documents issued by Mrs Gandhi's government after June '75 strongly argue that just these developments were taking place and were threatening to get out of hand. If that was all the evidence we had we might well wonder if and when India would return to democratic forms of government.

Right on the heels of the declaration of emergency Mrs Gandhi came down with *The Twenty Point Program*. This document seems to have for India something of the same significance as Mao's *Ten Major Relationships* for China. As with Mao's document, and for similar reasons of international relations, it is not a straight document. The Indian government have left no doubts in the minds of Indian administrators, industrialists, union leaders, politicians and the public that these twenty points set the priorities for national action. And here is the catch. For the past two decades India has followed the Soviet model of centralized planning, on a five year set of quantifiable targets and with prime emphasis on science and technology as the means to bring India up toward Western standards. Now, in these twenty points only point 8 on building super-thermal electricity stations looks like a piece of a 'Soviet model plan'. If the twenty points had been intended to highlight the key points in a current five year plan they would have centred on physical growth of the technology with an emphasis on heavy industry, investments in the scientific-technical base and target dates for achievement. Even the singling out of power generation may have been a specific response to the rise in world oil prices.

In contrast to such conceptions *The Twenty Points* represent a return to an Asian model of development; Gandhian of course, not Mao's, despite the similarities. At the heart of this Asian concept is acceptance of the fact that, as Gandhi always stressed, India is the India of the villages and will remain so for as far ahead as one can practically see. The points specifically directed to rural development give no comfort to the Hindu communalism movement.

Just about all previous attempts to legislate for reform at the village level have foundered on the rocks of caste, landlordism and lending of money. These forces have effectively corrupted the judicial system and the legislatures and got away with physical violence when all else failed. In these points there is evidence that the weight of government action is being progressively shifted from the legislative, judicial systems to the executive-administrative system. A similar shift can be seen in the points intended to bring under control the 'social parasitism' discussed above.

If we add together these trends toward strengthening the executive-administrative system and the rapid build up of the paramilitary forces surely there is a strong chance that Mrs Gandhi's India is on a path of nonreturn from totalitarianism? That she is taking India towards the end that we saw as pretty inevitable in 1973 rather than yield the rather dubious honour to someone else?

I now doubt this gloomy prospect. Not only is the government acting firmly to reduce the social base of Hindu communalism, with all of its repressive segmentalist implications, but in its points for industry it has come out firmly for debureaucratisation of government agencies and democratisation of work in the factories, mines and offices. Just how firmly can be readily judged from its action in setting up the National Institute for Labour in 1974 and the subsequent monthly bulletins of that Institute (under the leadership of the Nitish De we quoted above on social parasitism).

These developments have made the future path of India less predictable rather than more predictable. Thus, for instance, the world still hangs on what will happen after the death of Mao, although we think that has been settled for many years.* Allende in Chile seemed obviously

* Since these lines were written Mrs Gandhi has called off the Emergency and arranged for national elections. Mao has died. There is still uncertainty about the stability of the

to lack the base needed for survival.

Where is the social base from which Mrs Gandhi can swing her people back on to a neo-Gandhian path?

To reach out into the hundreds of thousands of villages and tens of thousands of urban areas that constitute India, Mrs Gandhi does not have anything like the 23 million members of the Communist Party that Mao had. But then Mao would hardly have called for a two-thirds reduction in the party if he had regarded it as the main means of producing change. Similarly there seem to be no way that she can take on an open battle with the kulaks of her villages in the way that Stalin did in the early thirties (nor any indication that she would wish to). Without the Gandhian ideals of trusteeship and 'first and last' it seems highly unlikely that Mrs Gandhi will mobilise the social support necessary to reverse the course that India has been on.

If she can, it will leave the Soviet Union in a very isolated position and greatly enhance the chances that that country will seek a new course. At very least the Asian scenario would look even better than what we suggested.

There is reason to believe that India will seek to mobilise social support through new forms of *participative* democracy.

The representative forms have proven too open to abuse in a country like India with a low literacy rate and powerful caste influences. Thus in the Gram Panchayats (the second level of elected village councils) it has not been atypical for the higher castes constituting twenty percent of the population to have seventy five per cent of the elected positions and for scheduled castes constituting twenty per cent to have no representatives (Mehta, 1975, pp. 39-45). This and the landlords' privileged access to the courts and lawyers have played havoc with legislation to help the poor, the landless and the tribals.

In the 1976 B.B.C. film 'Mrs Gandhi's India' she was asked how she saw India in 10 years time. She replied:

'That depends very much on what happens with the rest of the world, doesn't it. But I do think that we can get what we want – *we want a democratic system, but not confined to elections, but involving the people really in decision making processes. By people, I do*

---

new regime but at last the document on the Ten Major Relationships has been released to the Chinese people as *the* blueprint for China's future.

not mean a handful of intellectuals who live in the cities or sit in airconditioned rooms. I mean the vast majority of peasants and workers – actually the peasantry and the landless labour and tribals – these that form the majority. We want their voice to be heard in the planning of programmes of development for their areas' (Statesman, 2 April, 1976).

It seems clear that Mrs Gandhi is determined to take India to the edge of the wei-ch'i board, to the India of Mahatma Gandhi. But this is not the Gandhi that the West tends to think of as a village guru and romantic idealist who would take Indian industry back to the spinning wheel. It is much more the Gandhi depicted in Ram K. Vepa's *New Technology: A Gandhian Concept* (1975) as:

'realist enough to realize that it was impossible for him, or anyone else, to change everything and, therefore, he placed before himself short-term goals in the shape of the Constructive Programme with well-defined objectives. In each case he had formulated a plan of action and set up institutions to carry on the work ... his Constructive Programme represented not what was desirable but what was possible' (1975, pp. 39-40).

Permeating and giving coherence to such practical steps are of course the ideals of trusteeship, *etc.*, the strategic importance attached to the villages and to human resources, and Gandhi's acid test for the utility of any administrative measure, 'think of the poorest Indian you know and 'will it help him is the question'.'

7. Notes for a world scenario

The attempt in this last part to write a 'most probable' scenario for the world, needs to be prefaced by reflections on the earlier methodological notes.

The prime concern through all of the scenarios has been to identify qualitative transformations. The prediction of quantitative changes can best be left to the demographers, the Kahn's and McHales' of this world. Where the qualitative changes are equivalent to phase changes in an identifiable system some prediction is possible. The system, unless it is in its infancy will typically have some persistent characteristics. This is clear when one considers Japan. However, when we consider the current world scene we have social systems moving into degrees of interdependence that have not previously existed. The situation is that represented in figure 4, Appendix I. As stated there: If (systems) A and B survive the interaction, some of their system properties may predictably survive. What seems unpredictable are the processes set up by the interaction and the changes occurring in A and B if they become directively correlated to form a larger inclusive system. If we were discussing individuals the situation would be the same as two individuals marrying under Western free choice conditions: however well we knew the individuals there would be a great deal in their subsequent married life, public and private, that we would have had no way of predicting. There would in effect be an excess of genuine novelty. We expect an excess of novelty on the world scene in the next decade or so.

The 'future scenarios' we have reviewed show how little they are geared to other than more or less of what we already have. I have predicted that it is most unlikely that most people will allow their futures to evolve by default. I have further predicted that in general people will not simply react but will take advantage of their new freedoms from fear, want and ignorance to pursue more purposes and higher ends.

When systems that are themselves undergoing major qualitatative changes, become extensively involved with each other, their futures become close to unpredictable. It is almost the problem of predicting the outcomes of marriage between two who are both in the throes of adolescent change.

I am prepared, however, to sketch a skeleton of the emerging world: to identify the main lines of international stress and strain within which the social blocs will have to adapt the pursuit of their own ends.

The predominating polarity for some decades to come is that between East and West. What is basic to the scenario is that this is becoming a complementary polarity, as are male and female, red and green. This is not to exclude antagonistic incidents in the next few years but to assert that each such incident will lessen the probability of that kind of incident causing trouble in the future.

I have tried to be more specific than speak simply of 'East' and 'West'. In the 'West' it is clear that Scandinavia has played a leading role in confronting the problem of debureaucratising work. It is likely that the small Western countries like Scandinavia, Holland and Australasia will act in the role of skirmishing before the frontline of Western change. They carry little of the historical burden of feudalism and they are small enough and sufficiently culturally homogeneous to quickly reach a decision to move.

However, the key role of relating the development of Western ideals to Asia is most likely to be played by Germany and France. Insofar as they can continue to develop their own interrelationship, they carry the historical core of European culture in a way that could not be matched by any other countries, or combination of countries. They also carry the weight and muscle in the European Common Market. We suggest that they, and only those two nations together, could convince Asia that there was a genuine transformation in Western values. It would be unconvincing coming from the British, and incredible coming from the U.S.A.

We expect France and Germany to play the key role *within* the Western bloc. They will encourage parellel changes in the U.S.A., in Mediterranean Europe and Central Europe. They will confront the particular problem of reintegrating the ancient values of the Mediterranean cultures within the emerging values of the West. Throughout the Mediterranean peasant societies the matriarchial culture persists, thinly veiled; despite the gross forms of subjection to which women can be exposed. It seems very likely that the northern Europeans will need to absorb much of this culture if they are to overcome their masculine hero orientation and live with the more feminine pursuits of nurturance, beauty, *etc.*

There are some doubts about whether Germany and France can or will assume this leading role. I do not share these doubts. Both nations are as desperate to find a new national identity, one that surpasses their recent past, as is Japan. Both nations are as assured as Japan that the battle for 'plenty' is essentially won.

In 'the East', China has already emerged as the leading part. Within two or three years I expect that Japan will emerge in a new 'Greater East Asia Coprosperity' scheme; without the trappings of violence and direct domination that marked the first such scheme. This will not involve Japan in going Maoist. They will be able to relate to each other provided each scrupulously respects the self image of the other and both acclaim their common cultural roots, in ancient China. Japan can be expected to deliberately reduce her rate of economic growth in order to reverse the trend of environmental pollution and urban chaos. With Japan's aid China's economic growth will greatly increase but still with most of the people in agriculture. The effect of this aid will be most striking in China's transport system (shipbuilding, vehicles and aircraft) and communications industry.

The partnership between China and Japan will provide the umbrella for the realisation of 'Maphilindo' (probably including Thailand). Trade and aid will create rapid economic growth in this region. Land reform and stabilisation of agriculture are expected. Overall social and economic progress in this area throughout the late seventies and the eighties will be much faster than in any other major region of the world. This will apply also to food and fuel production.

Trading relations between the Eastern and Western blocs may take some time to stabilise. The East will try to control Western dealings in their markets and the West will seek to protect their own markets from more vigorous economic expansion of the East. Partly within and without this relation, the U.S.A. will be primarily occupied with its own transition to an active adaptive state. However, it may get temporarily embroiled in South America and Africa as it feels its interests being undermined by Asian penetration. Any U.S. military action is likely to be brief and limited as every effort will be made to avoid another Vietnam.

The most dangerous and unpredictable development on the world scene is the emergence of the Indo-Soviet alignment against China. Against their protestation that this is a defensive arrangement is the fact, that both are moving closer to an Orwellian solution of their social future. We suggest that so long as they move in this direction they need an external enemy. It is most unlikely that they will run the risk of a protracted war with China. There is some chance that the Soviet will try a 'pre-emptive' strike if they think there are Chinese leaders wishing to swing back from Mao's line after Mao's death. There is a real probability that India will try to seize back the territory of Aksaichin in Kashmir that China occupied in 1962. The perspective of the Indian leaders is suggested by their estimates, after defeating Pakistan, that the defense budget in the last half of the seventies will run at $ 2,500 million as against $ 1,600 million in 1970.

(Section 6.8. suggests that this threat has been considerably reduced; not, however, that the Soviet-China threat has disappeared).

7.1. The „Third World"

I have left consideration of the remainder of the so-called 'third world' till this point because the thing that most characterises them is lack of self-determination. It seems unlikely that any of these nations, mainly in South America and Africa, will determine the course of their evolution through the seventies. Even the eighties seem doubtful. Excluding the rich oil nations, such as Venezuela and Libya, the fate of the Third World seems dependent on economic aid and/or stable trade. Both are dependent on others.

Even Cuba and Chile[1] who have made major steps toward freeing themselves from direct political manipulation are little less dependent. They could put forward 5 year plans but we could not take them as reliable indicators.

Both Africa and South America suffer from a long standing rural crisis that seems to have no prospect of resolution. It is possible that the emerging East Asia bloc will offer stable markets in order to establish their

1. Already gone down since the time of writing.

influence in these areas. However, in South America major land reforms and rural investments would be necessary to reverse the trend, and it is not clear where either would come from.

In the meantime the most likely prediction is the continued mass migration from the country to the cities. Thus in South America there are now 17 cities over a million as against 9 in 1960. By 1980 there are expected to be 26. (U.S.A. at the present has seven). (Similar trends are operating in Africa e.g. Lagos and Ibadan). This urbanisation is a 'push' migration from the country. The cities offer little work. Whilst countries like Mexico and Brazil have made some progress with protected industries, the great mass of the population has been left behind, giving a dual character to the societies. The urbanisation of these workless, landless masses is bound to increase the social and political instability of these societies, increase terrorism and counterterrorism.

The U.S.A. will not readily keep out of attempts at changes of the social structures in South America. Whatever lessons seem obvious from Vietnam this will be seen to be different; this is America's backyard. As Salvador de Madariage put it:

'I only know two things about the Monroe Doctrine: one is that no American I have met knows what it is; the other is that no American I have met will consent to its being tampered with. That being so, I conclude that the Monroe Doctrine is not a doctrine but a dogma' (1962, p. 17).

Amusingly put but almost certainly true. There seems little doubt but that the U.S.A. will be increasingly drawn into an active role in South American affairs. The Chinese will take any opportunity to incite such intervention in order to preoccupy and isolate the U.S.A. The doctrine espoused by Lin Piao of 'encircling the cities from the countryside' was Mao's. It is certain to have a continuing role in Chinese foreign policy.

In Africa the source of strife lies in the continued tribal allegiances. Just as pan-Africanism took no grip in the fifties and sixties there is no chance that it will act in the 70's to override internal tribal dissensions. Similarly, there is no chance of these nations unifying against South Africa. South Africa is too stable and too strong.

The future in these parts of the world looks like more of the same. More of the pendulum swing between the small civil and military elites; more urbanisation; more poverty; more unrest and more repression.

The only possibility is that by the end of the seventies the East and West will see sufficiently eye-to-eye that they jointly coordinate aid and support to this 'Third World'.

This may be the acid test of whether East and West are both committed to pursuing ideals of homonomy, nurturance and humanity.

7.2. International cooperation about international concerns

The changes we have been predicting will not just effect nations and blocs of nations. We can expect that it will transform the climate within which international arrangements are made.

At the present the international arrangements for postal, tele-, and air communications provide a framework which is practically taken for granted. Similarly with the International Red Cross and the World Bank. At the apex, the U.N. Security Council and General Assembly have come in for considerable scorn for faults that essentially lie in the international order, not the U.N. Beneath this, however, is a web of international agreements and agencies that are now accepted as essential to *national* existence. Not even warring nations dispute the necessity to observe these arrangements.

Beyond this we have had the great effloresence of the 'multinational' firms in producing and marketing goods and servies. These have penetrated into all but the 'communist' nations. Their practice is basically to match market research and development and products to capabilities and requirements wherever the latter exist, regardless of national boundaries. The emergence of the multinational firms has been marred by persistence of national orientations of the dominating groups of share holders. Increasingly, however, there is the realisation that they can continue to operate effectively only if their local plans are subordinated to some degree to national development plans (Hill, *ibid.*).

More recent, but parallel to this, is the multinational, multifirm cooperation in resources development. The scale on which new physical resources have had to be brought into use has surpassed old forms of economic organisation. It is no longer enough for a rich corporation, for instance, to find a new oilfield, develop it and push the output onto the world markets. For any significant addition to the world's useful resources it is now necessary to envelope the development in a long term set of commitments by a multitude of organisations whose own commitments are but to one aspect or other of bringing the resources into being. Thus long term contracts from would-be consumers of the resources bring into being long term charters for bulk ships that have not yet been designed, let alone built. This development is not restricted to Western societies. The U.S.S.R. is regarding development of Siberian resources in the same light.

We can expect that the recognition by the East and West that they are starting to pursue common ideals will add a great impetus to defining 'common ground'. An obvious way in which this will be reflected is in world resource accounting, minerals, fuel and food. Shortsightedness is unavoidable in the multicorporation, multinational arrangements to develop resources, and conflict is incipient in the resource producers banding together to decide their policies. Only international agreement can reduce potential conflict over resources. If for instance the average U.S. citizen wishes to go on using the equivalent of 10 tons of coal per annum then he may have to work that out with his society; not assume that it will be automatically fed in from the world's resources. If the Russians assume that it is more important to add to their nuclear missile stocks than add fertiliser to their fields then they might not assume such ready access to the world's grain surplus.

Simply mentioning two hypothetical examples illustrates the development before an international in national consciousness that is necessary before an international resources policy becomes a reality. At the same time we must bear in mind that this now seems to be an achievable goal; in the first half of the century desire for unilateral control over resources was a prime source of antagonism between nations.

It is likely that the agreements banning nuclear weapon testing will extend to other forms of pollution. However important these agreements, the most important effects of the change in international climate are likely to be those on the masses of individuals who will be moving from one part of the world to another. If people get the feeling in other countries, as visitors, conference attenders or business men, that those people are concerned about the same ideals, then they are not about to be worried about differences in the ways they are pursuing those ideals. More importantly they are not likely to allow their governmental representatives to claim that there is no basis for seeking mutual understanding with the representatives of those people.

In composing this picture of the future I have made no attempt to be encyclopaedic about the present nor to exhaustively review all other views of the future. Hence the fact that I can see no more probable future is neither here nor there. Perhaps the future is neither here nor there, but elsewhere.

8. Epilogue:
social sciences and social futures

I have suggested, as strongly as I can, that people will make their own future. The question arises whether the new 'experts', the social scientists, will be advising and shaping this future. I think not. The concept of a 'social engineer' is, however, gaining such potency (usually as an agent of maladaptive strategies) that an explicit redefinition seems in order.

There is clearly a sense in which any science is or should be responsible to society. The resources that the sciences use, human and material, are part of the resources of society and remain so no matter what special privileged access the scientific institutions have to them. At any one time the decisions to allocate these resources are made by the existing power centres, for example, state bodies and industrialists. Since the Neuremberg trials, however, it has become clear that broader social interests may be invoked if these resources are misused.

This general problem has been ably explored by others. It is mentioned only to highlight the next point. Unlike the physical and biological sciences, the social sciences cannot be indifferent to their subject matter. They cannot expect to survive, let alone grow, unless they pursue purposes that are shared by their chosen objects of study. No matter how cunning or devious the social scientist became, it is almost certain that his subject matter would eventually outmanoeuvre him, as no physical particle could. This is not a new observation: 'Suppose the physiognomist ever did have man in his grasp, it would merely require a courageous resolution on man's part to make himself again incomprehensible for centuries (Litchenberg, 1788, quoted by Hegel, p. 345).

The survival and growth of social sciences presupposes a role in which they enhance the range and degree of purposeful relations that men can form between themselves and their environment. They may need to take account of a wider set of conditions and broaden their responses to them. They may also need to extend their awareness of goals they might successfully pursue.

In this way the social sciences would guard against sins of omission as well as sins of commission. This is not achieved by the usual codes governing professional ethics. Nor can they be achieved by legally constituted bodies set up, as in California, to examine all experimental proposals that intend using human beings as subjects. It is good, but still not enough, that the keystone of the *Ethical Standards of Psychologists* (American Psychological Association, 1967) should be the declaration that: 'The psychologist is committed to a belief in the dignity and worth of the individual human being'. These guidelines and sanctions may reduce the harm we do to people. If we are to fulfil our social responsibility, we must do more to help men to realise more fully their potential as human beings, whether this resides in individuals or groups. People can use their resources as human beings only in the conduct of their practical affairs, including 'contemplation of their conduct'.

The unique mission and responsibility of the social sciences is the mutual enrichment of social science and the important practical affairs of man. This concept rests uneasily alongside the older view that the primary task of a university is 'the disinterested pursuit of knowledge' (*U.G.C. Report*, 1930). Yet we must search out the implications of our social responsibilities wherever they lead us. The implications are particularly compelling because some critical areas of social science can be advanced only by actively collaborating with institutions and groups outside the universities. Our subject matter cannot always be put into a test tube, laboratory, or simulated on a computer. That is, the enrichment of social science and the enrichment of key affairs of men are not necessarily, nor usually, mutually exclusive ends. Mutual enrichment is not equivalent to doing a task (a) for practical purposes and task (b) for social science; mutuality implies something different from being jointly engaged in separate classes of activities directed to different goals. Mutual enrichment implies that one and the same class of activities serves to enrich both social sciences and the practical concerns of men.

This is not to say that all social scientists should be involved with the outside world in this way or that all of our research should be of this character. Rather, social science as a whole should take on this responsibility. This responsibility should be recognized and supported even by those social scientists whose personal interests and abilities lead them in other directions. There is no good reason why recognition of this responsibility should lead to denigration of the essential complementary tasks of pure research.

8.1. Social science roles

How are we to judge whether this responsibility is being fulfilled? As a first step table 8.1.1. presents a simple scale of the levels of mutual engagement, of what tasks are involved and of what enrichment can be expected for the social sciences and for society. This provides a framework within which to approach the morass of professional ethics and responsibilities.

Any elucidation of professional responsibility must proceed from a consideration of the roles within which the social scientist operates. Elsewhere Churchman and I have distinguished three major roles, the academic, the servant and the collaborative (1966).

In the academic role the social scientist is adequately guided by the traditional values of objectivity and disinterested pursuit of knowledge. How this knowledge is used by others is not his direct responsibility. We would hardly regard him as professionally responsible, however, if he allowed his scientific contributions to be misrepresented to serve the interest of one social group against that of another. An academic social scientist is not held responsible for selecting socially relevant areas for his research. It is enough that his research helps others towards greater conceptual clarity and more efficient methods.

The service role exists when a social scientist is employed by an organisation or is in the usual type of consultant relation. Here special problems emerge. His employer or his contractor may have interests that are inconsistent with those of social science. For example, his interests may best be furthered by denying 'the dignity and worth of the individual'. In this situation, the social scientists needs the protection offered by an explicit code of professional ethics. But it is his responsibility to ensure that his services are not utilised in ways that are contrary to the code.

Table 8.1.1. Levels of mutual engagement, task content and outcomes.

	For social science	Task content	For the society
1. Simple consultation	Deepened intuitive understanding and communicable knowledge of qualitative outlines of processes	Analysis and advice without systematic data collection for testing either	Extending the range of relevant variables
2. Level of so-called action research (study of operating systems in action)	A field experiment or systematic body of data for theory construction	A one shot study involving some systematic design for analysis	A weighted set of solutions to particular problems and administrative experience with a method of approach
3. Level of building new operating systems	Systematic data on the building of social systems	Designing and testing new social systems in the enterprise	More appropriate social systems and culture
4. Level of building social scientific procedures into administration	Creation of a stable growing point for social science or social scientific data	Building into the enterprise procedures for continued scientific analysis	A capability of solving a class of recurrent problems

Social science fulfils its responsibilities when it is engaged at levels 3 and 4. Implicit in this judgement is the paradox that the social sciences should work towards making themselves superfluous as special disciplines (Emery, 1960).

There does remain, however, a deeper responsibility. The capabilities of a social scientist in this role will be called upon only for the purposes of the institution he serves. Even if a professional code of ethics could protect him from sins of commission, what is to protect him from sins of omission? As Marcuse has said (Marcuse, 1964, pp. 107-120), the service role can negate the aims of social science.

Much present-day social science consultancy with industry carries this threat. It emphasises participative management and organisational development, assuming that the basic management-worker relations remain unchanged. Creating enlightened management is expected to bring about better human relations and the illusion of greater worker participation. By ignoring the scientific evidence that the management-worker relation markedly affects the kind of managerial climate that can stably exist, this movement comes close to being manipulative, both of workers and managers. This attenuates its own scientific base and threatens to alienate social science from its subject matter. Social scientists who enter this role must take responsibility for examining the purposes of their masters, as well as for their own contributions as social scientists.

The collaborative role is our main concern in this discussion, not only because it creates special problems, but also because it is critical for the engagement of the social sciences with society. Despite Marcuse's pessimistic appraisal, this role can be developed in industry. It frees the social scientist from having to operate within the assumptions of either management or trade unions and from the taint of manipulation. Two European examples are reported in Emery and Thorsrud (1976) and Hill (1971). Values of objectivity and disinterest or codes of professional ethics alone will not serve in this role. The mutual engagement that arises from genuine collaboration brings up value problems that the social scientist has no particular expertise or social sanction to decide on. The historical conditions under which the social sciences have emerged have not made them, like a priesthood, a sanctuary of social values. Nor are social scientists about to recognize any other institutions as having an unchallenged claim to wisdom about values. If collaborative research is to be carried through, there needs to be agreement on the values of the researcher and the researched and, preferably, some body able to sanction this inclusive set of values. This represents the ideal to which we must strive in order to attain a mutual enrichment of the social sciences and the practical affairs of man.

8.2. Examples of ethical problems

As social scientists we must work towards establishing ethical guidelines for our own conduct in the collaborative relation. As a first step we should begin to codify the ethical problems that arise in our research. To start this process some of the ethical problems encountered during 12 years at the Tavistock Institute will be briefly mentioned. Although the solutions may not be model ones, the ethical problems may be fairly typical. The cases are drawn from six research areas.

The first case concerned tobacco smoking (Emery *et al.*, 1968). The researchers believed that smoking would give valuable insights into the social and psychological sources of personal stress. Leading figures in the Tavistock Clinic, however, believed that there was an open and shut case against smoking on health grounds. From their view point no research into why people smoked was justifiable unless it started from the premise that people had to be stopped from smoking. As social scientists we had to insist that we respected the possibility that people have other aims than that of keeping healthy. Whatever peoples' priorities, social scientists can collaborate to obtain a better understanding of their motivations and to help them achieve or reconsider their purposes. It is not just that social scientists have no overriding hierarchy of values. More important, no single value can be wholeheartedly pursued without detriment to others. The social sciences can help people pursue their purposes in a more balanced way, lessening the chances of selfdefeating operations, for example, the U.S. Prohibition in the 1920s.

The second case concerned detergents. For several years we had resisted pressures to put our social science resources at the service of one of the two vast contenders in the U.K. washing powder market. It was feared that any social science input would be concerned with manipulating brand choices. As there appeared to be no brand differences, consumers would be forced to act irrationally. After finally agreeing, however, to study the mountain of research that had been done in the general field, we found grounds for continuing the engagement. Coming thinly through the noise created by the massive advertising of both parties was the voice of the consumer. They wanted not the 'whiter than white' offered by both companies but some product that would help them with the biological waste products that accumulate in most clothes. Here was a problem that we felt we could legitimately research.

The third case concerned a prison (Emery, 1970). We were asked by the U.K. Prison Commissioners to undertake an experimental redesign of a prison in order to improve conditions for the inmates. We refused this task unless we had equal freedom to redesign the prison to improve the working conditions of the staff. Despite the view of some people that men who voluntarily accept the role of prison officer are below contempt and abnormally motivated, we felt that prison officers should be accorded human dignity. Another ethical dilemma developed. It became necessary to stop some senior prison officials from sabotaging the experiment. What justification has a social scientist for interventions that endanger a person's career prospects? The only justification can be that an organisation has agreed with social scientists on the values to be pursued in the project. Those values then become a criterion for the judgment of the behaviour of both parties. If the social scientists happen to be in the best position to make that judgment it is their responsibility to do so. Alternatively, if no agreement can be reached, the conditions of the collaboration have to be redefined explicitly. Nonaction on the part of the social scientists is, in these circumstances, irresponsible.

The fourth case concerned group relations training. What is the responsibility of social scientists when they find that the methods they have devised to allow insight into group dynamics can create marked psychological disturbances in participants? Various *ad hoc* methods can be introduced to protect the individual but these all have the effect of clouding the microscope. The response of the Human Resources Centre of Tavistock was to withdraw for some time from this field. We made an exception where groups were composed of volunteer group trainers, that is, people who had had a good deal of exposure in this situation and were fully aware of the risks. Since this is rarely the case, we, in effect, temporarily opted out of an area of great scientific fascination.

The fifth case concerned organisational change in industry (Emery and Thorsrud, 1976). When, in the past, we had collaborated in producing organisational changes that affected operatives as well as managers, we had usually ensured that unions and employers were equally represented in a body controlling the research; we had also obtained the agreement of all parties including the researchers on a clear statement of purposes and procedures. In Norway and Ireland it was possible to go further and have the employers and trade unions contributing equally to the research funds. But in Britain the national union leadership did not feel able to be publicly linked with managerial efforts to develop their organisations. All we could do in this case was to spell out with top management a detailed statement of company philosophy and ensure that this was effectively diffused to all employees and local trade union leaders. In practice this seemed to protect the research from drifting into manipulatory practices (Hill, 1971).

The sixth concerned drinking and driving. An agency, hired by a government department, requested our help in polishing up an advertising campaign. This was designed to lower the frequency with which people drove cars while under the influence of alcohol. The advertising message relied on horror and the accusation that all of those who drank and drove were criminals and potential killers. Under existing law they were not criminal; nor were they all potential killers. We did not feel justified in making such charges against a large section of the adult population. On ethical grounds, therefore, we refused to help with the campaign unless its content was changed. This did, in fact, happen but we still experienced difficulty in getting quite high civil servants to see that they had no right to make these accusations.

8.3. Conclusions

What can be learned from these examples? At this stage we can only codify our experience since we are not in a position to draw up theoretical guidelines. A number of themes have emerged:

1. Ethical prejudgments of human behaviour based on data from physical and biological sciences cannot relieve the social scientist of the responsibility of looking at the issues from his standpoint.
2. The social scientist should avoid collusion with partners who assume that any interested party deserves less than the full measure of human

dignity. Expediency is no excuse for accepting such assertions as the following: the average consumer does not know what is good for him, criminals are inherently vicious, the ordinary worker is naturally lazy and irresponsible, and women are inherently irrational and neurotic.

3. In a collaborative relation both parties should seek to define the values that will govern their joint pursuits. This goes beyond the narrow operational terms of reference that usually satisfy a consulting relation. It also makes it much harder for either party to turn a blind eye on the grounds that it is none of their business.

4. In a collaborative relation the pursuit of immediate scientific ends must take second place to those ends that are mutually beneficial.

5. A social scientist cannot afford to let down his guard because he is dealing with a public authority. The latter are particularly apt to think that they are vested with responsibility for the people rather than being responsible to them.

It emerges that to take a responsible stand the social scientist is usually forced to go beyond the problem as it is defined by those who seek collaboration. More than that, where appropriate, he must insist on special arrangements for social sanctions and public commitments to protect his participation in matters of public concern.

In summary it has been suggested that social scientists carry a special burden of responsibility. It is necessary but not enough that the profession engages in the disinterested pursuit of knowledge. It must encourage and support within itself scientific work that has as its aim the mutual enrichment of social science and the practical affairs of man. This demands the emergence of a collaborative role than differs in essentials from the traditional roles of academic or consultant. It has been shown that the collaborative role crystallises the responsibilities that the professional social scientists must accept towards society.

Appendix 1. Social forecasting

A. Methodological premises of social forecasting[1]

The forecasting of social futures has to contend with emergent novelty, as one phase in development is replaced by another and as social processes of diverse nature first come to interact. To this problem of emergent novelty the social forecaster must add the difficulties which arise because:

1. the social systems are much more complex than the aspects studied by the separate social sciences; and
2. the sharing of parts between different subsystems is so great that their subordination to newly emerging processes can be very difficult to detect.

The perspective of futurology

A prediction of the future can always be challenged by the argument that we can only know what we have experienced or are experiencing; that is, the future does not yet exist and, hence, cannot be experienced, cannot be known. This scepticism reduces itself to the position that we can know only what is presently experienced, because the past is also non-existent and we have no way of experiencing and, hence, knowing whether what we think was experienced was actually experienced. These objections cannot be allowed to rest there. To be consistent one has to define the present. If one insists that past and future do not exist and, hence, cannot be known, then the present becomes the split second of immediate experience and knowledge; knowers and knowables disappear.

This attitude to prediction is no more useful to understanding what we actually do than is the other Laplacean extreme which suggests that the past and future are completely given in the present array of matter and energy. Our own experience of successful and unsuccessful prediction is a far better guide to what we might be able to achieve in trying to assess

1. This is an abridged version of the discussion of methodology in F. E. Emery, and E. L. Trist (1972).

the future requirements for the social sciences. Granting the compelling point that we cannot experience that which does not exist, we are still prepared to agree that we know something scientifically if we know we could, given present conditions, create the relevant experiences by experiment, test or observation. This copes not only with why we believe that we know something of the past, but also with why we believe we know something about the future. For example, we can experimentally demonstrate that exposure to present conditions will lead to a particular set of events at some point in the future. At a trivial level we can say that, given the numbers taking up sunbathing today, there will probably be many more with sunburn tomorrow.

These latter considerations give us good reason for rejecting a sceptical viewpoint about prediction and accepting the question, more usually asked by Everyman, 'how do you know that?' – allowing that only under some special circumstances will he ask 'how can you know that?' However, we have in our riposte implicitly redefined the notion of present, the present within which we can potentially carry out a confirmatory experiment or collect the ingredients of sunburn is not the immediate conscious present of the sceptic.

Chein (1948) suggested that just as much of the present is organised into spatial Gestalten, so the present is embedded in 'overlapping temporal Gestalten'.

Temporal Gestalten

The experience of a melody presupposes experience of a temporal Gestalten. A sneeze can be part of the present, but so is middle age part of the present of a middle aged person and the 1970s part of the present of a railway organisation. Any person or group is at any instant in many presents, each corresponding to what is a phase of the temporal Gestalten in which he or it is embedded. In dealing with living systems (whether species, population groups or individuals) we have been led to the viewpoint that there are laws corresponding to the whole course of a living process. This is so because we have identified in these processes parts which coexist throughout the duration of the process and, in their mutual interaction and interdependence, generate the causal relations characteristic of that process.

Certain, not all, of the characteristics of events arising within a process or the emergence of phases of a process will be determined and, hence, can be predicted by the laws governing that process. However, by the same reasoning, the phases will possess certain characteristics of their own (hence, laws of their own) arising from the mutual determination of their subparts. These characteristics will not be determined by the characteristics of the preceeding phases unless these arise from laws of the total process and except in so far as the preceeding phases determine the starting point of the phase in question.

Sommerhoff (1950) has stated these propositions in a more rigorous and exact way in his concepts of long, medium and short term directive correlations (corresponding to phylogenetic, adaptive learning and behavioural responses) and of the hierarchies which can arise between them. For our purposes, it is enough to note that it is consistent with the principle of contemporaneous causation to regard certain types of past and present events as causally related to, and predictive of, events which have yet to occur or to be experienced. These are the events which arise in the course of the process and which are mutually determined by the laws governing that process. In psychology, for example, the facts of maturation and learning are of this type. The prerequisite for prediction is a knowledge of the developmental laws. In the absence of the knowledge even the meaning of the immediately present facts cannot be understood: the gaining of this understanding through knowledge of every immediately present fact can even be regarded as theoretically impossible. This is the problem of Laplace's supermathematician and the illusion of some supercomputer schemes for integrated data systems. In addition to a knowledge of the laws governing different classes of living processes, we need a knowledge of earlier facts if we are to know how those laws are operating in a specific individual process and what the effects on later phases are going to be.

Overlapping temporal Gestalten
So far, I have considered only the case of a single process (temporal Gestalt, system or directive correlation) and its parts, and have implied that the whole burden of causation is within a process. This is, of course, a travesty of reality. Many of the phenomena we observe arise from the

interaction of processes that we are unable to treat as if they were parts of a more inclusive process. When such independent processes overlap, a new process emerges and a class of events is generated which has no history prior to that at the beginning of the interaction. There are clearly degrees of independence. The interpersonal life which will emerge in the marriage of a man and a women from the same culture is probably more predictable than that which would emerge if they came from different cultures. In any case, these hybrid processes seem to entail a special degree of unpredictability. The sufficient conditions for these newly emerged classes of events cannot be found in the prior history of the individual processes.

The main suggestions about the theoretical possibilities and limits for prediction can be spelled out more clearly with reference to simple diagrams. Throughout, I will be concerned with predicting the future of concrete individual processes for example, that of the United Kingdom or of John Smith. I will not be considering how one builds up predictive knowledge for a class of repeated or repeatable processes, nor will I consider forecasting techniques for processes which display only quantitative change.

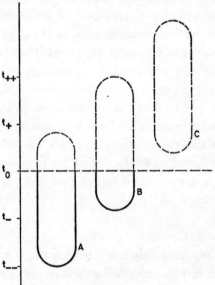

Figure 1
Four factors influencing the predictability of temporal gestalten

Let us assume that figures A, B and C in figure 1 represent the scope and temporal extension of three living processes, which could, for instance, be ecological, social or psychological. Let t_0 represent the present and $t--$, $t-$, $t+$ and $t++$ represent past and future points in time.

Four factors influencing the predictability of temporal gestalten
1. *Familiarity*: in the situation represented in figure 1, we would expect to be able to predict the state of A at $t+$ better than we could B at $t+$; provided, of course, than A and B are the same kinds of system.

The general principle is simply that for any system there is a minimum number of its component positions that have to be filled by parts before the system is recognizable. In practice, we do find that the more of its course a system has run, the easier it is to understand. On the same grounds we would regard C as unpredictable at t_0.

2. *Phase distance*: figure 2 represents a situation in which a and b are phases of A: While some prediction about the future part of a is theoretically possible, there is no basis for predicting the specific characteristics of phase b. Beyond phase a one could only make predictions of the kind discussed with reference to figure 1; that is, predictions about the more general features of system A.

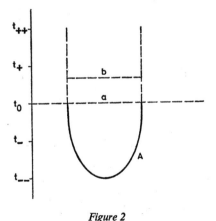

Figure 2

3. *Inclusiveness*: figure 3 represents a situation in which A and B are

coextensive in time, but in which *B* is a part process of *A*. One would expect that predictions about *A* would be theoretically easier than predictions about *B* taken alone. The basis for this expectation is the general property of part-whole relations. *A* sets some of the parameters of *B*; hence, whatever one knows of the values likely to be taken by *B*, one knows more if one knows how these parameters might change. The future of *B* is dependent upon the future of *A* in a way that *A* is not dependent upon *B*. At the same time, predictions about *A* will be less specific than could be predictions about *B*.

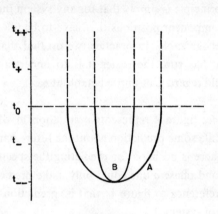

Figure 3

4. *Emergent overlap*: in figure 4 we have two processes which are presumed to interact after some point *t+* in the future. If *A* and *B* survive

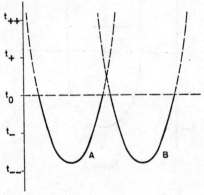

Figure 4

the interaction, some of their system properties may predictably survive. What seems unpredictable are the processes set up by the interaction and the changes occurring in A and B if they become directively correlated to form a larger inclusive system.

It would be too much to expect that the above mentioned situations constitute a complete set or that the interpretations are all equally defensible. It will be sufficient to make the point that there are genuine theoretical questions involved in predicting the future, as distinct from methodological ones, and to explicate the assumptions used. These assumptions guide the search for appropriate methodologies and the strategy for identifying future changes.

B. Forecasting social futures as a problem in reduction of complexity

Two difficulties in complexity reduction
Our concern is with modes of predicting future states of large complex social systems. Thus, it is relevant to discuss several special difficulties arising from the study of these systems:

1. their complexity is greater than that which we have so far learned to cope with in our separate social sciences;
2. the sharing of parts between different subsystems is so great that their subordination to newly emerging processes can be difficult to detect; that is, the parts appear to be still functioning as parts of the established familiar systems, although perhaps a little more erratically.

It seems to us that the social sciences cannot hope to cope with the complexities of large, complex social systems unless they take as their unit of analysis something larger than, and inclusive of, these systems. Specifically, the unit of analysis must be the social field or environment that includes the set of systems whose changes we are studying.

Analysis based on the leading part
This brings us to suggest the notion of the leading part. In this case

the reduction is not, as it were, a reduction across the board to pick out a key element present in all of the parts. Selecting the leading part seeks to reduce the total complexity by ignoring a great deal of the specific characteristics of all but one part. At its extreme we have the reduction to a figure-ground relation in which the leading part is considered in relation to all the other parts taken together as its ground; that is, as the internal environment of the total system. Throughout this range of possibilities the method is basically that of establishing which part it is, whose goal tend to be subserved by the goals of the other parts or whose goal achievements at t tend to determine the goal achievement of all the parts at $t+$.

Practical use of the other methods of value study or structural analysis usually involves an implicit assumption about what is the leading part, for example, McClelland's 1961 study of achievement values as a driving force in modern history and the Marxist mode of production theory. The values of the elite or the character of a central organisation (or set of like organisations) can readily form the basis for predictions about the future. There is a better basis for prediction when the intermediate step of selecting the leading part has an explicit methodological basis. One windfall from asking 'what part acts as the leading part?' is that major phase changes might be identified. Most studies of developmental phases in individuals or societies seem to identify a change in phase with a change in the leading part.

C. The problem of detecting emerging processes

Concealment and parasitism

The second major difficulty in predicting the future states of large complex social systems is that of early identification of emergent processes. This difficulty poses far more perplexing methodological problems. However, if social life is properly characterised in terms of overlapping temporal Gestalten, then many of those processes that will be critical in the future are already in existence in the present. If this were not the case, it would be difficult to see how such processes could quickly enough muster the potency to be critical in the next thirty years.

The early stages of a sycamore or a cancer are not obviously very different from a host of other things whose potential spatio-temporal span is very much less; so it is with many processes in social life.

One suspects that the important social processes typically emerge in this manner: they start small; they grow; and only then do people realise that their world has changed and that this process exists with characteristics of its own. Granted that they are genuine emergent processes (otherwise, why worry about futurology?), then we must accept real limitations upon what we can predict, and we must also accept that we have to live for some time with the future before we recognise it as such.

Yet, it is not simply foolhardy to think that we may enable ourselves to recognise the future more readily in its embryonic form. There are almost certainly some regularities about these emergent phases. Social processes which in their maturity are going to consume significant portions of men's energies are almost bound to have a lusty growth. They do not, by definition, command human resources at their infancy. Hence, their energy requirements must be met parasitically; that is, they must in this phase appear to be something else. This is the major reason that the key emergents are typically unrecognised for what they are while other less demanding novel processes are quickly seen.

A social process which passes for what it is not, should theoretically be distinguishable both in its energy and informational aspects. Because it is a growing process, its energy requirements will be substantially greater, relative to what it appears to do, than the energy requirements of the maturer process which it apes. Because it is not what it appears to be, the process will stretch or distort the meanings and usage of the vocabulary which it has appropriated. The energy requirements may be difficult to detect not only because we lack scales for many of the forms of psychic and social energy, but also because a new process may, in fact, be able to do not only as much as it claims (for example, television, to amuse), but to do it so much more easily as to be able also to meet its own special growth requirements. The aberrations of linguistic usage are, on the other hand, there to see.

Shared parts
Complex social systems, as does the human body, rely a great deal on

the sharing of parts. Just as the mouth is shared by the subsystems for breathing, eating and speaking, so individuals and organisations act as parts for a multiplicity of social systems. We think that it is this sharing of parts which enables social processes to grow for quite long periods without detection. If they could grow only by subordinating parts entirely to themselves, then they would be readily detectable. However, if their parts continue to play traditional roles in the existing familiar systems, then detection becomes difficult indeed. The examples which come to mind most readily are the pathological ones of cancer and incipient psychoses. Perhaps this is because we strive so hard to detect them. In any case, healthy changes in physical maturation, personality growth and social growth typically follow the same course. Once we are confronted with a new fully fledged system, we find that we can usually trace its roots well back into a past in which it was unrecognized for what it was.

Phases in the state of competing systems
If, in fact, most, or even some, important social processes are not detected for this reason, methodological approaches are suggested. Despite the redundancy of functions the parts tend to have with respect to the roles they play in any one subsystem, one must expect some interference in the existing systems as a new one grows. Angyal (1966) from his analysis of competing psychological systems within an individual, has suggested a general classification which can serve as a basis for analysing social systems. This is as follows:

1. When the emerging system is relatively very weak, it will tend to manifest itself only in the parasitical effects it has on the energies of the host system; that is, in symptoms of *debility*. The host systems will find it increasingly difficult to mobilise energy and or people, for their functions and there will be a slowing down of their responsiveness to new demands. The balance of forces may oscillate so that these symptoms occur in waves and make the functioning of the existing social systems less predictable.

At any given time, a social system experiences a fair amount of uncontrolled variance (error) in its operations. The reasons for an increase in this variance, of the kind being discussed now, will typically be sought within the system itself; measures may be taken to tighten up the system's integration. The unpredictable oscillatory effects are likely to encourage a wave of experimentation with new modes of system functioning. All these symptoms have behavioural manifestations, hence, are open to study. The methodological strategy of operational research is that of proceeding via analysis of the variance of systems, and this would seem particularly appropriate here.

2. When the emerging system is stronger, but still not strong enough to displace the existing system, we can expect to see symptoms of *intrusion*. Social phenomena break through, as in the case of the ghetto and student riots of 1967-1968. Clearly, these breaks are not simply errors in the functioning of the existing systems. At the same time, because of the relative weakness of the emerging social systems, they will usually only break through because they have shortcircuited or distorted the functioning of the existing systems. Their appearance will not obviously reveal the shape of the emerging system. However, if we are aware of the possibility that these phenomena can arise from emerging systems, it should not be beyond our ingenuity to develop appropriate analytical methods as has been done in psychology for detecting the existence of competing psychological systems from slips of the tongue.

3. When the emerging system has grown to be roughly in balance with the existing systems, there may be *mutual invasion*. At this stage it should be obvious that there is a newly emerging system, but mutual retardation and the general ambivalence and lack of decisiveness may still lead the new system to be seen simply as a negation of the existing system, for example, as a counter culture. The methodological task is to identify, in the chaotic intermingling of the systems, characteristics of the new system which are not simply an opposition to the old.

The fact that early detection may be possible does not in itself make it a worthwhile pursuit. The fact that early detection increases the range of responses and, hence, the degree of control a system has over its development does interest us. There are facts about the growth of social change which suggest that each unit step in the lowering of the detection

218 FUTURES WE ARE IN

level will yield a disproportionately greater increase in the time available for response – put another way, early detection would yield a disproportionately richer projection of the future from any given time.

Bibliogaphy

Ackoff, R. L., *A concept of corporate planning*, Wiley, New York and London 1969.

Ackoff, R. L. and F. E. Emery, *On purposeful systems*, Tavistock, London 1972.

Amber, C. H. and P. S. Amber, *Anatomy of automation*, Prentice-Hall, New York 1962.

American Psychological Association, *Casebook on ethical standards of psychologists*, Washington 1967.

Angyal, A., *Foundations for a science of personality*, Harvard University Press, Cambridge, Mass. 1941, reissued 1958.

Angyal, A., *Neurosis and treatment*, Wiley, New York and London 1966.

Arnheim, R., *Art and visual perception*, University of California Press, Berkeley 1954.

Arnheim, R., *Art and entropy*, University of California Press, Berkeley 1971.

Ashby, W. R., *Design for a brain*, Chapman and Hall, London 1960, 2nd edition.

Basu, R. N., The practical problems of assembly line balancing, *The Production Engineer*, October 1973, pp. 369-370.

Beer, S., *The brain of the firm*, Professional Library, London 1972.

Beman, L., What have we learned from the great merger frenzy, *Fortune*, April 1973, pp. 70-75.

Boguslaw, R., *The new Utopians*, Prentice Hall, New York 1965.

Box, G. E. P., Evolutionary operation, a method for increasing productivity, *Applied Statistics*, 1957, p. 6.

Boyd-Orr, Lord, World hunger, *Scientific American*, August 1950.

Brown, L. R., Human food production as a process in the biosphere, *Scientific American*, September 1970.

Buckminster Fuller, R., *Utopia or oblivion*, Bantam Books, New York 1969.

Burgess, A., *A clockwork orange*, Penguin, Harmondsworth 1972.

Burnett, J., *Plenty and want: a social history of diet in England from 1815 to the present day*, Penguin, Harmondsworth 1966.

Burns, T. and G. Stalker, *The management of innovation*, Tavistock, London 1961.

Butterfield (Emery), M., Towards equality through inequality in educational opportunities at the tertiary level, *The Australian University*, 1970, 8, pp. 169-192.

Caldwell, G., *Leisure cooperatives*, Ph.D. thesis A.N.U., Canberra 1972.

Carr-Saunders, L., *The population problem: a study in human evolution*, O.U.P., Oxford 1922.

Caudwell, C., *Further studies in a dying culture*, Bodley Head, London 1949.

Chapman, F. S., *The jungle is neutral*, Chatto and Windus, London 1963.

Chein, I., The genetic factor in a historical psychology, *J. gen. psychol.*, 1948, 26, pp. 151-172.

Chein, I., The genetic factor in a-historical psychology, *J. gen. psychol.*, 1948, 26, pp. pp. 115-127.

Chein, I., *The science of behaviour and the image of man*, Basic Books, New York 1972.

Churchman, C. W. and R. L. Ackoff, The democratization of philosophy, *Science and Society*, 1949, 13, pp. 327-339.

Churchman, C. W. and F. E. Emery, On various approaches to the study of organizations, in: Lawrence, J. R. (ed.), *Operational research and the social sciences*, Tavistock, London 1966.

Clark, Colin, *Starvation or plenty*, Secker and Warburg, London 1970.

Cohn, N., *The pursuit of the millenia*, Secker and Warburg, London 1957.

Coser, L. A., *see under* Weber, 1964.

Crombie, A. D., *Planning for turbulent social fields*, Ph.D. thesis, A.N.U., Canberra 1972.

Davis, L. E., Pacing effects on manned assembly lines, *International J. of Industrial Engineering*, 1966.

Davis, L. and J. Taylor, *Design of jobs*, Penguin, Harmondsworth 1973.

De, Nitish R., *Social context of organizational development*, Paper to second annual conference; Indian Society for Applied Behavioral Science, 1973.

Diet and coronary heart disease, Report 18, Australian Academy of Science, Melbourne 1975.

Dodds, E. R., *The Greeks and the irrational*, University of California Press, Los Angeles 1963.

Drucker, P. F., *Landmarks of tomorrow*, Harper, New York 1957.

Emery, F. E., Notes from discussion on Swiss Cottage proposal, *Doc. 702*, Tavistock Institute of Human Relations, London 1960.

Emery, F. E., Second progress report on conceptualization, *Doc. T 125*, Tavistock Institute of Human Relations, London 1963.

Emery, F. E., Report on a theoretical study of unit operations, *Doc. T 900*, Tavistock Institute of Human Relations, London 1966.

Emery, F. E., The next thirty years: concepts, methods and anticipations, *Hum. relat.*, 1967, 20, pp. 199-237.

Emery, F. E. (ed.), *Systems thinking*, Penguin, Harmondsworth 1969.

Emery, F. E., Research and higher education, Chapt. 9 in: G. S. Harman and C. Selby Smith (ed.), *Australian Higher Education*, Angus and Robertson, Sydney 1972.

Emery, F. E., *Living with work*, Australian Government Publishing Service, Canberra 1976.

Emery, F. E. and M. Emery, *Participative design*, Centre for Continuing Education, A.N.U., Canberra 1973.

Emery, F. E., M. Emery and C. de Jago, *Hope within walls*, Centre for Continuing Education, A.N.U., Canberra 1973.

Emery, F. E., E. L. Hilgendorf and B. L. Irving, *The psychological dynamics of smoking*, Tobacco Research Council, London 1968.

Emery, F. E. and E. Thorsrud, *Form and content in industrial democracy*, Tavistock Publications, London 1969, (Norwegian edition, 1964, Oslo University Press).

Emery, F. E. and E. Thorsrud, *Democracy at work*, Martinus Nijhoff Social Sciences Division, Leiden 1976.

Emery, F. E. and E. L. Trist, The causal texture of organizational environments, *Hum. relat.*, 1965, 18, pp. 21-32.

Farnsworth, H. C., *National food consumption of fourteen western countries and factors responsible for their difference*. Food Research Institute Studies, Stanford 1969, XIII, pp. 77-94.

Feibleman, J. and J. W. Friend, The structure and function of organization, in: F. E. Emery (ed.), *Systems thinking*, Penguin, Harmondsworth 1945.

Forbes, R. J., *The conquest of nature*, Pelican, Harmondsworth 1971.

Freud, S., *Civilization and its discontents*, Hogarth Press, London 1949.

Fromm, E., *Escape from freedom*, Routledge and Kegan Paul, London 1950.

Galbraith, J. K., Technology, planning and organization, in: K. Baier and N. Rescher (ed.), *Values and the future*, Free Press, New York 1969, pp. 353-367.

Gardner, M. R. and W. R. Ashby, Connectance of large dynamic (cybernetic) systems: critical values for stability, *Nature*, 1970, 228, p. 748.

Glazer, N. and M. Moynihan, *Beyond the melting pot*, M.I.T. Press, Cambridge 1963.

Grazia, S. de, *Of time, work and leisure*, Anchor Books, New York 1964.

Greco, M. C., *Group life*, Philosophical Library, New York 1950.

Harcourt, G. C. and N. F. Laing, *Capital and growth*, Penguin, Harmondsworth 1971.

Hegel, G., *Phenomenology of the mind*, Allan and Unwin, London 1949.

Heider, F., Attitudes and cognitive organization, *J. Psychol.*, 1946, 21, pp. 107-112.

Heider, F., *The psychology of interpersonal relations*, Wiley, New York 1958.

Heilbronner, R. L., *An enquiry into the human prospect*, Norton, New York 1974.

Hill, P., *Toward a new philosophy of management*, Tavistock, London 1972.

Hirschman, A. O. and C. E. Lindblom, Economic development, research and development, policy making: some convergent views, *Behav. sci.*, 1962, 7, pp. 211-222.

Hise, C. R. van, *Concentration and control*, Macmillan, New York 1962.

Huxley, A., *Island*, Penguin, London 1962.

Ingall, E. J., A review of assembly line balancing, *J. of Industrial Engineering*, 1965, 16, p. 4.

Jay, A., *Management and Machiavelli*, Penguin, Harmondsworth 1970.

Jordan, N., *Themes in speculative psychology*, Tavistock, London 1968.

Jones, W. O., *Manioc in Africa*, Stanford University Press, 1950.

Jungk, R. and J. Galtung (ed.), *Mankind 2000*, Allen and Unwin, London 1969.

Kahn, H., *The emerging Japanese super state*, Prentice Hall, New Jersey 1970.

Kahn, H. and B. Bruce-Briggs, *Things to come*, Macmillan, New York 1972.

Kahn, H. and A. J. Weiner, *The year 2000*, Macmillan, New York 1967.

Kildridge, M. N. and L. Wester, The assembly line model-mix sequencing problem, *Proc. of Third International Conference on O.R.*, Oslo 1963.

Kingdom, D. R., *Matrix organization*, Tavistock, London 1973.

Kirk, D., *Prospects for reducing birthrates in developing countries; the interplay of population and agricultural policies*, Food Research Institute Studies, XI, Stanford 1972, pp. 3-10.

Kristol, I., About equality, *Quadrant*, 1972, 16, pp. 72-80.

Laing, R. D., *The divided self; a study of sanity and madness*, Tavistock, London 1960.

Lewin, K., *A dynamic theory of personality*, McGraw Hill, New York 1936.

Lewin, K., *Resolving social conflicts*, Harper, New York 1948.

Liddel-Hart, B. H., *Thoughts on war*, Faber, London 1944.

Macarthur, M., Some factors involved in estimating calorie requirements, *J. Royal Statistical Society*, 1964, A, pp. 392-408.

Mackie, I. E. et al., *Fermented fish products*, F.A.O. Fisheries, Rome, 1971.

Madariaga, S. de, *Latin America between the eagle and the bear*, Praeger, New York 1962.

Mao Tse Tung, *Selected works*, Jarrold and Sons, Norwich 1954.

Mao Tse Tung, On ten major relationships, *Current Background*, 1956, p. 892.

Marcuse, H., *Eros and civilization*, Routledge and Kegan Paul, London 1956.

Marcuse, H., *Soviet civilization*, Routledge and Kegan Paul, London 1962.

Marcuse, H., *One dimensional man*, Routledge and Kegan Paul, London 1964.

May, R. M., Will a large complex system be stable?, *Nature*, 1972, 238, pp. 413-414.

McClelland, D. C., *The achieving society*, D. van Nostrand, Princeton 1961.

McGregor, D., *The human side of enterprise*, McGraw-Hill, New York 1960.

McHale, J., *The future of the future*, Ballantyne Books, New York 1969.

McHale, J., World facts and trends, *Futures*, 1971, pp. 216-301.

McLuhan, M., *Understanding media*, McGraw Hill, New York 1964.

McLuhan, M., *Culture is our business*, Ballantyne, New York 1970.

Mead, M., *Sex and temperament in three primitive societies*, New American Library, New York 1952.

Meadows, D. et al., *The limits to growth*, Earth Island, London 1972.

Mehta, B., *Bureaucracy and change*, Administrative Change, Jaipur 1975.

Mellor, D. P., *The role of science and industry*, Australian War Memorial, Canberra 1958.

Mollmann, J., From pursuit of happiness to solidarity, in: *Science and absolute values*, Vol. 1, The international cultural foundation, Tarrytown, New York 1974.

Mumford, L., *The myth of the machine*, Secker Warburg, London 1967.

Neumann, E., *The origins and history of consciousness*, Routledge and Kegan Paul, London 1954.

Odend 'hal, S., Gross energetic efficiency of Indian cattle in their environment, *J. of Human Ecology*, 1972, I, pp. 1-27.

Orwell, G., *Nineteen eighty-four*, Penguin, Harmondsworth 1960.

O'Toole, et al., *Work in America*, M.I.T. Press, Cambridge 1973.

Parker, S., *The future of work and leisure*, Paladin, London 1972.

Patmore, J. A., *Land and leisure*, Pelican, Harmondsworth 1972.

Pawley, M., *The private future*, Thames and Hudson, London 1973.

Perlmutter, H. V., Some management problems in spaceship earth; the mega firm and the global industrial estate, in: W. P. Scott and P. O. Le Breton, (eds.), *Managing complex organizations*, University of Washington Press, Seattle 1969.

Pierce, W. H., Redundancy in computers, *Scientific American*, February 1964.

Popper, K. R., *The open society and its enemies*, Routledge and Kegan Paul, London 1945.

Roberts, D. *Victorian origins of the British welfare state*, Yale University Press, New Haven 1960.

Roe, D. A., *A plague of corn: a social history of pellagra*, Cornell University Press, Ithaca 1974.

Rogers, C. R., *Encounter groups*, Harper Row, New York 1970.

Schon, D. A., *Beyond the stable state*, Temple Smith, London 1971.

Schram, S. R., *The political thought of Mao Tse Tung*, Pelican, Harmondsworth 1969.

Schurmann, F. and O. Schell (ed.), *Communist China*, Vol. 3, Penguin, Harmondsworth 1968.

Selznick, P., *Leadership in administration*, Row Peterson, Evanston 1957.

Seth, G. R. et al., *Sample surveys of mango and guava in Uttar Pradesh*, Indian Council of Agricultural Research, New Delhi 1971.

Sharp, I. G., Arbitration system, *Building Forum*, September 1972, pp. 75-80.

Simmonds, W. H. C., Planning and R & D in a turbulent environment, *Research Management*, November 1975, pp. 17-21.

Skinner, B. F., *Beyond freedom and dignity*, Knopf, New York 1971.

Sommerhoff, G., *Analytical biology*, Oxford University Press, London 1950.

Sommerhoff, G., The abstract characteristics of living systems, in: F. E. Emery (ed.), *Systems thinking*, Penguin books, Harmondsworth 1969.

Sommerhoff, G., *Logic of the living brain*, O.U.P., Oxford 1972.

Stevens, L. C., *Est*, Capricorn Press, Santa Barbara 1970.

Swaminathan, M. C. et al., Nutrition of the people of Ankola Taluk (N. Kanara), *Indian J. of Medical Research*, November 1960.

Taylor, F. E., *The principles of scientific management*, Harper, New York 1911.

Terreberry, S., The evolution of organizational environments, *Admin. Science Quarterly*, 1968, 12, pp. 590-613.
The effect of (national) income on the structure of the diet, *Ceres*, 1970, 3, p. 11.
The world banana economy, *Commodity Bulletin Series*, 50, F.A.O., Rome 1971.
Third World food survey, F.A.O., Rome 1963.
Toda, M., The design of a fungus-eater: a model of human behaviour in an unsophisticated environment, *Bahav. sci.*, 1962, 7, pp. 164-183.
Toffler, A., *Future shock*, Bodley Head, London 1970.
Tomkins, S. S., *Imagery, affect, consciousness*, Vols. 1 and II, Springer, New York 1962-1963.
Trist, E. L. and K. W. Bamforth, Some social and psychological consequences of the longwall method of coal-getting, *Hum. relat.*, 1951, 4, pp. 3-38.
Trist, E. L. et al., *Organizational choice*, Tavistock, London 1963.
University Grants Committee, *Returns from Universities and colleges in receipt of Treasury grants*, U.K., 1930.
Vepa, Ram K., *New Technology: a Gandhian concept*, Gandhi Book House, New Delhi 1975.
Weber, M., Some consequences of bureaucratization, in: L. A. Coser and B. Rosenberg, (ed.), *Sociological Theory*, Macmillan, New York 1964, pp. 472-473.
Wild, R., Group working in mass production, Part 1: flowline work, *The Production Engineer*, December 1973, pp. 457-461.
Winnicott, D. W., Some thoughts on the meaning of the word democracy, *Human relations*, 1950, 3, pp. 175-186.

Index

Achievement 77
achievement values 214
adaptability 96
adaptation XV, 2, 11, 13, 41, 43, 79, 169, 176
adaptation
  active – 124
  passive – 124
adaptiveness 23, 95
adaptive
  – control 96
  – learning 209
  – planning 176
  – responses 13, 67
  – social planning 143
  – state 192
  – strategies 12
  – system 7
administration, system of – 16
advertising 17, 203, 205
affluent 152
agricultural cooperation 157
agriculture 49, 51, 61, 64, 157, 165, 171, 177, 183, 192
  industrialized – 62
  – and industry 27
aid programs 51
Asian culture 27, 166
Asian and Western culture 176
assembly line 100, 102, 106-109, 112, 114
authoritarianism 30
autonomy 73, 121

Balance of power 36
beauty 70, 71, 76, 77, 87, 88, 91, 97, 154, 181, 192
behaviour 6, 7, 34, 35, 42, 43, 70, 82, 99
  active – 33
  adaptive – 10
  conformity in – 35
  human – 205
  ideal seeking – 100

outcomes of – 86
purposeful – 100
simulated – 9
birth rate 49
braking
  – distance 49
  – period 55
  – phase 60
building block, organizational 108
bureaucracies 24, 28, 52, 58, 99, 151, 183
bureaucracy 16, 26, 168, 171, 172
  centralized party – 158
bureaucratic
  – controls 177
  – educational institutions 140
  – organisations 24, 29, 102
  – society 146, 176
  – structures 58, 137
bureaucratisation 16, 25, 26, 28, 33, 45, 150, 151, 174
  – and urbanisation 44
bureaucratised 30, 42
building block 109
  socio-technical – 112

Catastrophe theory 10
causal texturing 4, 5, 8, 9
centralized planning 186
change 150
China's future 164, 168, 172
choice 31
  – behaviour 81, 83, 85, 88
  – of purposes 91
class mobility 150
collaboration 202, 206
collaborative role 202, 206
command planning 39
commitment of resources 38
competing systems 216
complexity 12
communication(s) 11-13, 15, 16, 110, 130

communications industry   192
community   150
concentrations   63
concrete productive relations   116
conditioning   6, 90
conglomerates   19
consumer(s)   203, 206
consumption   55
control   107, 166
   – and coordination   106
   – systems   25
cooperation   130, 177
cooperatives   62
coordination   104, 107, 112
   – control   130
corporate growth   17
counter culture   28, 217
cultural
   – heritage   172
   – heterogeneity   117
   – identity   173
   – mechanisms   XIII, 92
   – revolution   170, 173-175, 180
   – roots   117
culture   119, 156, 172, 182, 210

Decision making   118, 127, 184
democracy   58
   industrial –   119
democratic   133
democratisation   187
dependence
   asymmetrical –   92
   symmetrical –   92
design-criterion   111
design philosophy   23
design principle   97, 101
dissociation   13, 32, 41, 43, 45, 46, 184
developing nation   60
diets   54, 64
dietary pattern   57
dimension of choice   31, 73
directive correlations   2, 3, 209
discipline   94
disjointed incrementalism   123
dominance   78
domination   151
doomsday scenarios   XIV
dynamic equilibrium   87

Economic
   – development   161

   – growth   183, 192
   – planning   4
   – and technical aid   181
education   14, 119, 132, 134-138, 144,
   145, 151, 171, 173, 174
   continuing –   143
   – and family   133
   – and leisure   137
   – for leisure   152
educational
   – body   143
   – certification   142
   – institution   140, 141
   – resources   143
   – results   140
   – systems   142
employment   150
enlightened management   210
environment   1, 2, 4, 5, 9-11, 14, 15, 34,
   42, 67, 86, 90, 122, 153, 173, 213
   causal texture of the –   3
   clustered –   47, 91
   controlled turbulent –   137
   disturbed reactive –   47
   electronic –   15
   humanised –   133
   institutional and organisational –   4
   internal –   214
   organisational –   121
   randomized –   12
   reactive –   20, 121, 123, 169
   shared –   130
   social –   2, 3, 67, 125, 147
   social and natural –   3
   turbulent –   40, 47, 73, 121, 145, 151,
      169
   undifferentiated –   6
environmental
   – contingencies   42
   – designs   146
European culture   191
evangelicism   30, 32, 45, 46
expertise   129, 141
experts   36, 119, 125, 131, 198

Familiarity   70
family   30, 43, 44, 49, 59, 72, 119, 132,
   134, 135, 145, 153, 154, 166, 171
   – and education   153
farming   54
flow line production   110
food   192

– bank 61
– industry 59, 64
– inputs 60
– intakes 60
– processing industry 63
– requirements 55, 60
– resources 49, 63, 64
forecasting
social – 1
– technique 210
fractionation 35, 107, 109, 114
– of production 106
future XIII, 15, 44, 48, 167, 176, 208, 210
models of the – 158
probable – 197
– changes 213
– planning 160
– scenarios 190
– shock 15, 31, 151
– states 213, 214
futurology 215

Gestalt 209
Gestalten, spatial – 208
giant corporation 20
goal seeking behaviour 100
goal seeking system 7
GOER 62
government 16, 18, 25, 186, 187
– and religion 132
green revolution 185
group dynamics 204

Habitats 80
health food 60
homogeneity
cultural – 156, 170
social – 170
homonomy 72, 73, 77, 85, 87, 89, 91, 99, 102, 128, 142, 154, 176, 181, 195
host systems 216
human
– consumption 58
– dignity 204
– foods 61
– ideals 81, 88
– management 103
– planning 48
– potential 123
– potentialities 115, 118, 120
– relations 101, 119

– resources 38, 189, 198, 204, 215
– system 3
humaneness 99
humanity 75, 77, 85, 88, 154, 176, 181, 195
humanity and beauty 102, 129
hunger 48

Ideals 68-71, 73, 76-80, 85, 91, 96, 102, 133, 154, 176, 181, 195, 197
ideal, adaptive – 77
ideals of nurturance 142
ideal seeking systems 80, 87
individuals 34, 80, 166, 177, 204
individual
– behaviour 41
– shift-work 111
– systems 4
industrialized food 57, 62, 63
industrialists 198
industry 165, 171
information 18, 148
– overload 15, 78
institutional values 81
institutions 10, 34, 80
intellectual pursuits 154
intelligence XIV, 7, 138
intention 85
interdependence 77
international agreement 195, 196

Japan 181
Japanese culture 155, 181
job enrichment 101, 109

Knowledge 7, 28, 70, 73, 82, 86, 125, 127, 131, 136-139, 143, 145, 148, 182, 206, 207
expert – 125
pursuit of – 199, 200
scientific – 74
knowledge-based industries 143

Labour
– power 148
– requirements 108
– reserve 167
land reforms 194
leadership 29, 115, 122, 131, 160, 170, 174, 176, 184
collective – 157, 159

learning   6, 8, 23, 28, 83, 85, 93, 95, 98,
  127, 136
  meaningful –   7
  – groups   140-142
  – on the job   108
  – to learn   125, 129, 131, 138
  – and planning   90
  – process   139
  – requirements   138
leisure   132-136, 147, 152-154
  – choice   153
  – market   152
leisure's future   154
linguistic usage   215
living systems   2, 6
loss of power   41

Macro-economics   18
malnutrition   50, 53
management sciences   8, 19
market power   16
mass
  – aggregation   44
  – flow line   110
  – flow production   110
  – flow production lines   113
  – markets   103
  – media   XIV, 34
  – production   107
matriarchial culture   191
matrix organisation   101, 121, 122
megamachines   24, 92, 93, 95
mergers   17
military power   175
mobility   150, 151
  – for leisure   149
modern societies   117
motivations   9, 84, 128
  understanding of –   203
M.T.M.   105, 107-109, 110, 112
multinational(s)   11, 15, 63, 67, 99, 121,
  195
multinational arrangements   196
multinationals, super-super –   19

Nazis   173
Nazism   44
neighbourhood   59, 146, 147, 151
non-human resources   72
nuclear
  – assault   180
  – capability   172

– deterrent   185
– family   146
– power   179
– program   170
– shield   182
– strike   178
  testing, banning –   196
– test program   179
– umbrella   185
– weapons   162-164, 168, 178
nurturance   59, 60, 74, 77-79, 85, 86, 88,
  99, 102, 128, 154, 176, 181, 192, 195
nutrients   56
nutrition   49
nutritional
  – intake   57
  – requirements   49, 50, 53, 55
  – standards   65

Open society   79, 80
operational planning   8
operations researchers   127
optimiser   35-39, 124, 128-130
organisations   10, 15, 18, 34, 79, 80, 110,
  123, 216
  acquiring –   16
  bureaucratic –   100
  central –   214
  great monolithic –   101
  matrix type –   123
  monopolistic –   121
  structure and function of –   92
  unstable –   110
organisational
  – designs   22, 95, 100, 111
  designs basic –   91
  – development   46
  – theory   8
organised systems   81, 82
overarching corporations   21
over-eating   53, 57, 58
overmanning   114

Parameters of choice   81
parasitism   184, 214
participative democracy   188
participative management   78, 201
party
  – bureaucracy   159
  – control   170
pecking orders   58, 59
personal

– mobility 149
– resources 146
planners 37, 39, 42, 127
planning 6, 7, 11, 35, 37-39, 105, 123-125, 129-131
adaptive – 123
corporate – 121, 124
modern – 124
social – 125
strategic – 123
technology of – 123
– bodies 40
– model 169
– process 128, 139
– structure 165
– tool 107
population 49, 55
– explosion 48
– forecasts 48
– pressure 147
– trends 55
power 14, 15, 19, 37, 47, 82, 130, 131, 176, 186
– centres 198
prediction of the future 207
probability
– of choice 70-72, 82-126
– of outcome 70, 75, 83, 85
probable effectiveness 70
problem solving 8, 90, 125, 126, 136
process industries 102, 134
production 107, 192
productive
– enterprises 130
– organisations 145
– process 116
– systems 3
project type organisations 73
pseudo war 41
purposeful systems 13, 42, 69, 82

Quality control 105

Rational decision making 126
recreationalists 152
redundancy 68, 92, 95, 98, 216
– of function 99
– of parts 99
redundant 25, 27
relative value of intention 70
requirements, human 68
resources 74, 99, 122, 134, 148, 198

consumers of the – 196
control over – 196
human – 38, 189, 198, 204, 215
material – 198
– development 195
use of – 129
world's – 196
– allocation 36, 129, 163
– of expertise 140
response 92
adaptive – 92
behavioural – 209
maladaptation – 12, 29, 30, 41, 123
responsibilities 15, 43, 44, 71, 199-201, 204-206
responsibility, social – 199
retiring age 137
rote learning 7

Scenario 44
science of organisations 25
scientific management 8-10, 22, 23, 26
search 127, 129, 130
– conference 130, 143
segmentalism 184
segmentation 13, 31, 41, 43, 46, 185
segmentative processes 40
selfactualisation 77
selfexpression 77
set of futures 37
shift work 134
social
– behaviour 40
– engineer 198
– engineering 42
– forecaster 207
– future 193, 207
– islands 131
– orientations 29
– parasitism 184, 187
– resources 19
– sciences 199, 208, 213
– scientist(s) 127, 198, 200-206
society 146, 148
sociological forecasting XII, XIII
stability 122
state bodies 198
strategic planning 168
strategies (y) XIII, 5, 7, 8, 14, 46, 91, 122, 130, 162, 184, 213
strategy
active maladaptive – 32

adaptive – 145, 151, 177
maladaptive – 42, 120, 150, 184, 185, 198
passive maladaptive – 32
– of segmentation 123
– in war 163
strategies for change 131
strategies of superficiality 43
structure 137
subculture 184
subjective seriality 92, 97
super ego 72, 146
superficiality 13, 32-35, 40, 41, 46, 184
– in human relations 151
life strategy of – 36
supervision 106, 107
supervisory control 108
survival 2, 3, 7, 10-12, 42, 81, 88, 96, 99
symmetrical dependency 99
synoptic idealism 29, 32, 33, 35, 123
system 4, 8, 9, 11, 113
design 114
emerging – 217
purposeful – 13
systems redundancy 23
systems thinking 115

Task fractionation 109, 110
technological determinism 27
television 18, 34, 37, 42, 43, 46, 153
– screen 151
temporal gestalten 208, 211, 214
third world 48, 49, 60-66, 71, 174, 193
trade unions 114, 135, 170, 202, 205
transience 33

Uncertainty 12, 13, 67
underdeveloped
– areas 140, 171
– countries 50, 53-57, 174
– nations 51
– societies XIII
understanding 70, 80, 83, 86, 176
– through knowledge 209
unions 204
unit of analysis 112

urban
– concentration 63
– conglomerations 56
urbanisation 194

Values 68-72, 76, 78, 87, 91, 121, 127, 128, 202-206
– and ideals 67
social – 122

War 48, 162, 164, 176, 178, 180, 193
– mentality 42
warring nations 195
wei-ch'i 163, 167, 168, 179
welfare state 97, 119, 148
western
– agriculture 65, 66
– culture 27, 166
work 24, 59, 68, 100, 111, 118, 132-137, 142, 144, 145, 150-153, 173, 187
– assignment 108
– education and family 131, 151-153
– force 27, 118, 136
– load 22
– organisation 21, 25, 27
– pace 106
– problems 114, 136
– roles 22
– situation 110
– standards 106
– station 114
– times 106
bureaucratisation of – 100
conditions of – 27, 204, 150
democratisation of – 101, 102, 115, 120, 136
hours of – 152
involvement in – 153
quality of – 133
semi autonomous – 111
worker participation 202
working week 137
works council 139
world food bank 62
world food reserves 66
world food supplies 48

9 3 2 8